SONG OF AMERICA

Books by George M. Mardikian

DINNER AT OMAR KHAYYAM'S

SONG OF AMERICA

GEORGE M. MARDIKIAN

SONG OF
AMERICA

McGraw-Hill Book Company, Inc.
New York   Toronto   London

SONG OF AMERICA

Library of Congress Catalog Card Number: 56-8179

EIGHTH PRINTING

40302

Published by the McGraw-Hill Book Company, Inc.
Printed in the United States of America

TO NAZ

who has shared
so faithfully
the work and the wonder

PREFACE

SOME WRITE FOR art or money or posterity or a girl, but if you asked me if I wrote this book for any of those things I would have to say I'm sorry; it was nothing like that.

The reason this book was written was that there were some things I wanted to say about America, and a friend or two encouraged me to say them, and I listened to them and thought that it was time somebody did. Maybe it was meant to be me. And maybe, too, that was the way I could help pay a debt to the beautiful Lady with the Torch, whom I first saw more than thirty years ago from the steerage deck of the *Meghali Ellas.*

One of those friends I mention was DeWitt Wallace, editor of *The Reader's Digest.* In the summer of 1954 we spent some time at the Bohemian Grove, 60 miles north of San Francisco. We used to talk late in the evenings, around a flickering campfire and under the tall, quiet redwoods.

We talked mostly about America.

When we came back to San Francisco, he made Naz promise to make me write down what had happened to me in America, and the way I thought and felt.

It was not easy. It took more than Wally's encouragement and Naz's belief. It took moral support from my old friend Frank J. Taylor, the magazine writer. It took the urging and prodding of Julie Medlock, whom I had first known as a San Francisco reporter and then, later, admired as the brilliant New York newspaperwoman and feature writer that she is today.

And it took the technical writing and editorial assistance

of another old friend, Robert O'Brien, whose *This Is San Francisco* is still the best book that has ever been written about our romantic City by the Golden Gate.

So I must say thanks from the bottom of my heart to all of them, and to literally hundreds of others whom I wish I could name, whose trust, faith, and love have sustained and guided me.

I hope that a lot of people read what I have written. I hope that Americans read it, because sometimes I think that many of them take their country too much for granted. I hope that people living in the lands across the sea read it, because I know and have lived what is written here. It is the true America.

She may not be perfect. Her people may not always live up to their ideals, but they try, and they'll go on trying.

I hope that this book will help people everywhere understand why we Americans are so proud of America, why we believe in her, why we know that God was smiling when He made this land, and why we live and die knowing that she is the hope of the world.

George M. Mardikian

CHAPTER ONE

Few people, I think, have burned their fingers as often as I have. I was always lifting up the cover of the pot to see what my mother was cooking, and trying, if I could, to steal a piece of delicious-smelling meat. I guess my cooking experience goes back to before I was ten years old, for when we first moved to Scutari, across the strait from Istanbul, I loved to run down to the shore of the Bosphorus and find mussels along the rocky beach, make a fire, and throw them in. I cooked shrimps that way, too.

They called me Shishko—Armenian for "chubby"—because I loved to eat. Some children like to pull their parents into toy shops, but I used to tug on my father's arm whenever I smelled the warm, savory aroma of the *ishkemba chorba* stands.

1

"All right, little Shishko," Father would say, "we will go and eat a bowl of tripe soup," and we would turn aside from our walk and follow the smell and the rhythmic tap-tap from the chopping block, and they would lead us to the tiny outdoor soup stall.

A great black kettle would be steaming on its tile platform above a blazing fire. The *chorba* maker would be skillfully chopping the tripe and tossing it into the pot. The stand would be crowded with customers, and we would push our way in and order our soup, and I would be in seventh heaven.

Then, too, the streets of Istanbul and Scutari used to have *mekhanas*, or cafés, where for five cents you could get fried liver, with onions and parsley. Many times, after a big dinner at home, I would sneak down to the forbidden corner by myself for five cents' worth of liver *piaz*. I would always get caught, because my mother would catch a whiff of the onions —or maybe it was because of my guilty look.

One of my earliest cooking experiences took place after we organized the boy-scout movement in Scutari. For the three weeks of our summer vacation, we camped in the forest of Tchamlija, in the hills back of Scutari. There we tried to live like savages, on wild berries and turtle meat. This experiment ended quickly, for long before the three weeks were up, we were back on a diet for civilized boys, and I found myself in charge of the cooking for the camp.

Later, when I fought with the Armenian Legion during the First World War, food was a desperate problem. We Armenians were sort of stepsons to the Allied Armies; if there wasn't food enough to go around, we were the ones who didn't eat. The only time we had a decent meal was when we captured a town. Even though I was still a youngster, most of the cooking was left to me. I would find a lamb, kill it, and put it on the fire. We could never wait until it was properly cooked. As soon as it was hot through, we ate it with our bare hands.

But perhaps, before we go any further, we should leave this talk about food and eating, a subject which has been so much a part of my life, because I would like to tell you something about my people.

2

Almost everyone has the idea that all Armenians are dark-eyed and dark-haired, but this is untrue. The Armenians came from Macedonia and, under the leadership of Armeneus, crossed the Hellespont, as they called the Dardanelles in ancient times. There they intermingled and intermarried with the Hittites, the wheatgrowers of antiquity. And today, in some sections of the Caucasus country, off the highways and back in the hills, you still find Armenians who resemble Germanic or Celtic types. In fact, you find many Sunday or holiday costumes made of knitted wool that looks like the iron mesh of the Crusaders.

I tell you all this so that you will understand it and believe me when I say that my mother was an Amazon of a woman, with blue, blue eyes and hair that was as golden as the wheat fields of Erzerum in the summertime. Her name was Haiganoush, and her family, the Amirians, who numbered forty-five or fifty, were important citizens in the village of Xanta.

"Village," they always called it, but for those mountains it was really a large community, having some three hundred families and homes, and probably as many as two thousand people. It was southeast of the Black Sea port of Trebizond, high on a 4,000-foot plateau in the Caucasian mountains, near Bayburt, or Papert.

The word *Xanta* means "twenty-domed" or "twenty-crowned," and the village was called by this name because its largest church had twenty domes and towers. In ancient times it was famous as the place where the Greeks brought their long-limbed mares and mated them with the deep-chested stallions of Xanta, so that Xenophon and his generals would have mounts that had the speed and beauty of the Greek strain and the stamina and power of the Armenian horses.

My father's name was Magar. Like my mother, he was born and raised in Xanta and he, too, was blond and fair-skinned. He wore a proud, thick, curving mustache, and I have heard it said that everyone in Xanta called him Shag, which means "the golden-haired one." But with all his blondness, he had large brown eyes, which could snap and sparkle with good humor or flash with anger or shine with love.

3

My father's people were warriors and the descendants of warriors. That is how we came to be called Mardikian, for in Armenian the word *mardik* means "warrior." We were very proud of our name.

My father's father was a landholder in Xanta. He owned many acres of the Papert plateau, and 2,000 sheep. The sheep of the country were called "fat-tailed." Their tails grew so fat and heavy that my grandfather's men made little wheel carts for their favorite sheep to pull their tails around on.

The Mardikians were almost as prominent in Xanta as the Amirians. My father, for example, had an uncle who was a priest. He was Derhair Haroutun Mardikian, the Derhair standing for "Father." He had soft, silvery hair and a long, silvery beard, and his dark eyes showed his compassion and tolerance. Derhair, or Der Haroutun, had been educated in the fine schools of Istanbul. He had attended the seminary in Tiflis, and had studied at the great Armenian college at Echmiadzin. But more impressive than all these, Der Haroutun had read the *Vetz-hazaria*.

To understand how important this was, you must know that the title means "six thousand secrets of wisdom." There are only four or five copies of the *Vetz-hazaria* in existence. They are all ancient and massive volumes, that have been written by hand on parchment. Very few are ever allowed to see and read them. Their whereabouts is a secret. In the history of my country, the readers of the *Vetz-hazaria* have formed, down through the centuries, almost a mystic order, to whose members has been handed down the wisdom of the ages. And Der Haroutun, my father's uncle, was one of them.

This accomplishment—the reading of the "Six Thousand" —set him apart, as a star is set apart from the earth. It made him almost a god of learning. When the villagers wanted advice on family or spiritual matters, when they wanted important letters written or needed medicine for their children —in short, in the crises of their lives—they came to see my father's uncle, because he had read the "Six Thousand."

Even as a young man, my father had traveled as far as Trebizond and Batum and Istanbul. He was a dashing fellow,

4

and a bold one, with a reputation in the village as a rake, a man of the world, and a lover of spirited music. The stern-faced Amirians would have nothing to do with him. When he swept off his hat and bowed to my mother in the streets of Xanta, they pulled her along and forbade her to look back.

They called my mother "Dudu," and one evening she was attending the wedding of a friend, and my father sent a little girl to the house where the wedding was to give my mother a "message."

"Dudu," said the little girl, "your grandmother wants you to come right home."

My mother excused herself. A short distance from the house of the wedding, my father swooped down on his horse out of the evening shadows, gathered my mother in his arms, and galloped out of the village.

Some children playing nearby ran into the wedding house. "Magar has run away with Dudu!" they screamed. "He has kidnaped Dudu!"

A band of angry Amirians leaped on their horses and thundered out of the village. My father had with him cronies who were armed to the teeth with scimitars and pistols. A few miles from the village, the Amirians caught up with them. Both sides were bristling for a fight.

The spokesman for the Amirians aimed his cocked pistol at my father's chest. No one moved. He spoke very slowly. "Either you will marry her—or we shall kill you both."

This matter of honor among young unmarrieds was very important. For instance, it was the custom for a committee of the bridegroom's relatives to examine the newlyweds' bed sheets the morning after their wedding night. If there were no blood spots to prove that the bride had been a virgin, she was disgraced for life.

The demand of the Amirian spokesman was just what my father wanted. It was like a scene from an operetta. He took Dudu in his arms. "I shall save your daughter's honor," he said. "The sooner we are married, the better."

After two hectic weeks of preparations, they were married at my Grandfather Mardikian's house. Der Haroutun per-

5

formed the ceremony, and the entire village took a four-day holiday. They say it was the biggest and most joyous wedding party that Xanta had seen in many a year.

That was in 1894, and the villagers of Xanta were happy that year. But then, according to my mother and father, they were always singing in the fields and the meadows. They were happy people. In the springtime they were the first to plant their wheat of all the farmers in that region of the Black Sea, and they were the first to reap their harvests. A branch of the Jorokh River ran through Xanta and turned the huge, dripping, creaking water wheels of the mills along its banks, and at certain times of the year the air was always filled with the warm, rich smell of ground wheat.

The year after my father and mother were married, their first child was born. It was a boy, and they named him Zakeos, after the wealthy publican of Jericho who befriended Christ. And in that same year Abdul Hamid II, the Red Sultan, set out to massacre every Armenian from the Caucasus to the Dardanelles.

The villagers of Xanta were armed and organized. They fought off the Ottoman invaders for three long months, and then the Turks sent word that they wanted to negotiate a truce. My father's father and my mother's father were chosen to meet the Turkish officers outside the village limits. The two men said they would be back at nightfall, but they did not return.

The next day, the barking of their dogs led the villagers to the bodies of my grandfathers. They had been shot in the back and left beside the road. My mother helped carry them back to the village, where they were given Christian funerals and buried.

A few months later, little Zakeos died of pneumonia, and Xanta became such a sad place that my father and mother could stay no longer. My father had been selling grain and wool in the ports of the Black Sea, and he had friends in Batum. So that is where they went.

They did not stay long in Batum, but went on west to Istanbul. Strangely enough, Armenians were always safest from
6

Ottoman sword and gun in Istanbul. That was the seat of the foreign embassies and large colonies of British, French, German, American, and other nationals. Atrocities in the hill country could be blamed on "bandits" or brushed aside as incidents of the interior, but atrocities on the streets of Istanbul or Scutari would have caused indignation all over the world.

In Istanbul, in 1898, my parents' second child was born. They called her Arshaluz, which means "the sunrise." Many years later, with a strange melancholy in her voice, my mother told me that Arshaluz was the loveliest and happiest baby she had ever seen, with hair like spun gold.

When the baby was a year and a half, my father decided to move to Tiflis, in the heart of the Caucasus. They traveled to Tiflis through Xanta. While they were there, Grandmother Amirian, my mother's mother, fell in love with her little granddaughter. She begged my mother and father to let her stay for a visit. She hugged Arshaluz to her breast and wouldn't let the little girl out of her sight. Finally, my parents gave in. They left Arshaluz behind for a stay of several weeks, while they went on to make a new home in Tiflis.

You can still see today that in many of the mountain villages the houses have flat roofs. That was the way they were in Xanta. One day my grandmother put Arshaluz on the roof to play in the sunshine. Around the edge of the roof was a low wall, and although one of her cousins was there to watch after her, the little girl pulled herself to the top of this wall and looked down.

On the ground two stories below sat a group of boys. They were laughing and playing. The oldest, another cousin of Arshaluz, was cleaning his rifle. He held it in his lap, muzzle to the sky. He was sure the chamber was empty. But when his rag caught on the trigger, the rifle fired. Above him, on the roof, the cousin reached Arshaluz' side and caught her arm and pulled her back.

"Come back here, you naughty girl," she said.

For such a merry, wriggly little girl, Arshaluz was strangely limp. She dropped on her back to the roof. The cousin saw

7

her face and ran away screaming. Arshaluz had a bullet hole in her forehead, above her right eye.

The child's death made a tragic wound in my mother's heart. For many years, at the sight of a little girl with golden hair, her eyes would become sad, and she would grow silent. So it must have been a blessing that my sister Baidzar was born soon after in Tiflis, on the last day of the century. My brother, Arshag, was born there eighteen months later. Eighteen months after that—on November 7, 1903—I came along, and the three of us spent our earliest years in Tiflis.

Tiflis was a mountain city. It was very lovely, and through it tumbled the white waters of the Kur. I remember particularly its wonderful theater, with groups of traveling players and musical shows. But my most vivid memories are of the fishermen, the *kintos*. They were humorous, quick-on-the-trigger fellows who caught fish in the Kur and sold them in the street bazaars. They always wore baggy pantaloons, and you could always tell the wealth of a *kinto* by the richness and heaviness of his belt, which was made of pieces of silver, with churches and cathedrals engraved upon them.

When I was five was the year of the *Huriyet*—the liberation, we Armenians called it—when the *Ittihads*, or Young Turks, deposed the Red Sultan. That was the year we left Tiflis and went to Scutari.

Baidzar was a pretty girl of eight, with long curls down about her shoulders. Arshag and I were her dolls, and she was our "mother." She was very grave, and Arshag was brown-eyed and serious, too, and I was the smallest and chubbiest of the three of us. I had red cheeks, just like apples, and everybody wanted to reach out and pinch them. It made me angry, and I would run to my mother and hide in her skirts.

Father went on ahead to Scutari, and my Uncle Krikor, my mother's brother, came from Papert, where he was a school-teacher. He took us to Batum, and there we boarded a Russian steamer and sailed to Istanbul. Everywhere Uncle Krikor went, we followed him, like cubs following a father bear. He was a good-humored man in his twenties who laughed a great deal and bought us *lokoum*, which is a Turkish candy, and

8

carried us around on his broad shoulders. Like my mother, he was blond and blue-eyed, and straight as an arrow. We worshiped him then, and always would.

Our house in Scutari was on a hillside in Ejadiye, the Armenian district. From its windows we could see the shining domes and minarets of Istanbul. Then, below them, the dark blue waters of the Marmora and the strait that led to Istanbul's Golden Horn and the Black Sea. They were alive with little ferries, called *shirket* boats, and also with sailboats, rowboats, and long, slender *kayeks*.

The thrill for us children was when we all went running and charging down the hill to the beach and rocky sea walls of Scutari. We loved, most of all, to watch the foreign ships go by. The ones that always left the biggest wakes to break over the wall were the Rumanian boats steaming to Greece, or east for Odessa.

And we loved to watch the *yazmaji*, the scarf washers, who brought bundles of beautiful colored scarves, which were worn by Turkish ladies, and washed them there on the sea wall, and then hung them out to dry in the breeze—green, blue, red, yellow, purple, and many other bright, gay colors, like the strings of signal flags on parading ships.

And the fishermen! In Istanbul and Scutari all fishermen are either Armenian or Greek. No other land has such fascinating and picturesque fishermen. They are happy-go-lucky people, with hearts as big as the sea in which they fish.

Twice a year there is a big run of two different kinds of fish. One is small and silvery, like smelts. The other is large and strong and tough-looking. The small ones are called *khamsi*, the big ones *palamoud*.

The steel-blue *palamoud* swim down from the Black Sea to the Bosphorus and Marmora in great schools late every fall. When you smell the aroma of roasting chestnuts in the air from the street braziers, you know that soon the *palamoud* will run. The day comes when the water is alive with them, and the waves scatter them along the beach and leave them flashing on the sand.

9

The fishermen roll up their wide, bell-bottomed pants and gather up the fish and pile them on huge wooden trays. Balancing the trays on their heads, they distribute the fish free of charge to the poor all over the city. No rich man can buy the fish; when the sea casts them on the sand like that, they are a gift from God, sent for the poor alone.

Then, in the early spring, with the first blowing of the south wind, which is called the *lodos,* the little silver fish swarm around the shore. You don't have to go to the markets or wait for the fishermen to come to your door to know that the *khamsi* are running. The smell of fish broiling over outdoor charcoal burners and the smoke hanging over the city will tell you. Everybody has set up his *manghal*—his brass cooking stove—out of doors, in order to keep the odor out of his house.

Another thing that we often feasted on down at the beach was eels. A little way off the shore was a tiny island. On this island stood a high-walled stone building that, as far back as anyone could remember, had been called *Kiz Kulasi,* the Castle of the Princess. How we used to boast that some day we would swim out to that island, scale those walls, and climb through the castle's dark, barred windows!

The legend about *Kiz Kulasi* was that the Sultan of Turkey once had a beautiful young daughter. From infancy, this lovely girl was terrified of snakes. Because she was his favorite, her father ordered a castle built especially for her—high on this rock out in the water—so that no snake could ever come near her. But one day a snake hid in a fruit basket. The servants of the princess carried it to the castle. That night, it crawled to the young girl's bedroom and sank its fangs into her throat. They found her dead in her bed the next morning.

Our eyes grew wide and serious whenever we told each other this story, and then, among the great rocks of the sea wall, we would catch eels that squirmed like snakes. These very eels, we said, were blood relatives of the snake that had bitten the princess; they must die to pay for what it had

10

done. And so we would kill the eels and cook them. They tasted much better than ordinary eels, for we were avenging the death of the beautiful princess of *Kiz Kulasi*.

Father went to work at his commission business in Istanbul every morning, crossing the strait with thousands of others in the *shirket* boats, and Baidzar, Arshag, and I walked down the hill to Sourp Khatch, the parochial school of the Holy Cross Armenian Apostolic Church. Now in the afternoons, Baidzar had another doll to take care of and play with, for our little sister Alene, my parents' last child, had been born shortly after we came to Scutari.

Sometimes during the summer months Arshag and I worked. I became a delivery boy for a grocery store and for twenty-five cents a week carried a grocery-filled basket up and down the Scutari hills on my back. One summer, I was an employee of a jewelry store in Istanbul's famous Closed Bazaar.

My job was to stand in front of the store and watch the passers-by very closely. Whenever I saw a likely-looking victim for my hawk-nosed employer, I grabbed him by the arm, pushed him quickly into the jewelry shop, and locked the door. From then on, it was up to my master. I kept my eye especially peeled for swaggering, well-to-do Turks from the interior. I could always tell them by the heavy gold or silver watch chains that dangled across their big stomachs and by their droopy pantaloons. If my master fleeced them, so much the better.

Arshag worked in a much more daring manner. Not far from Ejadiye was the Jewish section. Because of their religion, the Jews would not touch anything after sunset on Friday evenings. On these nights Arshag went from house to house to light fires for them. After he had kindled their fire, they would point to the money—five *para,* or about two and one-half cents—which they had placed on the table. "There is your money," they would say. And Arshag would take it, and go to the next house.

The streets were very narrow and crooked in the Jewish

district, and they were dark in the evening, so that I thought it was a brave thing for Arshag to do. I admired him for it, more than he knew.

When I mention fires, I remember the *neubetji*, who, in those days before the signal system, was Scutari's two-legged fire alarm. The *neubetji* wore a flaming red shirt and tight white trunks. When a fire broke out, he went streaking from one firehouse to another, telling the fire fighters where to drag their apparatus and put out the blaze. Every once in a while, to alert them that he was coming, he would stop short in his tracks and let out a weird, high-pitched howl, "Ooo-ow-w-ooo!" It sent shivers up and down your spine. It was the cry of the fire demon itself.

Then sometimes in the middle of the night the distant whistling of the boats down along the strait would grow silent, and all at once, through the stillness, you would hear a terrifying sound: a heavy, slow knocking, "Takh!—Takh!"

This was the *bekji*, the night watchman, roving the streets and calling out the hours of the night. He carried a large, heavy bludgeon that was covered with iron, and, like doom knocking, he pounded the hour against the cobblestones with this huge stick. Sometimes he reported a fire. You heard a ghostly cry, "*Yan-gin vah-h-r-r!* [There is a fire!]" And then he would give the district of the fire in either Istanbul or Scutari, so that relatives could get up and go to help the victims.

For entertainment Father sometimes took us to the top of the hill to the theater, to see an episode in a thrilling French movie serial. It must have been one of the first ever made. It was a melodrama of the sewers of Paris called, after its hero, *Judex*. Almost as stirring as the adventures of Judex himself was the accompaniment of the hunchbacked violinist who played his heart out in the flickering beam of light from the whirring projector.

Every week I went to the Turkish bath with my mother. She scrubbed me with a *kassa*—a rough, heavy mitten—until I was raw and almost bleeding. While this humiliation happened to me, Arshag went to the men's bath with my father

12

and drank sweet, bubbly *gazos*, like Seven-Up, out of bottles. One day the bathhouse keeper came into the women's baths with an armload of towels. She was very dignified, the widow (as most bathhouse keepers were) of a Turkish general, who had left her a small pension. I was stark naked. She stopped and held herself stiff and studied me carefully. "Next time you come, you might as well bring your father along with you," she said sarcastically.

On the way home my mother said she thought the bathhouse keeper was right. I was getting too old for the women's bath. Next week, I would start going on Friday nights with my father and brother. And, I added silently, drink six *gazos*, all by myself!

Often on Sundays we packed our picnic baskets, and all of us, including Uncle Krikor with baby Alene on his back, would go down the hill to the wharf and board an excursion boat for Prinkipo, the "big island" in the Sea of Marmora. The blue water would sparkle in the sunshine, the breeze would caress us, and I would be happy, until we steamed past Keopek Adasi.

Keopek Adasi means "Island of the Dogs," and it was a strange place. It was against the religion of the Turkish people to kill dogs or get rid of them when they were puppies. Consequently, the streets of most Turkish cities swarmed with mongrels of all ages, sizes, shapes, and colors. Every so often, police rounded up stray curs by the dozen, put them on a boat, and took them to this rocky little island. There they turned them loose to be killed by the pack or to die of disease or starvation.

The ferry always went too close to Keopek Adasi, and the breeze carried across the water the pitiful howling of the exiles, begging us, it always seemed to me, to stop and rescue them from their island prison.

Pleasanter Sunday afternoons came when we all gathered in the yard behind our house. Almond trees grew there, and plum trees that burst with blooms in the springtime. But my favorite was a high, spreading mulberry tree. Father and Uncle Krikor would stand under it with a large sheet

13

stretched between them. Then Arshag and I would scramble into its branches and shake and shake, and showers of mulberries would go sailing down into the sheet.

But our good times and our laughter stopped after Turkey entered the World War on Germany's side, against France and Great Britain and Russia, and, later, against the United States. The big guns of the British fleet grumbled in the distance every night and rattled our windows. My mother and father, and even Uncle Krikor, grew quiet, and their faces became sad and serious, and so did those of all the Armenians in Ejadiye, because with the sound of guns our heritage haunted us once more—a bitter heritage of homeless wandering, wars, persecution, and murder.

We no longer walked down to the warm Marmora with our father to watch the running of the *palamoud*. Instead, we drew our curtains and darkened our rooms and locked our doors. When I had to go out at night to buy food, I walked in the middle of the street, as my father told me, and carried sharp stones in my pockets to fight back with if I were attacked. We heard there were Turkish massacres in Cilicia to the south, and our people—refugees from Cilicia —came into church with their arms or legs or ears cut off by Ottoman scimitars.

In April, 1915, the Turks said that the Armenians were aiding the Allies. With this as their excuse they set out once more to exterminate my race. They "deported" thousands of Armenians, driving them from their homes and leading them into the deserts to die there like the abandoned dogs of Keopek Adasi.

One night toward the end of that month there was a terrible pounding on our door, and the Turkish officer came in and took my father. He was one of hundreds they seized in Scutari and Istanbul that night—the élite of Armenian manhood. I never saw my father again. The month after that my mother's mother, Vartanoush Amirian, and her whole family were driven from their home in Xanta and marched with many other Xantans to the town of

14

Erzingan. There, driven half insane by grief and suffering, she threw herself into the Euphrates River.

A fire of hatred burned in my breast. To take revenge for the wrongs done to my people and to make my mother proud of a warrior son, I ran away from our home in Scutari to fight against the Turks, as my ancestors before me had done for 3,000 years.

I was fifteen, and there were hundreds of others my age and younger, and the ragged legion we marched and starved and fought with helped to win Armenia's first independence in seven centuries. What a wonderful achievement that was! But it was only one of many breath-taking changes: the mighty Russian Czar overthrown, Russia torn by the Bolshevik revolt, and Turkey, her sovereignty lost, in the hands of Allied occupation forces. Our world had been shaken apart.

The Caucasus country was in chaos. Although I tried to get word through to my mother and Uncle Krikor that I was alive and safe, they never heard from me. Nor could I take a trip back home. How could I leave for one day, let alone a week or a month, our baby republic that needed every bit of help she could get? Unification and the training of her youth were essential. I pitched in at Kars to organize Armenian boy-scout troops.

One day in summer, 1920, I called on Captain Eddie Fox, district director of Near East Relief at Kars. I don't know what I expected from this man, or what I expected him to be: a conqueror, a Tamerlane? or a cold, stern-faced man of steel, like some of the German officers I had seen? Certainly, I was not prepared for this kindly, firm-spoken man whose gentleness seemed to come, not from timidity or weakness, but from strength.

On his office wall hung the picture of a strange-looking man. In Armenia, grown men wore full beards and big mustaches, but this man had a little stubby beard, and no mustache at all. When we began talking about my country, Captain Fox pointed to the picture and said, "What Armenia needs is a man like him—an Abe Lincoln."

This was the first picture of Abraham Lincoln that I had ever seen. As I studied it and saw what was in his face, my heart was filled with awe and reverence. He would have understood my country and her heartbreaking struggle for freedom. The boys who might have become her Lincolns seldom survived until manhood.

Then I met another American, another Near East Relief official, George D. White. He opened his warehouse door and said, "If there is anything here you need for your scouts, take it. It's yours."

He found footballs and baseballs for Armenian boys who wouldn't have known what to do with them, because they had never learned how to play football or baseball, or any other game.

Before we ever had a chance to use those footballs and baseballs, there came another war, with the Turks in front of us and the Russians behind us. It destroyed the last hopes of the Armenian nation and left it a Soviet vassal.

The Turks captured two hundred of us and threw us into a foul-smelling sauerkraut factory in Kars. We were packed in so tightly we couldn't lie down at night. By day we chopped ice on the Kars River. The Turks didn't need the ice; it was their way of killing us off. Every night some of us died from cold and exposure. When I was taken prisoner, I was a husky athlete; within three weeks I weighed 110 pounds. Only my hands and feet looked plump; they were puffy and swollen because they had been frozen.

Over the centuries Kars had had its fill of death. For invading Turks, it was the southern gateway to Russia; for Russian armies on the march to the south, it was the pass to Kurdistan. But even now, in the twentieth century, it was still one of the most heavily fortified cities in the Caucasus. It had been one of the prides of Czarist Russia to have the heights there bristling with heavy guns, and, underneath the city, deep tunnels stocked with food and ammunition.

Before I was captured, I had been in the barracks there and in private homes. In both you saw evidence of how the city

16

had changed hands—from Russian to Turk and back to Russian again.

I remember a painting which showed a clash between Russian Cossacks and Turkish cavalry. The canvas covered one entire wall. Fierce, screaming hordes charged each other across a wide plain. But there was something very queer about this picture. None of the thousands of horsemen had eyes. They had all been marked out.

"The painting was originally commissioned and executed here when Kars was under Russian control," the owner of the house explained. "Later, when the Turks reconquered the city, Turkish officers garrisoned here, with their bayonet points, put out the eyes of all the Cossacks. Then, some years later, when the Russians captured the city back again, they hired a painter to go over the canvas and paint out the eyes of every Turk in the picture."

One morning in Kars my spirit broke and I gave up to despair. There comes a time when you know you are finished. I had a desperate desire to send a last message to my mother. My only chance was to bribe the Turkish guard.

I went up to him on the way to the river ice pack.

"Let me stand by the road until the Near East Relief official drives by, and I will get you some condensed milk," I said. To sweets-loving Turks, condensed milk was manna itself.

He was going to kill me eventually, anyway; what did he have to lose? He growled and told me to hurry.

Too weak to stand, I lay shivering in the snow by the river bridge until a Near East Relief car came past. Luckily for me, Mr. White and his wife, Elsie, were in it. I was so thin he could hardly believe me when I told him I was Scoutmaster Mardikian. Tears came to Mrs. White's eyes. She wrapped me in her fur coat. They promised to rescue me.

"It's too late," I said. "I'm going to die. All I want is to send word to my mother, to say good-by." I gave them my mother's name and address. "Now, if you really wish to help me—this minute—give me two cans of condensed milk."

17

Mr. White shook his head. "We have carloads at the warehouse. Can you wait until we go get some and come back?"

I would gladly wait, I said. But I didn't think my friend over there, the Turkish guard, would be that patient.

"Pardon, sir." It was the Whites' Russian chauffeur. He opened the door to the back seat. On the floor beneath a fur robe was a wooden box filled with precious cans of Borden's condensed milk. "I forgot to deliver it to the commissary," he said, smiling. "I was going to take it there later in the day—"

Mrs. White clapped her hands with joy. Her husband reached into the box and took out three cans—one extra, for good luck—and pressed them into my hands.

I thanked the Whites, and their chauffeur. Then I said good-by quickly, so they wouldn't see me crying, and plodded across the snow to the waiting guard.

CHAPTER TWO

That night the heavy door of the factory rattled open. A guard yelled my name. We were used to these visits after dark. The prisoners the guards took with them never came back. I said good-by to my comrades. My time had come.

But instead of leading me behind the little Armenian church, where the executions took place, the guard marched me into the office of the Turkish commandant. Behind him stood Mr. White. The guard left us alone.

"Mardikian, why didn't you tell us you're an American?" roared the commandant.

As I stared, dumbfounded, Mr. White winked and nodded. From somewhere the right words came. "I'm sorry, sir. You didn't give me a chance."

19

"Just being an American doesn't release you, but we're going to send you to the hospital. Thank your friend here for that." And he jerked his head at Mr. White.

After three weeks in the American-supervised hospital, I worked in Near East Relief warehouses. When my strength returned, Mr. White slipped me and another prisoner canned food, shoes, and blankets, and one night we ran away. We hid in caves by day and traveled by night. It took ten nights to make our way through the snow to Erivan, on the Transcaucasus border.

There Dr. Clarence Usher, an American physician turned missionary, defied Bolshevik threats of death to anyone harboring a prisoner or an "enemy of the state," and gave us shelter. The next morning, my companion got safely away, hidden in a wagon carrying orphanage supplies and food.

I stayed with Dr. Usher in the American Mission House until my frozen feet were healed. Then, disguised as an American in a Near East Relief uniform, I went by train to Alexandropol. There I was made chief guard for the barracks in which 21,000 Armenian orphans were housed and fed.

Those who lived in more fortunate countries had forgotten that people in our section of the world had no food—all but the Americans. They came to our rescue, though sometimes in a way that seemed both tragic and funny. In one food shipment, for instance, we received tons of Cream of Wheat. The recipe on the package told us to boil it and serve it with cream and sugar. All very well, but we had no cream or sugar. There it was, all that tempting and very much needed food—food that would actually save hundreds of young lives—but it was very unpleasant to eat just boiled and served plain.

Frantically we experimented, trying this way and that to make it tasty. Finally, by adding pine nuts and a simple syrup made of honey and baking it, we invented the beautiful dish called *imrig halva*. To this day it is a favorite among Armenians everywhere.

It is very difficult to describe orphanages housing 21,000 children. Some of these children, because of shock, fear, and

20

the terrors they had witnessed, had lost the ability to speak. Probably 2,000 were going blind from trachoma, that dreaded disease which is the result of filth—inescapable because of the lack of soap—and, of course, malnutrition. They had escaped the massacres. They had survived like wild beasts in the forest. And the Americans, with the help of the newly formed (and short-lived) Armenian Republic and the Armenian relief societies, had gathered them together in Alexandropol, 50 miles from Erivan.

They lived in three fine old Cossacks barracks. The largest was Kazachi-Post. The second was Baliconn, where most of the girls were housed—it was very important to keep them separated from the boys. The third dormitory was the Seversky barracks on the bank of the Arpay-Chai, the river that flows through the outskirts of Alexandropol.

In this orphanage we learned the best way to teach the orphan boys respect and discipline—through boy-scout training. They responded wonderfully. What made them happiest were the long boy-scout staves. An American boy scout doesn't use the scout staff very much, because he doesn't need to. But that stick was everything to those orphans. They used it for jumping over gulches and fences and protecting themselves from wild animals—including some called "human beings."

We were all very upset when they decided to transfer our director, Capt. Milton D. Brown, to Erivan, the capital of Armenia, as chief of all operations for Near East Relief. He rode down the streets of Alexandropol on his black stallion, with his American-made gun at his side. Somehow, he gave us assurance that no Bolshevik or Turk was going to molest our children. He was our American knight on horseback.

They sent as his replacement the scholarly W. W. Rankin. Mr. Rankin was not the same type as Captain Brown, but you could see that he meant business. He was there to help, and exact discipline. And he got it.

Once, when Mr. Rankin was away, the Soviet commissar came with his men and took my superior, Vahan Tcheraz, and me to Soviet headquarters. There non-commissioned

21

underlings charged us with indoctrinating the orphanage boys with anti-Soviet, anti-Bolshevik, and anti-state teachings. Naturally, we denied the charge. Our only concern was to see that the boys stayed healthy and alive. The only subjects we taught were the alphabet and correct speech.

The hearing-room door swung open. In strode the commissar. He carried a silver-tipped swagger stick. His high, polished *sapogs* rapped on the floor. His face was familiar, though I could not remember where I had seen him before, and I could see that Vahan recognized him instantly.

He glared at us with such scorn, I thought he was going to spit in our faces. For ten minutes he gave us a tongue-lashing for teaching the future generation of the Soviet world the ways of the "decadent *bourgeoisie*." He called us every insulting name he could think of.

Then, after all this shouting, he commanded his officers to take us to his private quarters. He wanted secret information. He gave them the impression he might torture it out of us.

When we were alone, he made sure his men were out of hearing. Then he locked the door, threw his arms around Vahan Tcheraz and me, and started crying like a child.

"Please—" he said with a choking voice. "Forgive me—"

Suddenly I realized why I thought I had seen him before: he was the brother of little Hagop Hamdilian, one of our orphans. Vahan had taken a special interest in the boy, because he and this older brother—now a Soviet commissar—had fought shoulder to shoulder for the freedom of Armenia from the Turks. In spite of all this, Commissar Garo Hamdilian practically had to kick us and spit on us and call us names, for now he could not dare to show any love or friendship toward us.

His own superiors had forced him to arrest us. The only way we could regain our liberty was through an official protest from an American of standing, such as Mr. Rankin. Then, he said, he could release us.

He permitted us to send one of our boy scouts to Erivan, to tell Captain Brown what had happened. But before we

22

heard from him, Mr. Rankin was back in Alexandropol, protesting that American territory had been entered without his consent and that we should be released immediately. Commissar Garo Hamdilian was more than happy to let us go.

It was in the summer of 1921 that a group of distinguished Americans came to Armenia to visit our orphanages and survey the relief situation. We all marched to the railroad station to greet these men—senators, representatives, and others—who were coming from America with good tidings, with hope and cheer. There were about twenty of them. On the parade ground, we raised the American flag, as we did every morning. That day it seemed to wave higher and stand out more proudly than ever before.

The orphans paraded on the field and, with the help of us leaders, spelled out, "Thank you, America and N.E.R. [Near East Relief]." Dr. John Voris, who was in charge of the education department of Near East Relief, stood on a platform beneath the flagstaff and the American flag and gave a talk. None of us would ever forget it, for it filled us with faith.

"Do not give up hope," he said. "America knows about you and loves you. America will see to it that you Christian boys and girls—you youthful survivors of the tragedy of Armenia—are fed and clothed and kept warm."

Americans, the most humane people in the world, had saved my life and sheltered me when my own people could not lift a hand. Men like Mr. White, Captain Brown and now Dr. Voris, made me lie awake in my bunk at night, dreaming about the bright country across the Atlantic. I pictured life as it must be in that wonderful land—the happiness, the freedom, the opportunity to earn money to send back to my mother, much more money than I could ever hope to make in Istanbul. And the luxury: think of boarding a streetcar, dropping a nickel in the box, and riding like a pasha!

After our experience with Commissar Garo Hamdilian, we knew, Vahan and I, that we could probably not be safe much longer staying where we were. But I felt that I had a better chance at Alexandropol than he. I got along better with people. He had a wide stubborn streak. This, combined with a cold reserve, made him appear haughty and aloof.

I hold Vahan I didn't think that two of us could get through, but that one, traveling alone, could make it. He had graduated from Oxford, and as the nephew of the great Armenian patriot Minas Tcheraz, he had an inspiring name. I argued that he would have greater influence than I and so he must be the one to escape to Istanbul and tell our people about the plight of Armenians under Soviet rule.

But Vahan refused. He insisted that I was the one who should go. So, disguised again as an American relief worker, I rode a supply train north to Tiflis. Somehow, N.E.R. supervisors smuggled me into the wax-sealed freight car of a train bound for Batum. There, with a gang of other relief workers, I walked aboard a French supply ship. Her sailing whistle blew. My comrades hurried ashore. But I stayed below and hid among the crates and bales of the cargo. The sailors pulled in the gangplank and cast off, and the ship steered west—for Istanbul.

Everyone had told my mother that I must be dead. But she kept insisting that it was not true. Beside the front door in most Near Eastern homes, at about shoulder height, is a small sheltered niche for the burning of the *gantegh*, which is a little oil lamp. When you see one of these burning at night, you know that a loved one is far away. It is a sign that those in the house are thinking of him and anxiously awaiting his return.

Every night since the night so long ago when I had run away, my mother had lighted the *gantegh,* as a symbol of her hope that I would come back safe from the mountain battlefields of Armenia. My Uncle Krikor and Arshag thought that maybe she was losing her mind.

When I arrived in Istanbul, I telephoned the Armenian newspaper, *Azadamard.* They told me that Uncle Krikor was the director of a large Armenian orphanage, housed in a Turkish palace that the Allies had turned over to Armenian relief workers.

Fortunately, I was able to reach him on the telephone.

I asked him to go to Mother's and prepare her for my arrival; it must not be too great a shock. He left the orphanage and went to Scutari. He told Mother that one of my old friends had arrived from Armenia; she was going to enjoy a great surprise later that evening. To get ready for it, she was to cook all the things that her little Shishko had loved—stuffed mussels and okra stew and *topig,* made of garbanzo peas, and *gatahs,* which are fine Armenian cakes.

Uncle Krikor had had to tell my little sister Alene that I was coming home, and she had whispered the news to some of her friends in the neighborhood. So, although it was dark when I climbed the hill to home and stood beside the lighted lamp—a little choked, because I knew who had kept it lighted—I could feel in the darkness that many eyes and faces were watching me as I raised the brass knocker and rapped three times. Alene came flying out the door. She cried my name and threw her arms around me.

Over her shoulder, through my tears, I saw my dear mother, drying her hands on her apron and saying softly, "I knew this day would come. I knew God would be kind—" Then her arms were around me. Neither she nor I could speak.

As usual, it was Uncle Krikor who saved the situation. He herded us all into the dining room and invited everyone to have a glass of wine. I asked if I could be excused and went upstairs and took a bath and dressed up. I put on my *tcherkeska,* the Caucasian Cossack uniform of coarse black wool, and set it off with gold-tipped cartridges and a silver *kinto* belt that I had brought from Tiflis. To make me even more dazzling, Uncle Krikor went to his house next door and brought back a *khanchal*—an engraved Caucasian dagger—to hang on my silver belt.

I was a dashing figure when they were through with me, but I was still starved, and not for food alone. After we ate the wonderful supper Mother had cooked, we sat around the table and laughed and cried and talked, late into the night. For a long time we talked about my brother Arshag and my sister Baidzar, who had gone together to America, where

Baidzar had married a successful tailor named Aram. Mother had read their letters over and over, but I made her read them again, out loud. The letters told how happy they were and how they were living for the day when we could join them. Arshag said he was going to send me money to help me go to America.

Then I told Mother and Uncle Krikor about the Americans I had met—about how kind they were and how strong and just. She pressed my hand. "I want you to go—soon, my son," she said. She smiled down at Alene. "And we shall follow, and Krikor will come, and we'll all be together again in the New World."

Many visitors from the neighborhood came and called the next day to hear my adventures. One was a tall and very shapely girl with blue eyes and light blond hair. Her name was Victoria. I had known her since our school days, but in the five years since then, how she had grown and blossomed!

From the moment I took her hand, I seemed to know that she felt the same way I did. A few days later, when I had a chance to talk with her alone, I told her that while I had been in the Caucasus I had missed very much walking down the promenade of the *Frenginler,* the "Mountain of the French," and sitting under the plane trees and looking out at the castle ruins along the Bosphorus.

"When you go there, could I go with you?" she asked.

"I would love to have you come with me," I replied, and so our romance began.

But soon a letter from Arshag arrived, telling me to hurry to America, to where he was in San Francisco, California. With the letter came some money. That first week in June, 1922, I managed to book passage on the Greek steamer *Meghali Ellas,* which means "mighty Greece." Its destination was New York—and the land of my dreams.

My mother polished the brass *gantegh,* so she could burn it beside the door again for me. Neither of us said anything about it, but I know we were both praying that it would burn, not until I came home again, but until she shut the door of that house forever and started the long journey to me

26

and her other loved ones in America. She stood straight and tall in the doorway that morning, waving good-by. Her shining face was filled with love.

"Until we meet again, my son!" she called.

My little sister Alene buried her face in Mother's skirts. I couldn't say a word. I waved back and hurried down the street, down the hill, for the last time.

An hour after the ship sailed, Turkish *jandarmas*—armed police—pounded on my mother's door. When she answered, they pushed her aside. "We have come for your son," said their leader. "The one who has been masquerading as a Near East Relief worker."

My mother smiled. "Search the house if you wish."

Something in her voice—amusement, or pride, or contempt, or all three—made them hesitate.

"You are too late," she said. "He has escaped you forever."

They thought I had died, that that was what my mother had meant. It was the only way I could escape them that they could think of.

"No," my mother said, still smiling, "he has not died. He has just begun to live."

They ransacked the house from attic to cellar. Then, grumbling, they went away.

CHAPTER THREE

You must picture me some thirty-five years younger, at the age of eighteen. My hair was darker than either my father's or mother's, but my eyes were the brown of my father's. I was tall and—would you believe it?—slender.

A snapshot I remember shows me standing self-consciously against the steerage rail of the *Meghali Ellas,* awkward in my new, store-made suit, my wide-toed, heavy-soled shoes, and the round felt hat that perched squarely on top of my head. You could just barely make out, against the dark wool of my lapel, the tiny boy-scout emblem that I proudly wore at all times.

Although eighteen was my age in actual years and a certain

28

eagerness in my face and bearing showed this, I was rather an old man at heart, having seen so much suffering, so much misery, and so many things that shouldn't happen to human beings—things that resulted from oppression, intolerance, hatred, and the wars and conflicts that my generation, still so young, had already lived through.

There had been quite a few of these: the Italo-Turkish War, the Balkan War, the First World War, the Russian Revolution of 1917, and the Armeno-Turkish War. Then, when my country finally disappeared from the map of Europe, she had the crushing humiliation of being made a state in the U.S.S.R., which she still is today.

Until you know how much blood Armenian patriots shed for freedom, how many children were shot or starved to death during the fight for freedom, and how many brave hopes and ideals were murdered in those last days of the life of Armenia, you will never know how ironic it is that we had struggled and suffered only to have our country handed over to the tyranny of Communist Russia.

I remembered the bitter days, the thousands of brave patriots and the thousand shining dreams that had died.

Do you know that it is hard to grow with all this to think about? You may grow in size, in outward appearance, but inside, your heart stops growing. In those bitter days something was missing from my life. I was forced to do without many things that were rightfully mine as a human being. I was like a tree in an endless winter, without warmth, without sunlight.

The *Meghali Ellas* steamed west across the blue Mediterranean. The days and nights were without wind. It was very hot. The steel sides and deck of the ship made a huge oven. Two or three hundred of us were crowded like cattle in the gloomy hold. We had no berths.

Sometimes we worked. "Hey, you—there! Wash down these decks!" the mate would shout, and we'd scramble for brushes and mops. It was good to have something to do in the fresh air of the deck.

Arshag had sent me the money for my passage and five

29

dollars extra. I became friendly with a Greek, and when he learned I had five dollars, he said that he would make me wealthy. He had been to America before; what he said must be true, I thought.

"I have a bagful of American coins which I will sell you for your five dollars," he said. "They are getting too heavy for me to carry."

Amazed and pleased by his generosity, I pressed the five dollars on him and took the bag of coins. I carried it behind a big coil of rope and counted them. There were 500 of them—all pennies. Later, when I knew the meaning of the word, I could always say that I was one immigrant who didn't arrive in New York "penniless"!

The *Meghali Ellas* plowed slowly across the calm sea. Black smoke poured from her stack. She rocked easily on the long swells, her woodwork creaked, and she carried us all toward our destinations beyond the horizon.

I learned that a whole lifetime can pass by as you sit on the deck with the warm sunlight on your closed lids and listen to the waves and smell the salt air and hear the beat of the old machinery of a ship. We all thought the days would never end, and when it was night it was too hot to sleep; so we lay on the deck and looked up at the low summer stars. An Italian would play softly on his concertina, or my Greek friend would pluck the strings of his *oud*, and sing sad, homesick songs about the hills of Thessaly.

I was very happy and filled with hope and ambition when I thought ahead to the end of the passage and America; yet as the old world vanished on the horizon, I started thinking of all the things I had left behind.

The tall poplars and dusty roads of Armenia in the summertime came back to me; the storks flying high over the Golden Horn to Ayub; the far-off night songs of the *ulufar* fishermen and the little faggot fires that twinkled on the prows of their rowboats as they came down the Bosphorus; the perfume in the air when the laurel and lavender gypsies peddled their seeds and leaves along the Scutari streets; and

30

the poppies in the meadows where Arshag and I used to romp and run.

And as I closed my eyes and the concertina played, I remembered the last night with Victoria and felt again her tears upon my cheek and heard our whispered promises never to forget each other and to be true, always. I could see that she was trying hard to be brave and to show me that she had all the faith in the world in me, that she knew I would make good in America and send for her . . .

The twelve days that seemed endless ended at last. We immigrants stood upon the decks of the *Meghali Ellas* at dawn, struck dumb with awe at the dim, shadowy outline of New York and her famous skyscrapers. What lay ahead of us in this alien land so far from home?

It was very still there on the deck. Sailors passed among us, getting the lines ready and preparing for the arrival at the pier. A light morning breeze blew off the bay. Sea gulls circled and cried. Tugs and other small boats came down the harbor toward us. The bridge of the *Meghali Ellas* was dark. We were standing forward and could see behind its windows the bearded faces of her Greek master and mate and the clean-shaven face of the American pilot.

"Look!—Look!"

A dozen voices cried it at once. There across the water, in the soft, pearly light, was the Statue of Liberty—her crown and torch.

We stood there, unable to speak. Many of us were weeping. This one moment held all the meaning of what we had done. We were the huddled, the oppressed, the poor that she had asked for. We had left our homes and crossed the sea to her, and now here we were at last.

I closed my eyes and prayed, and as I prayed, I thought I heard her speak: "Welcome! Believe in me as I believe in you, for together we are the hope—and dream—of the world!"

Bells clanged. The engines of the *Meghali Ellas* suddenly stopped. The decks were no longer trembling. Then we

31

heard the chains rattling and the anchors plunging into the bay.

The tugs and the other boats came alongside. We were all ready, and eager, to get off. I had my bag of pennies, an overcoat, a package of *lokoum*—our homemade "Turkish delight" candy—that I was going to deliver to General Sebouh in New York, and a straw suitcase that my mother had packed. With the others, I pressed toward the rail.

The Immigration Service men ordered us back.

"All third-class passengers stay below!"

Obediently, we returned to our quarters. The first-class passengers left the ship and then the second-class passengers, and finally a large launch came and took the rest of us to Ellis Island.

The Greek and the others who had already been in the United States grumbled. They resented going to Ellis Island. It did not matter to me. I wasn't afraid, for most of the men in uniform were like the Americans I had met in my own country. Their faces gave me strength and confidence.

"Get in line," they said. "Follow us."

As we entered a huge dormitory-like building, we were shown to our beds. We were handed large white towels and big bars of soap. We were taken to the shower rooms and shown how to work the hot and cold water taps. The attendant spoke several languages.

I had taken showers before, in the barracks at Kars.

"How much hot water can we have?" I asked in French. This was important. You had to know when they were going to cut it off, so you wouldn't be standing there and suddenly get hit with a million stinging needles of ice water.

"How much?" the attendant grinned. "All you want."

I didn't believe him. Surely a guard would come in a moment and scowl at me and make me turn it off. But the minutes passed, and there I was—in heaven!

I began to sing. I stopped singing to splash and laugh, and then sang some more. The soap and the beautiful, plentiful

32

hot water were washing away the sweat and dust and grime of the steerage. I scrubbed harder and harder. I washed away the grime, and I washed away the years. I washed away the Old World. I washed away all the hatred and injustice and cruelty I had known, all the hunger, all the weeping, all the pain.

As I dried myself with the thick, heavy towel, and saw my clean skin and felt my blood tingle, it was as though I had been reborn, as though I were a completely new human being, a taller, stronger, prouder man—an American. Every year since, I have celebrated the day of the Ellis Island shower —July 24—as my birthday.

After the bath we were allowed to visit each other. We were as excited as children. I said good-by to one good friend who told me, "You are not the only one with a brother in the New World. I have a brother here, too. He is a man of importance in Toronto, Canada. See—?"

From his suitcase he took the photograph of a husky young man in a smart, well-cut uniform with gleaming buttons. I raised my eyebrows.

"An official of the city," he said in an offhanded manner, as if it were of no consequence to have such an influential brother. "Regard." He pointed to the tiny brass letters on his brother's cap. They spelled "Motorman," but neither one of us knew what the word meant. "His rank," my friend said carelessly.

I handed the picture back to him and looked his way with new respect. What a fine, modest fellow he was to have for a friend! How proud he was of his brother's success! And how grand his brother looked in his shining cap and polished buttons!

With my hands under my head, I lay on my bed, on the rough, friendly, gray blanket, and looked out the window at the sky over New York. Being up so early and all the excitement and the long warm shower had made me drowsy. I could barely hold my eyes open. But I didn't want to miss the freedom I felt in the air around me and over me and on

33

the other side of the window. The skies of this new land were clearer and bluer than any I had ever seen. I struggled, as long as I could, to stay awake.

It was seven o'clock the next morning when we were taken into the dining room. Now we were all anxious to set foot on our new homeland. A few talked and laughed nervously through breakfast; most of us ate silently and kept our thoughts and feelings to ourselves. They offered us Cream of Wheat—which made me smile and remember the orphanages and *imrig halva*—and oatmeal and eggs, and only two pieces of toast. We Armenians are bread eaters; I could have eaten at least twenty. Some of those who had been in America, like the Greek, had adopted a curious American custom: they poured ketchup over their eggs. How could anyone pour a sauce made of tomatoes—and sour tomatoes at that— over fine, well-cooked eggs?

The attendants let us mingle and look at newspapers. Now, we talked about everything but leaving Ellis Island, because that was what was foremost in our minds. The morning dragged on.

Finally the official called out, "Mardikian!" I knew that the time had come. To me, it sounded as though he had blown a bugle.

I was led to a small examining room, where, at a desk, sat an interpreter who spoke fluent Turkish. Through him they questioned me about my family and my past. They examined my passport from cover to cover. All was in order.

Now, I thought, I could go to New York City and deliver the *lokoum* to General Sebouh, a national hero of the Armenians and a great friend of my father, but the interpreter said, "You cannot go just yet. You have an appointment with some American ladies."

Then I met for the first time those true angels, the ladies of the Travelers Aid Society. I spoke Armenian, Turkish, French, and Russian, but there wasn't a word we could use that both of us knew. In spite of that, I discovered that they spoke a language that I and all the other immigrants could understand—a universal language of kindness.

34

"We have some things for you," their faces and manner said. It was my train ticket to San Francisco and twenty dollars more from my brother, Arshag.

I showed them the letters I had to friends in New York and the *lokoum* for General Sebouh. The ladies shook their heads and pointed to their watches and my ticket. I wouldn't have time to deliver them. My train was leaving too soon.

It was a disappointment, but one soon buried beneath impressions of the great seaport: the blocklike masses of the skyline and the tallest buildings in the world, as we saw them from the deck of the launch that took us up the harbor from Ellis Island; then the noisy, teeming streets of New York; and finally the tremendous size of Pennsylvania Station, with its clocks and rushing crowds, its wide, palatial stairways, and bewildering passageways.

Now there were only a few of us left together, a small handful of the hundreds who had crossed the ocean on the *Meghali Ellas*. My friend the Greek had gone to Brooklyn. I didn't have his bag of pennies any longer. I was such a nuisance to the candy vendors in the station, buying candy and peanuts and then digging down into my penny bag, that one of the Travelers Aid ladies thought I would be better off without it and gave me five dollars for it.

The ladies also gave me some sandwiches and a box of fruit, and pressed my hand. "You are safe now," their smiles were saying. A man from the railroad hung a card in my lapel. It had my name on it and my destination, "San Francisco."

I followed the man and the others down a ramp to a long lighted platform under the ground, where our train stood waiting. I carried my suitcase and overcoat and the box of *lokoum* and a little bundle of neckties that I couldn't get into my suitcase. I found a seat in the coach. The other seats filled. People were saying good-by. Those who were leaving sat in their seats and waved through the windows to their friends and relatives on the platform outside. All at once the car jerked. The train began to move. I pressed my nose against the glass and looked out at the lights and the many

35

tracks. We were on our way. I felt lonely and scared. New York was left behind, but the loneliness remained. There didn't seem to be another passenger who spoke the languages I knew. I kicked myself and blamed my teachers, my parents—everybody. Why couldn't they have taught me English, instead of forcing me to learn Turkish and Russian, as well as Armenian and Greek, by the time I was ten years old?

The trip to San Francisco was to take eight days, and it seemed as though the train were flying. It *was* flying, compared with the trains in Armenia. Several times I had missed an Armenian train. All I had to do was hire a horse and catch up with it.

For my meals and expenses I had Arshag's twenty dollars and almost all the five dollars from my bag of coins, but I spent very little. In the station restaurants, where we coach passengers ate, I saw a curious sight—grownups sitting on stools, eating ice cream by the scoopful or drinking ice-cream sodas. In Europe, ice cream was for children. It was scraped off on a very flat spoon, and there was hardly any of it to a helping. The only item on the menus I could read was "Potato Salad," which in Armenian is *"patates salata."* I didn't have the nerve to ask for anything else. Morning, noon, and night, I ordered potato salad. Usually, it was very bad potato salad. I made up my mind that some day I would invent a better potato salad than they served in railroad-station restaurants in America.

All day long, I flattened my nose against the window, looking out and trying to see everything that was America, or American. Oh, the shining cities and the winding rivers and the green meadows as far as the eye could see! Oh, the sweet villages and the trees and the peace! All day long I looked out the window at the beautiful country.

I must have read my books three or four times on the *Meghali Ellas.* Now, I started them all over again. At night, while the other passengers talked or played cards, I lost myself in Raffi's *Samuel,* which is about the ancient glory of the Armenian nobility in its wars against the Persian hordes

36

—how the Queen Mother of the Bakraduni rallied the Armenian princes and led them into battle against the armored elephants of the Persians.

That is the reason Raffi is so inspiring, and you can read him over and over again. He tells how small people, for the sake of freedom, became giants of courage, defying not only nations but forces a hundred times bigger and stronger than themselves.

And then I would read the nationalistic *Voice of Revenge* by the Armenian poet Varoujan. But the one that was most interesting to me was my third book, Teotig's *Everybody's Almanac*. It told me about everything and everybody, about world personalities and events that had taken place everywhere. It was the almanac for that year, 1922. By the time I reached San Francisco, I knew every article in the book.

There was one moment that I shall never forget, one panic-filled moment when my mind flashed back to the horrors of the sauerkraut factory and the ice packs at Kars. I broke out in a sweat.

The train stopped in Kansas City. As I looked out the window, I saw a bloodcurdling sight. Men in Turkish fezzes and pantaloons were marching by the thousand down the streets of Kansas City toward the railroad station!

My God, the Ottoman Turks! In my terror, I remembered the Cilicians with their scimitar-slashed ears and severed arms. Instinctively, my hand went to my pocket for my protective rock.

But as they approached, I heard the music of their band. It was not Turkish music. Their clothes seemed Turkish, but there was something about them—a newness, a richness of color and material—that I had never noticed in Turkish garments. And their faces—they were light-skinned, most of them. More than this, they all looked too happy to be Turks.

They marched past the station. The band music faded in the distance. I breathed easily once more. When I reached San Francisco, I told Baidzar that I had seen regiments of strange-looking Turks parading past the depot in Kansas City.

37

"Turks?" she repeated, with a puzzled frown.

"Well, I'll admit they didn't act much like the blood-thirsty Turks we have known," I said. "But these men certainly looked like them."

All at once she burst out laughing. "They weren't Turks. They were Shriners. They had a big convention here in San Francisco. The ones you saw must have just arrived home." And she told me all about this organization which does so much good in America and which probably does not have a real Moslem in its entire membership.

People were very kind to me on that long ride. When they walked down the aisle past me, they would lean over and read my name and the words "San Francisco" on the tag in my lapel, and speak to me in English. I could tell by their expressions that they were kind people and interested in a young immigrant who had come so far to make America his home.

The seat was soft and covered with mohair. But as we got closer to San Francisco, it seemed to grow harder and harder. It was so dusty and made my clothes and hands so black that at least ten times a day I went to the washroom and tried to wash my hands under a very difficult faucet that shut off the minute I let go of it. I watched what the others did, and so learned for the first time the trick of filling the metal bowl and then washing in the water that I had trapped in the basin.

Hour after hour, day after day, we traveled west. I had never known a country so big. I had never known a sun so bright, or landscapes so bare. The pioneers crossing it were marvels of courage and adventure.

They were immigrants like me, crossing the country to their promised land, just as I had crossed the ocean to mine. They didn't know what was waiting for them—death from thirst or an Indian's arrow, from cholera, or from blizzards in the mountains. But they went anyway, in their covered wagons, to fight through to their promised land and to build a new home there for themselves and their children. I did not know very much about them and the real hardships they

38

faced, or I would have respected them even more. But I knew that much.

The train reached California. We went through Bakersfield and then Fresno. I wanted to get off there, because even in Scutari we had heard about Fresno—how it was the home of one of the biggest Armenian colonies outside of the homeland. But Arshag and Baidzar were waiting for me in San Francisco.

Through the vineyards and past the rolling wheat fields of the San Joaquin Valley raced the train. In a few more hours we would be there. My old suitcase was packed. My overcoat and bundle of ties and General Sebouh's *lokoum* were on the seat beside me.

I pressed my face against the window and looked out at the rich landscape of California. The sky was that clear, bright blue, and the sun was high and hot, and far to the east I could see the hazy outlines of the Sierra Nevada.

I was proud of something. In a little way, those plains crossers and I were partners. I didn't share their hardships, but I did share their dreams.

Most of them, in their own ways, made those dreams come true. Did I have the same strength and courage? Were there still opportunities left? Could I do what they did? Or was I too late?

A thousand hopes and fears chased through my mind and heart as the train raced north, through the late summer afternoon, toward our destination.

CHAPTER FOUR

On the ferryboat that was taking me across the bay from Oakland to San Francisco I couldn't help thinking of the ferry building in Scutari, near the *iskala*, where many *kayeks* were moored—the long, slender rowboats that cross the Bosphorus to Istanbul.

The charge for the *kayeks* was more than that for the regular ferries—the *shirket* boats—but a ride in a *kayek* was very thrilling. Many times, when my schoolmates and I had twenty cents in our pockets, we would purposely miss the *shirket* in order to go to Istanbul in a *kayek*. If the *kayekji* was a kindly man, he would even let us row.

These *kayekjis* were fearless mariners. Sometimes the strait—a mile or so wide—would be shrouded in dense fog. Nevertheless, they would cross without compasses and without being able to see 3 feet ahead of them. It was a weird trip for us crouched there in the seat—nothing in the watery world of gray but the splashing of oars, the moaning of foghorns, and the thick mist.

Sometimes I would meet my father at the *iskala* when he returned home from work. Instead of taxis you hired *eshegs*, which were donkeys, or horses, with blue beads woven in their manes as charms to ward off the Evil Eye.

Father would swing me up on the horse ahead of him, and the horse would carry us up the hill. How proud I was as we rode along, with the Turkish boys running by our side, to take the horse when we got home and lead him back to the *iskala*. The horse, in my imagination, became a magnificent charger. My father and I, we were knights in armor—Crusaders!

As I stood at the railing of the upper deck on the ferry boat taking me across the bay to San Francisco, I heard the gulls and smelled the salt breeze, just as I had in New York and just as I had so many times back home. It was good to remember the horseback rides in the Scutari dusk. It was like feeling my father's hand on my shoulder.

It was in the evening, Saturday evening. I could see why they called this strait the "Golden Gate." Beyond the channel to the sea, a rich, trembling light—the afterglow of the sunset—filled the sky. Already, lights were twinkling on the hills around the bay. The scene reminded me very much of home, except that there were no minarets on the hills, no domes of mosques, and the city lights were more numerous and much brighter.

The ferry building waiting across the water was all lighted up. Its tower clocks glowed. All above the waterfront, electric signs hung in the air and flashed on and off. Many were colored.

The wind gave off a fresh tang. It was a blessing after the days on the train, the heat of the desert and the long California valley. My heart beat faster. Only this narrowing stretch of water separated me from the warm embraces of Baidzar and Arshag and Baidzar's husband, Aram.

41

A bell rang down below. Timbers cracked and groaned and gave way. The ferry slid along the slip into her berth and, with her wheels foaming in reverse, came to a halt. Gangplank chains rattled. On the deck below, the passengers hurried into the big shed. I picked up my suitcase and coat and packages and followed them.

A moment later, I was in bedlam.

"Hotel St. Francis!—Palace Hotel!—Fairmont!—Step this way! Right this way!" shouted the hotel runners.

"Taxi! Taxi!—Cab, mister?"

"Evenin' pay-puz! Getcha evenin' pay-puz!"

It seemed as though thousands of friends and relatives had come to meet the passengers from the train. While all the shouting was going on and the streetcars clattered away from the loop in front of the ferry building, they were greeting people on all sides, throwing arms around them, laughing and crying, hugging and kissing and talking, all at the same time.

I searched every face. I looked behind every pillar. Nowhere did I see Baidzar's familiar figure or hear Arshag's greeting. Frantically I paced up and down amid the noise and confusion.

There was only one thing to do. All our letters had been sent to the address of the men's shop where Aram worked as a tailor: 48 Powell Street. I found an empty cab and climbed in.

"Where to, mister?"

"Forty-eight Po-vell Street."

The driver stood in the door. " 'Po-vell' Street?" he repeated.

"Po-vell Street."

He shook his head. "Never heard of it, buddy." He glanced at my suitcase and bundles, read the tag in my lapel. Then he grinned. " 'Po-vell' Street, eh?"

The door slammed. We shot out past the streetcar loop into Market Street. Never had I seen so broad a thoroughfare. Four sets of streetcar tracks, two for cars going in one direction and two for cars going in the other. As I looked,

42

the cars raced each other recklessly up and down the street. And the big shop windows, and all the jitneys and autos and people! They made my head swim.

"I think this is your street," said the driver. "Powell Street."

We turned off Market. At the corner, for the first time, I saw the quaint cable cars. One was on the turntable and a man leaned his back against it and pushed it around, like a toy. Half a block farther on, the cab pulled up at the curb. "Forty-eight Powell Street. See if this isn't right."

Yes, there was the sign of the store where Aram worked. I got out of the cab. The driver lifted my suitcase to the sidewalk. I looked more closely at the store. It was dark.

I handed the driver some money. A man standing under the store awning came over to me. He started speaking English. I couldn't understand a word he was saying, but I almost hugged him when I heard him say Aram's name.

"Aram! Aram!" I repeated eagerly.

The cab pulled away and started up Powell Street. My overcoat and ties and General Sebouh's *lokoum* were still in the back seat. I ran after the taxi. "*Sbasse! Sbasse!* [Stop! Stop!]" I shouted.

But the driver didn't hear me. I had carried those things 9,000 miles, and all I could do was stand there on the sidewalk and watch them disappear. I felt like weeping, but what good would that do? I turned back to the man who knew Aram's name.

He took out his watch and gave me to understand that Aram would soon be there to meet me. Sure enough, a few minutes later another taxi stopped at 48 Powell Street. The door opened.

"Baidzar!" I cried.

"Brother!"

My sister smothered me in her embrace. I held her at arm's length. I had to see her to believe she was there. Yes, it was my same dear Baidzar, with her rosy cheeks and laughing dark eyes. As I read the welcome and tenderness in her face, I realized for the first time how much I had missed her.

43

Then Arshag's arms were around me in the Old World greeting of brothers. Arshag, I noticed as I caught my first glimpse of him, had lost weight, and his hair was thinner. His American clothes, for an instant, made me feel awkward and crudely dressed.

And like another brother I greeted Aram, whose face I knew from his picture. He was a heavy-set man with black hair and he wore glasses with black rims. The lenses were very thick and were exact circles. He had on a long gray overcoat that made him look like a comfortably-off business-man or merchant of the middle class.

What had happened? They had gone to meet me at the San Francisco railroad station, at Third and Townsend Streets. They had left Aram's friend there at 48 Powell Street, in case something went wrong.

But it didn't matter now. We were acting just like those people at the ferry building, laughing and crying at the same time, too, right there on Powell Street, in all the lights, hardly noticing the smiling Saturday-evening crowds around us.

The four of us climbed into the back seat of the taxi that had brought Baidzar and Arshag and Aram and rode to the flat where they lived together, at Bush and Webster Streets. It was up three flights of stairs. There were two bedrooms, a living room, a dining room, and a kitchen.

I dropped my luggage and ran through it, exclaiming at the marvels of the New World. Running water! And no sputtering gas mantles, but real electric lights that didn't need any matches! And a wonder of a gas stove, instead of the benzine contraption that we used in Scutari! And a telephone!

"What are you?" I asked, laughing. "Millionaires?"

We were too excited to eat supper. We sat around the dining-room table and celebrated our reunion with cinnamon-flavored tea and white Armenian cheese. We laughed and cried again, and all talked at once. For years after I had gone back to the Caucasus, they had thought I was dead.

It was past midnight when we went to bed. We were all

44

exhausted, but I was very happy—happy because my long journey was over and because I had brought some joy into the lives of my sister and brother and brother-in-law.

Arshag had missed me. Even though I was younger, he always looked upon me as the leader in the family after Father died. I had been out in the world more than he, and he thought I knew more and was more experienced. He regarded me, with a brother's pride, as a man of the world, as one who appreciated the niceties of life, whereas he was too roughhewn to care much for that sort of thing. He, too, was happy that I was there at last. The night I arrived I had my first real rest in eight days, and I was longing just to sleep and sleep. But several times during the night a movement of my blankets awakened me. It was Arshag, bending over me in the dark, covering me up so that I wouldn't catch cold from the night air blowing in from the sea.

The next thing I knew church bells were ringing. The bedroom was flooded with sunshine. I could hear Baidzar calling from the kitchen. "Get up, lazy brother. Breakfast will soon be ready!"

I had taken a bath before going to bed, but now I took another, just to enjoy the luxury of lying there in the tubful of warm water. Then we had breakfast—my first taste of bacon and eggs, cooked American-style in a home kitchen, and some beautiful, light, flaky pastry that Arshag had bought in a German bakery on Fillmore Street.

More alert now and rested, I listened carefully to all the spoken and unspoken things that passed between Baidzar and Aram. I noticed their smiles and gestures, the quality of them, as you must if you are to know what they really mean. What I sensed about them made me very happy. When I tell you the story, you will know why.

Aram was much older than I or Baidzar or any of us had been led to believe by the picture we had seen in Scutari. Aram was a *Bitlistzi*, a native of Bitlis, a town in lower Armenia, west of Lake Van. He had fled to the United States after the first Armenian massacres, in 1896 or 1897. He had then been about sixteen.

45

He had been a tailor's apprentice in Bitlis, but in California he settled near Fresno and worked hard in the fields and eventually bought 20 acres of vineyards of his own. In the depression that followed the First World War, he decided he could make more money in the city. So he turned his vineyard over to his brother, Puzant, and moved to San Francisco and took up his old trade again. It went well with him. There was only one thing wrong: he was lonely.

Aram had a distant cousin, named Haroutun Kermoyan, who owned the flower stand on the corner of Geary Street and Grant Avenue. This cousin had been in America for many years, but he could speak only seven words in English: "Lady, this flower is just like you."

Aram's cousin made his living off these seven words. To any woman who passed his stand, whether she was a pretty girl of eighteen, a stout, middle-aged tourist, or a tottering great grandmother, he held out a rose or a carnation. He bowed and smiled. And then he said, as though he had a mouthful of sugar, "Lady, this flower is just—like—you."

The ladies bought his flowers by the dozen, and so he made his living.

This cousin, in 1921, decided to return to Scutari to marry his childhood sweetheart, who lived not far from my mother's house.

"I wish I were going with you," Aram said. "If I could only marry a nice Armenian girl, life would be complete."

Aram's cousin was shrewd. "If you cannot go, we will do the next best thing. I shall take your picture with me."

For members of various racial minorities in California and other states, this way of arranging marriages was not unusual. Later I discovered that even Americans, the Forty-niners, had done it during the Gold Rush.

But this practice had been the cause of much misery. Sometimes the men in America lied. A shoeshine man or a small florist or a very small farmer would send a twenty- or thirty-year-old picture of himself back home to the old country and write that he was a wealthy businessman. Then his relatives would find a girl for him and show her the photo-

46

graph. She would go all the way to America—California, perhaps—and marry him, only to move into some shack or one-room tenement apartment. To most of these girls, marriage was a sacred institution. In spite of the lies, they stayed married and brought up their families as best they could, although they were cheated out of many of the joys of life.

So the day came that summer in 1921 when Haroutun Kermoyan had been introduced to my mother and Baidzar. He showed them the picture of Aram. In the photograph he was a fine-looking young man of about twenty-four or twenty-five.

"My cousin is a God-fearing, Christian man," Haroutun Kermoyan said. "He is a prosperous professional man in San Francisco. He will make a very good husband for your daughter."

My mother had many misgivings, but at length she drove a bargain with Haroutun Kermoyan and his cousin in San Francisco. She wanted her son and daughter to have the opportunities of the New World, but only in an honorable fashion. This was the bargain she made: The cousin, Aram, would pay the fares of both Baidzar and Arshag all the way to San Francisco. If Baidzar liked him and wanted to marry him, and Arshag approved, she would become his bride, and the debt would be canceled. But if Baidzar did not want him, Arshag would go to work and pay Aram back every penny it had cost to bring them to America.

My heart sank when I first saw Aram that night on Powell Street. He was at least twenty years older than his picture. But I knew that Arshag had given his approval; so I decided to wait and see for myself.

And now, this Sunday morning, as I saw them together at the breakfast table after more than a year of marriage, I could tell that they were really in love.

"Baidzar!" I said sharply. She looked across the table at me, over her coffee.

"Yes, brother." Her brown eyes were serious. Something had displeased me.

47

"You are a young woman, twenty-five years of age, and have been married for more than a year—is that not so?"

"Yes, brother, it is so."

"Then tell me this: Why have you no children?"

Arshag glanced at me and winked. Aram shifted in his chair and looked both pleased and embarrassed. Baidzar's lovely red cheeks grew redder and redder. All at once, we began laughing together. We laughed until the tears came to our eyes. Something told me that pretty soon there would be a baby in this house. (And before too long there was—my little niece, Mary.)

I wanted to see the Pacific; so we took a Sutter Street car. It was a bright, beautiful Sunday, and the car was crowded with families on their way to Ocean Beach. First we passed streets and houses and then mile after mile of sand dunes. But at last we reached the end of the line—the carbarn by the Sutro Baths and the Cliff House.

The sunlight flashed to the west, and I started to run down to the Cliff House, so that I could see the ocean.

"Wait!" called Arshag. "It's better from up there." He pointed across the road to a parklike bluff.

A strange warm smell filled the air. Aram went to a booth and paid some money and came back with paper bags filled with rich-smelling white stuff. I had my first unforgettable taste of popcorn.

We crossed the highway and climbed to the summit of the heights. Statues stood in groups, white against the trees. The gravel drives were neat and clean. Flowers bloomed. It was like walking through a palace garden. The mansion had burned down, Arshag told me, but this beauty remained for all the people to enjoy. Mr. Sutro, the millionaire whose estate it had been, was an immigrant from Germany, Arshag said.

By a parapet that might have crowned a height at Tchamlija, overlooking the Bosphorus, we stood and gazed west to the shining Pacific. In spite of its name and the gentle day, the breakers came rolling in and pounded themselves against Seal Rock and the rocks below the Cliff House,

48

and against the long beach that stretched south as far as we could see.

We could hear barking above the sound of the surf. It came from the sea lions on Seal Rock, Baidzar said.

"Well," Arshag said, "there is the Pacific."

His voice rang with pride. He was inhaling deep, slow breaths of the sea air. There was a smile on his lips. It does not take long to become an American, and proud of the things that are America's.

"Yes—there is the Pacific," I said with a tone that tried to match his. But my heart was strangely heavy as I spoke. I was remembering the day, long ago, when my mother and Uncle Krikor took us from Tiflis to Batum. At Batum we got into a horse-drawn carriage and started for our lodgings. All at once we rounded a corner and there, reaching from the end of the street to the end of the world, was the Black Sea. It burst upon us all at once, as if God had suddenly given a cry. I could never understand, and never begin to describe, the feeling that I had when I saw that beautiful sea for the first time. Now, I was waiting to feel something like that here, on the edge of the Pacific. But it didn't come.

"Don't you like it?" Aram asked.

"Yes, of course. It is very beautiful," I replied. But Aram knew I was disappointed.

Was there something wrong with me?

The people on the streetcar had disappointed me—all those mothers and fathers, and children, too, chewing gum as fast as they could and talking at the same time. In Europe this was very bad manners. And now this let-down feeling, this heavy weight in my heart about the ocean. I don't know what I had expected, but it had been something wonderful and special and romantic—something flashing, with waves of the deepest blue and foaming snow-white crests, like the manes of the snow-white stallions of Xanta; something with the hint of the South Seas about it; something with the air of the Orient; something with the movement and life of ships and sails on it. But not this emptiness, this flat, gray-green emptiness, this desert of water.

49

We left the heights and walked through the amusement park and along the beach. The farther we went, the more shocked and disappointed I was. To the others, I smiled as best I could and agreed with the observations they made, but inside I was getting angry. Were they blind?

Here were adult men and women doing the most childish things—racing up and down the chutes, talking, laughing, screaming at the top of their lungs. They were throwing balls at wooden milk bottles in canvas-covered stalls and walking around with dolls under their arms and carrying toy balloons. Across the highway on the sands of the beach grownups played leapfrog and chased each other in and out of the water.

Were these the Americans, the brave, gentle, generous Americans that the missionaries and the relief workers had told us about? the liberty-loving Americans who had fought for and won their independence? the courageous Americans who had crossed the plains? the warmhearted Americans who, at that very moment, were helping to feed hundreds of thousands of starving Europeans?

I was shocked and hurt and angry, all at the same time. I couldn't believe my eyes. These people—my American heroes—were clowns. How could I have made so tragic a mistake?

Aram knew. "George does not like America."

"I do!" I protested, trying to make my words sound honest and sincere.

Aram shook his head and looked disgusted.

We started home through Golden Gate Park. For a moment there was a sharp feeling of gratitude at the sight of the buffalo and deer and elk; they were roaming free across a green meadow instead of being locked up in cages the way they were in Europe. They looked healthy and contented.

Arshag showed me the statue of General Pershing. "It was done by a countryman of ours, Haig Patigian, who is now a famous San Francisco sculptor," he said.

That made me proud for a bit, but I could not shake myself out of this depression. Even when Baidzar came and put her

50

hand in mine and smiled at me, I could only look at her helplessly and try not to show my disappointment and my misery.

"He does not even appreciate this beautiful park," Aram said bitterly. "Come—let us go home and have our supper."

We walked in silence beneath the eucalyptus trees. We came to a little glen. Down at its end were two picnickers, a boy and a girl. They had finished eating and sat close together, leaning back against the trunk of a tree. They had their arms around each other and were kissing. I knew they could hear our footsteps, but they just stayed that way. It was a shameless thing that Armenians would never do.

I asked Arshag, "Is this the way they behave?"

He shrugged. "They're harmless. They know when to stop."

I thought his reply cynical. It all made me sadder than I had ever been. At the end of the walk, at Fulton Street, we got on a streetcar and went home.

Baidzar started setting the table for supper. I think she was going to prepare some of the Armenian dishes she knew I loved. This tenderness, now, would have been more than I could stand.

"Please forgive me, sister, and excuse me," I said. I went to my bedroom and shut the door.

I heard the murmuring tone of Aram's voice, and I knew that he was reproaching me. Then Baidzar defended me. She said I was exhausted from my long journey and upset and probably homesick. Maybe I would feel better in a few days. Arshag said nothing. I knew he was disappointed, too —in me and in the way I silently judged and condemned these people he had come to love.

Hour after hour I lay in the dark. I tossed from side to side. Could I accept these people? Did I want to? Was it only the Americans abroad who were serious and dignified and respectable, like Dr. Voris and Mr. Rankin and Captain Brown? And were the Americans who stayed at home all clowns and children who never grew up?

When daybreak came, I could stand it no longer. I got out

of bed and dressed, crept silently down the stairs, and went into the street. I wanted to walk and walk and walk, and become so exhausted that I would go to bed and sleep until all this disappointment had gone away.

I walked south a block, to the Sutter Street car line that we had taken to the beach the day before. After you have traveled a great deal, you learn that one of the best ways to keep from getting lost in a strange city is to follow a street-car line, so that when it is time to return, you can retrace it back to your starting point. I walked down Sutter Street toward Van Ness Avenue. It was another clear, bright morning. The sun was already in the sky, but the old houses were still asleep. The drawn blinds of their bay windows made them look as if there eyes were closed.

At the end of the block, I saw a man in the gutter with a broom.

"Even here in this great country of America," I said to myself, "they cannot get along without the lowly street sweeper."

As I came alongside him, I stared in amazement. He looked happy. And he was humming a tune. I was stunned. A man in such a job and happy about it?

Two big policemen strode down the street toward me. Perhaps they had been working together on the night shift and now were on their way home. They were big, brawny men and swung their clubs and walked with a swagger, as though they were proud of their uniforms. They had smiling blue eyes.

"Good morning," they said pleasantly, as they passed me.

I smiled back. I was feeling better. I had never heard of policemen who smiled before.

By the time I reached the end of the next block, more people were in the streets. A scavengers' truck went by, loaded to the top after a night's work. High on the rubbish sat three fellows with flowers in their hats, singing "Santa Lucia." They waved at me. Then I noticed men in working clothes coming out of the houses and down the side streets with lunch pails in their hands. They laughed and talked among themselves and hurried to the corners to catch the streetcar. The streetcar swayed and clattered toward us. The motorman waved and stamped his footgong, not to warn everybody that he was coming, but just to make music.

At a house on the corner of Octavia Street, I saw what to me was the most wonderful sight of all. A milk wagon stopped before an old-fashioned San Francisco home that had ten or twelve steps leading up to the front door. Out stepped a young milkman. He was bareheaded and whistling a gay tune. He took two bottles of milk from his rack and ran up the stairs. Without even knocking, he left the milk on the porch beside the front door. It stood there, white and precious, for anyone to steal and carry off. Without so much as a backward glance the milkman went whistling on his way. Was it safe? In my heart, I knew that it was. And in my heart, I knew that out of all the people I had seen on the street that morning, I was the only one who would ask that question.

My head began to spin. I stopped in the middle of the sidewalk and turned around and looked back down the street. Sounds began running through my brain, one by one, then all mixed up together: the humming of the happy street sweeper, the pleasant "Good morning" of the two smiling policemen, the clanging of the motorman's gong on the crowded streetcar, the running footsteps of the men hurrying to work, the happy voices of the scavengers, the cheerful clip-clop of the milk wagon's horse, and the quick, gay tune that its driver was whistling.

They all mingled in my ears into the most beautiful music that I had ever heard. All at once, standing there in the bright morning sunlight on the street of that lovely city, I understood. I was hearing the song America sings. I was hearing the Song of America.

I turned around and started running. I wanted to shout my new happiness to all the world. Before I knew it, I was back at our house and racing up the stairs two at a time. I burst into the living room. Baidzar came out of the kitchen. She seized my hands. "George! Where have you been?"

53

"Nowhere, sister—nowhere and everywhere! All over America!"

I threw my arms around her. "Give me a kiss!" I started singing in Armenian. I danced her around the room.

"Get Arshag. Get Aram, and tell him I apologize for yesterday."

Baidzar looked at me, wide-eyed.

"I'm all right, sister, I'm all right. I've just heard the most beautiful music in the world—the Song of America. No more sad songs for me, only happy American songs. And do you know something?—They aren't crazy over here. It's the people in Europe who feel so sorry for themselves that are the crazy ones."

Aram stood there with a big smile on his face, and Arshag threw his arms around me and hugged me, and over his shoulder I shouted, "All I want is to be an American— another happy American!"

CHAPTER FIVE

Aram's sister's name was Apisag. She was the wife of Mampre Korkmaz, a successful businessman of Fresno. Korkmaz means "fearless," and that is what everybody called him.

When he heard of my arrival, Korkmaz came to San Francisco and stayed two weeks at his brother-in-law's. His only reason for coming was to ask me questions about Armenia and talk about the old country. Although he had lived in the United States for many years, he, too, like Haroutun Kermoyan, could speak only one sentence in English. All Korkmaz could say was, "That's all right."

Korkmaz was a delightful person, but he might as well have been back in Bitlis. He spoke Armenian with other *Bitlistzis* all day long. He had been a trustee of the Armenian

55

church in Fresno for many years and attended all the functions of the Armenian colony. But I don't think that he ever went to an American theater or political rally or sporting event. Nor did any of those who were like him.

While Korkmaz was staying in San Francisco, he decided to go to Oakland to collect $150 that a man had owed him for a long time. He had the man's address on a piece of paper, and he took me with him.

It was my first trip to Oakland. We left the ferry and rode for miles on a streetcar. The conductor told us where to get off. With the paper in my outstretched hand, I would approach a pedestrian, hold it out and say, "Please—where?"

The pedestrian would point and motion and talk, all at the same time. I would bend forward, trying to understand what he meant. Then Korkmaz, right behind me, would bob his head and say politely, "That's all right. That's all right."

The pedestrian would smile back at him as if to say, "Well, I'm glad *you* understand, anyway," and then go his way. And we would be just as much in the dark as before. Finally we went home without ever finding the man who owed Korkmaz the $150.

It took days to get adjusted to San Francisco. At first I walked the streets and up and down the steep hills by the hour looking for silver dollars, for I had been told in Europe: "All you have to do over there is walk around and pick up money in the streets." Naturally, I did not expect to find a fortune lying in the gutter—just a dollar or two, or maybe five. Anything was possible in America.

During my walks I learned about the city and about Americans. One day, in Golden Gate Park, I rounded a curve in the path and came upon a fist fight between two boys about fourteen. One was short and wiry and had red hair. The other was rangier and clumsy, and his nose was bleeding. The redhead put his head down and bored in. His flying fists hit the big fellow on the chin and down he went.

To my astonishment I saw the redhead bend down, take the other fellow's hand, and help him to his feet. He took

56

out his handkerchief and held it to the fellow's nose. With their arms around each other's shoulders, they went to a bench. Half crying and half laughing, they began talking, each asking the other if he was all right. It was all over—the tension, the anger, the desire to hurt and conquer. They were friends again.

They showed me something I had never seen before. If the fight had happened in my country, the redhead would have jumped on the other fellow, or kicked him, to make sure he stayed down. But this was the American way. This was the way of forgive and forget.

When more than a week went by and I hadn't found a single penny, I realized that I couldn't go on being a burden to Aram and Baidzar and Arshag. I would have to get a job.

My friend Vahram Yeramian got me work washing glasses at Coffee Dan's. I worked from 7 P.M. until 7 A.M. and had every other Sunday off. For those twelve hours every night I washed glasses—by the thousand, it seemed—under hot running steam. Every hour or so the boss would check up on me. He would glance at the back of my jacket. If it wasn't damp with sweat, he would growl, "You ain't got enough to do." Soon the waiters would bring me dishes to wash, too. But how could I complain? Wasn't I earning a fortune— twelve dollars a week?

Coffee Dan's was a flight of steps below the sidewalk on O'Farrell Street, next door to Powell. It was a prohibition night-life restaurant that specialized in ham and eggs, "country" style, and hamburgers on buns. But it was also a speakeasy. San Franciscans flocked there all night long to drink bootleg wine and whisky in coffee cups. They loved to sing and beat on their tables with little wooden hammers.

The sound of them still knocking in my ears would keep me awake in the mornings when I went to bed. Even more than that, I couldn't forget the sight of full orders of ham and eggs and sandwiches being thrown away because the patrons who had asked for them had lost their appetites or decided they weren't hungry after all. I used to remember the hungry orphans of Alexandropol, and get on my knees

57

beside my bed and ask God to find some way to send this wasted food to Europe.

Down O'Farrell Street a block, at the corner of Stockton (where Macy's stands today), was Clinton's Cafeteria. I heard they were paying dishwashers thirteen dollars a week. I went to my boss and asked permission to leave Coffee Dan's for this better job. To my surprise he grinned cheerfully. "I'm too much of a slave driver for you, eh? Well, go ahead and take it. I don't blame you."

I knew that I would never have a chance to become a real American—to act and talk and think like an American—until I could speak with other Americans. And you don't get much of a chance to practice the language washing dishes twelve hours a day, and I still had to work this long even after I left Coffee Dan's for Clinton's Cafeteria.

There was no time, of course, to go to school. My only schooling those first months was in the Alcazar Theater, where Miss Winter and her husband, Henry Duffy, had their theater company. Holbrook Blinn starred in a Mexican bandit play. Leo Carrillo played in *Lombardi, Ltd.* I paid twenty-eight cents for a seat high in the peanut gallery and saw the shows over and over again, so I could hear English spoken.

Some evenings I bought the cheapest seat at the Orpheum Theater, across the street from Coffee Dan's. My favorite star was Fanny Brice. How I cheered when she came on the stage as a Russian immigrant with a shawl over her head, like the immigrants I had seen on Ellis Island. I loved her unhappy melodies and her wailing songs. They were actually supposed to be very funny. The audience howled with laughter. But they struck me in a different way, and while the rest of the people doubled over laughing, I sat there and cried my heart out. I could not tell you why it was. And I used to think that many of those who were laughing were really laughing to keep back the tears.

About a month after I arrived, Aram's mother came from Fresno and moved in with Aram and Baidzar. Although Baidzar did not want us to leave, Arshag and I found a room

58

for ourselves. It had one double bed. It was on Ellis Street near Buchanan.

Arshag was a fine shoemaker, an artist in leather who made gentlemen's boots that cost seventy and eighty dollars a pair. When I came home from work, it was time for him to get up. The first year of my stay in San Francisco I can say was the year that I never got into a cold bed.

But it was a long trip from our room to the restaurant, and the day came when I wanted to live downtown, closer to my job. So I moved into the Fairfax Hotel. My room cost $2.50 a week. I got meals free at the restaurant, and sent my mother $5.00 a week. That left $5.50 to spend on clothes, theater tickets, meals on my nights off, and everything else.

My friend Vahram Yeramian, who always wanted to be an actor, lived at the Fairfax. I had known him in Scutari. His brother and I, in fact, played together in the Raffi Band of Scutari. I love music, but I cannot read a note or carry a tune. I got into the Raffi Band by playing a tuba. All I had to do was go, "Oom-pah! Oom-pah! Oom-pah!"

Vahram was a carpenter and cabinetmaker, but never in your life did you see Vahram in coveralls. He rushed to the hotel after work and took a bath and immediately dressed up like a fashion plate and went out. He would rather pretend that he was an actor and tell people that someday he was going to Hollywood and be a big star than be proud that he was one of the best cabinetmakers in San Francisco.

Though he got older and older, he never gave up this daydream. I can imagine that when he got killed on Wake Island during the war, the bitterest thing to him about the bullet was that it ended his beautiful dream. It deprived him forever of "someday."

You must not think of the Armenian colony in San Francisco as a separate little community within a community, like the Italian settlement of North Beach, for instance. It was just the opposite. Armenians were spread all over the city. Some seem to have lost their way. They were the paradoxes. They were very proud of America and proud to be Americans, but somehow they lacked the ambition or whatever it took to jump into American life and sink or swim. So they continued to speak Armenian, put off learning English, and went around feeling somehow disappointed or cheated. They were people without a country.

While I did not think that I had earned my place as an American yet, I still did not feel right among these who hung back, who clung to the shore and would not get into the swim. So I joined the others, who were trying to adapt themselves and give something to America. These people were happier.

One of the bright spots in the day-to-day life of these Armenian-Americans was the talented Mrs. Melikian and her family. Mrs. Melikian, her beautiful daughter, Varia, and Varia's husband were stars of the Armenian theater who had escaped the Bolsheviks, fled to America, and settled in San Francisco. From time to time they staged plays in a hall on Fulton Street. The small admission fees were their only livelihood.

Once the play was Shirvanzadeh's *Tcharvoki*. I played the part of "Crazy Dan." In this role I loved a little girl who reminded me very much of my own daughter who had been killed in a terrible Armenian earthquake. My daughter's name had been Manoushag, and although this little girl's name wasn't Manoushag, I always called her that and took her presents of nuts, raisins, and figs.

Unfortunately, she had a foster mother who made her life miserable. Every time I heard the little girl crying, it was more than I, Crazy Dan, could bear. I would creep near her door and, to soothe her, would strum on my Armenian *taar* and sing to her:

> *Yes bulbul nem Gulistani bagheroun,*
> *Yes baykhoush nem Daghistani lerneroun!*
> (I am the nightingale of the Armenian meadows,
> I am the owl of the Daghistan peaks!)

When this failed to quiet the poor little girl, I would roar, "*Manoushagis tebchogin badar badar gunem! Hoom hoom goodem!* [Whoever touches or hurts my Manoushag will be mincemeat! I'll tear him to pieces! I'll eat him raw!]"

In the midst of this scene opening night I became so carried away that I seized Vahram, who was playing the part of the girl's father, and threw him down on the floor and started choking him. I banged his head against the boards. Finally he tore himself loose. "I've had enough," he said. "I'm through."

With great presence of mind, Mrs. Melikian rang down the curtain. Out front, the audience applauded. They thought it a wonderful scene, the climax of the second act. I apologized to Vahram.

"I really didn't mean it," I said. "I just forgot myself and was showing what I would do to anyone who hurt my Manoushag."

But Vahram started pulling off his costume. His eyes flashed. "No! This is the end!"

"Please, Vahram," begged Mrs. Melikian, "I implore you —this is the biggest crowd we've ever had. Almost 110 people, and we've never had more than 50 before. Please, Vahram! George didn't mean it—"

Vahram could not resist her. He put on the jacket of his costume, I gave him my solemn promise that Crazy Dan would never touch his throat again, and the play went on.

These plays entertained us and helped Mrs. Melikian and her daughter and son-in-law pay their bills, but the real reason for them was that we hoped Americans would come to see them. Then maybe they would understand and make real friends out of the Armenian people in their midst.

We found another way of trying to win this understanding: we organized the Masis Club. Mount Ararat, Armenia's Biblical mountain, has two peaks, one called "Little Masis" and the other called "Big Masis." To Armenians "Masis" is a symbol of a height, a peak that you scale, a goal that you work for and strive to achieve, something big, something wonderful, some beautiful ideal or dream to which you dedicate the best there is in you.

We tried hard to live up to this symbol, and what we were

trying to achieve was a pure understanding between the living America—the America of homes and streets and industries and schools and churches—between that and us. We wanted to be part of it all, and at the same time we wanted Americans to know us and our background and culture better.

We were very proud of our Armenia. She had fought for freedom for hundreds of years. So when we were invited to take part in a great international festival, we were both honored and eager to do our part.

But I ran into trouble right away. We wanted everyone to know that, with all her centuries of history, Armenia was keeping up with the times.

"We have no better way of doing this," I told our committee, "than to present a group of Armenian boy scouts. I know. I have just come from Armenia last year. I will train them myself."

My friend Armenag Hairenian, the Sacramento Street coppersmith, made me twelve belt buckles for my twelve scouts. Each buckle had the "Little Masis" and the "Big Masis" of Mount Ararat stamped on it. On their caps Baidzar stitched the motto of the Armenian Boy Scouts: *Partsratzir, Partsratsour!*, which means, "Excelsior!" or "Ever upward."

One evening I got my boys together—all American-born sons of Armenian parents—and hiked with them to Alta Plaza, a grassy park on Pacific Heights. I placed them in formation. Then, like a drill sergeant, I bellowed orders.

"*Badrasd!* [Attention!] *Haratch!* [Forward march!]"

Not one of them moved.

"*Haratch!!!*"

Still no one budged. Several evening strollers stopped to watch.

"*Kayl Haratch—Onn!!!*" I roared. This was really telling them to "forward march."

My boy scouts couldn't hold it in any longer. They fell on the ground and rolled in the grass, they were laughing so hard at me, standing there yelling like a bull in Armenian. When I realized how ridiculous I must have looked and

62

sounded, I couldn't keep a straight face, either. I laughed as hard as they did. They turned around and taught *me* the American commands. We made a fine showing on the day of the festival.

We had made big plans for a glorious Armenian program. We brought Zarouhi Elmasian, "the Armenian nightingale," from Fresno. Our big tableau was going to represent the four major dynasties of Armenia. The main character would be the great King Haig, played by Misag Kermoyan, Haroutun's cousin. He was also a florist, and a huge, strapping fellow. In the armor and helmet that we rented for him at Goldstein's costume shop on Market Street, he looked just like King Haig.

All along he had refused to march. At the dress rehearsal, we saw why. He had fallen arches. His big feet were as flat as pancakes, and in his heavy costume he plodded along like an elephant. We made a throne for him to sit on all through the festival. It wasn't illogical, we argued. After all, King Haig was the greatest king Armenia ever had. Why shouldn't he sit on a throne?

Vahram was a prince of the Mamigonian dynasty, and our Mother Armenia, without which no patriotic Armenian observance would be complete, was played by the statuesque Mrs. Calfayan, wife of the tailor at the Fairmont Hotel. My assignment could not have made me happier. After I was through drilling the boy scouts, I was to carry the Armenian flag, for which I had fought on the battlefields of the Caucasus. Before the thousands upon thousands who would witness the festival, I was to hold the tricolor of Hayastan aloft, for all to see and remember as a symbol of her brave struggle for freedom.

The day before the festival, I went to Dan Attell, the manager of Clinton's Cafeteria. I explained about the pageant and my part in it. "And now," I said, "I am here to ask you for tomorrow off.

He smiled. "George, I'm sorry. This festival has brought many tourists to San Francisco. I need every man."

Mr. Attell was a wonderful person. He had been very

63

good to me. It took me a moment to understand. "You aren't going to let me off—?"

He shook his head.

I threw my chest out, my shoulders back. "But I am to carry the flag of Armenia—the tricolor of Hayastan!"

"I can't help it, George. I need every man."

I held myself even straighter. "All right, then, Mr. Attell. I quit!" I strode out of his office and slammed the door after me.

The next day, there was no prouder—and no poorer—flag bearer in all the International Festival than the fellow that carried the tricolor of Hayastan.

They say that things happen for the best. I believe it; I know it's true. Three days after the festival, I got a better job than ever at Compton's Cafeteria, at Kearny, Geary, and Market Streets. Here they paid me eighteen dollars a week, with every other day an eight-hour day instead of a twelve-hour day. That was more than I had dreamed possible.

I worked hard. I kept remembering the thoughts I had had on the train about the pioneers and the promised land and opportunities. I studied nights—or days, when I worked nights—because I wanted to be an American, a genuine American like those pioneers.

Once a counterman called me a foreigner. I invited him down into the cellar. He was bigger, but I was mad. He had no right to call me a foreigner. My people and I had gone through a great deal to make me an American. I knocked him back against a big plate-glass mirror. It shattered into a hundred pieces.

"There goes my job," I thought.

When Eugene Compton, the owner, found out about it, he went up to the fellow. "I hear you called George a foreigner and you had a fight and broke the mirror in the basement."

The fellow said that was right.

Mr. Compton said, "Did George give you a good beating?"

The fellow grinned. "He sure did."

"George—" Mr. Compton turned to me. "Forget about

64

the mirror." He walked away and never mentioned it again.

The fellow I beat up and I met halfway across the kitchen. We shook hands. From that moment on, he was one of my best friends.

When Mr. Compton opened another cafeteria at Ellis and Powell Streets, he sent me there with the hope that I might work myself up to counterman. "You can, if you will learn English," he said.

Not long afterward, one of the countermen didn't show up for work. The manager came back into the kitchen.

"George," he said, "get behind the counter. Start serving the customers."

You can imagine my happiness.

But you can imagine my embarrassment, too. I still couldn't speak English very well. Anyway, I had my lifesaver—my ability to smile. When, at three the next morning, I put on my hat and coat and walked down the street to the Fairfax, I scarcely realized that I had worked twenty hours that day. I was walking on air.

All the way down the street, I practiced calling orders: "Vee-al Coot-let! Corn-ud Bee-uf Hush! Pasht Ekks! Butt-red Toss-t!"

Every day after that I practiced calling orders in my hotel room, until the people in the rooms nearby hammered on the radiator pipes to make me stop annoying them.

Perhaps you think I'm exaggerating the trouble I had with English, but I assure you that this matter of speech is an important thing. When you are a native of your country, you take your language for granted. You do not think about how necessary it is to understand others and make them understand you because you have been able to do this from nursery days on. But learning to use a new language is very hard. It takes years of work. Many immigrants do not try. To them it's not worth the effort. But they, in the long run, are the losers.

I served the customers who went to work early in the morning. I always gave them free with their breakfast a cheery "Good morning" and a smile.

65

One man in particular always ordered oatmeal, buttered toast, and coffee. Whenever I saw him coming, I got his tray ready for him. As the days went by, he began striking up conversations with me. I tried to follow him. He talked very earnestly. He used long words which I did not understand. All I could do was nod every once in a while and say, "Yes, sir," or shake my head and say, "No, sir." Sometimes, when it seemed appropriate, I would say Korkmaz' words, "That's all right."

One day he slowed down, then stopped altogether. He glared at me. "Can't you say anything but 'Yes' or 'No'? Is that all you can say?" He brought his fist down on the table and spilled coffee all over his tray. All I could do was stammer, "I—I'm very sorry."

It happened that I was put on night duty after that, and for a long time I did not see this customer. Finally, Mr. Compton promoted me to the position of night manager. A morning came when the day manager did not come to work, and so I stayed on duty. At his usual hour, I saw my old customer enter the cafeteria. I beat him to the counter and gave his order: oatmeal, buttered toast, and coffee.

"Would you mind," I asked, "if I had coffee with you?"

He gave no sign that he remembered me. But he said, "Not at all."

We sat down near the window. "You don't remember me," I said, "but about six months ago you became very upset when I couldn't answer you and speak English with you."

Now he knew who I was! He laughed. "Why, yes! But I wasn't mad at you. I was mad at myself. I was running for supervisor and trying to drum up a few votes from you and your friends. Suddenly I realized how much time and effort I had been wasting because you didn't even understand what I was talking about."

He held out his hand. "I'm sorry I blew up. My name's Havenner—Franck R. Havenner. Maybe you'll vote for me some day, when you're a citizen and I'm running for Congress." I did, and he won, and went to Washington.

Even then, I made mistakes. When silverware was needed

at the counter, the counterman would call, "Silver's out!" and then more knives, forks, and spoons would be brought from the kitchen. It seemed to me that this was grammatically wrong. The next time we ran out of silverware I cleared my throat and announced loudly, "Silvers are out!" Everybody in the restaurant, help and patrons alike, looked at me and laughed.

I never said it that way again. And that is the way life is. Sometimes you must be hurt in order to remember.

CHAPTER SIX

One of the first things I had done on reaching America was to send a long, long letter to Victoria that I had written on the *Meghali Ellas,* so many pages each day. Then, on the train to Philadelphia, I wrote her my first letter from America.

And so it went all the way across the country. Each day I wrote to Victoria, sometimes just a page, sometimes four or five pages, or even more. I wanted to share America with her, and this thrilling adventure. I wrote to my mother, too, telling her that I was well and safe, but the letters I wrote my sweetheart were filled with love and enthusiasm and promises. They were touched with sadness, too, because every second the speeding train was taking us farther and farther apart.

But at last, I wrote triumphantly from San Francisco, the

68

journey was over; no longer was a ship or train taking me away. I covered page after page with impressions of San Francisco. I shared with Victoria cable cars and the beautiful palm trees of Union Square, hills and the summer fog that drifted up the bay, the pagodas and tinkling wind bells of Chinatown, all the motorcars, the splendor of the shop windows, the lovely mansions of Pacific Heights, the beautiful trees and meadows of Golden Gate Park and the tall, tall buildings downtown.

Then, when I had finished telling her about all these things, I had to tell her of my undying love for her, of my loneliness, and of how I longed to look into her blue eyes and whisper the things I was writing, and how I yearned to caress her light, lovely hair.

One morning, worn out after twelve hours at Coffee Dan's, I fixed Arshag's coffee. I could hardly keep my eyes open.

"Why don't you go to bed?" he asked.

"I want to, but I can't."

"Why not?"

"Victoria."

He put down his cup and looked at me severely. "You've written her every day. Sometimes twice a day. Are you afraid she doesn't love you?"

"Of course she does!"

"Then if a day, or even a month, goes by and you don't write, she should understand."

Today I do not think I would agree, but that morning I was so tired I needed little encouragement to put off my letter and go to bed. I told myself I would write when I woke up. Then I got undressed and slid between the covers and was asleep in an instant. I slept almost ten hours. When I awoke, it was time to eat and go to work. That was the first time a day went by that I did not write to Victoria.

The next time, it was easier. After a few months—and it happened so slowly that I did not realize it—I was writing once a week. There were so many new things to do and see. And every day the ties with Scutari and my old life grew weaker and weaker. Surely, Victoria would understand . . .

69

But I still went along as if things between us were settled forever. Someday I would send for her. When girls I worked with at Clinton's, and later at Compton's, winked at me and talked about going out, or when a girl customer became familiar, I couldn't help blushing and thinking of Victoria. After a while, I could joke with them about it, but I never took them out. And once a week I wrote to my blonde sweetheart in Scutari.

Almost two years went by like this before I looked at another girl. Proff Calfayan, the Armenian composer, brought from Fresno a group of singers—all intelligent, dignified, and cultured Armenian-American girls. With them came some young men from Fresno. To fill out the group for a concert at the YMCA auditorium, Proff Calfayan asked some of us San Franciscans to take part. Arshag, Vahram, and I, and three or four others, said we would help out.

Among the girls were two sisters, Nazenig and Lucie Ruzvanian. Nazenig was a member of the choir of Holy Trinity Church in Fresno and the most professional of all the group, and to show off her talents Proff Calfayan would turn his baton over to her for one or two selections.

On the stage the girls were all seated; standing behind them on one side were Arshag and I and others who had recently come from Europe; in the center were the older professional and businessmen; and on the other side were the young men from Fresno. When this Miss Ruzvanian was leading us, she would gaze at the young men from Fresno, in their American-made suits and with their nice speech and accents, and she would give them a warm, delightful smile. Then her head would turn toward the center. To these men her expression would say, "How solid and dignified you are, and what rich, beautiful voices you have."

Then she would come to us. Her head would go up in the air. Her face would freeze. Although she was shorter than any of us, she gave the impression of looking down upon us from a great height and saying, "Peasants!"

After the concert, Arshag and Vahram and I were the leaders in taking them all to a place where we danced for the

70

rest of the evening. I danced once with Miss Ruzvanian. I was still smarting under the look of scorn she had given us.

"Maybe my English isn't so good," I said. "But my Armenian is better than yours."

She stopped in the middle of the floor and frowned at me, as if to wonder if she had heard correctly. The rest of the dance seemed to last a hundred years.

I was very hurt. I tried forgetting it with some of the other girls, and it didn't help any when, later, Vahram said that the two Ruzvanian sisters really thought we were amusing. They called Arshag and me "those two nice boys from the old country."

Someday, I thought, I would show this Ruzvanian girl who was "a nice boy from the old country." But I had already been in the United States, working hard, for two years. How long was it going to take for me to be an American? How much more work, how many more hurt feelings? I tried to console myself with thoughts of Victoria, but it only made matters worse.

Looking back, I can see that by that time our romance was already over. America, the experience and the life there that we told ourselves were going to bring us together forever, had already divided us so far that we could never go back, for instance, to Tchamlija.

Still I was neither brave enough nor strong enough to see the truth then. Instead, I reasoned that two long years had passed since we said good-by. In a little while longer she would really be a *dunmena*—a "left-at-home." In the eyes of the Armenian people a man can be thirty or even forty and still be marriageable. But a girl who reaches the age of twenty-two or twenty-three and still remains single is in real danger of being a *dunmena* for the rest of her life. And the man responsible for making a girl a lifelong *dunmena* is almost as bad as a criminal.

After sleepless nights which left me more weary and confused than ever, after long walks alone in Golden Gate Park, I decided that I had no right to ask Victoria to wait any longer. I didn't want her to be a *dunmena*, and I didn't want

71

to be to blame for letting her run the risk of becoming one. I wrote a long letter and told her this and said that it was the end of our romance. She must try to find someone else.

"I am sorry—more sorry than I can ever tell you," I wrote. "I shall never forget you. . . ."

It was the truth. I wrung the words out of my heart. I could no more forget Victoria than I could forget my own dreams and hopes. As long as they haunted me, so would she.

The reply that came from her, in her fine and sensitive handwriting, was very sad and heartbreaking. She was saying good-by. I could close my eyes and see her face, tears in her eyes, and wearing an unhappy look—not a girl's look, but a woman's look of love and grief, and sorrow for us both. Her letter told me that no matter what happened, no matter whom she met and loved and married, she would always, in some little corner of her heart, be my *dunmena*.

Even though I was certain that it was better for both of us, I was ashamed of what I had done.

Some men drown a guilty conscience in alcohol; others drown it in work. I was one of these. I worked harder than ever at my job as night manager in Compton's Cafeteria on Ellis Street. But I couldn't keep away from the stoves. I knew without looking how much salt or seasoning to put in a stew. I loved the smells of the food on the broilers and grills, and I loved to take a number of ingredients, all different, and blend them together and cook them into one delicious dish that would taste good and at the same time give strength, health, and energy for another day of living. I could handle a skillet or a pastry whip as skillfully as a painter handles his brush, or a sculptor his mallet and chisel.

One day I made an appointment with Mr. Compton in his office. He looked at me sternly as I walked in.

"I can tell you right now, George, the answer is no."

I must have looked puzzled.

"Your work is satisfactory," he said, "but, for the present —no raise."

"But, Mr. Compton, I didn't come to ask for more money."

72

It was his turn to look puzzled. "I came to ask if I could be a cook."

His eyebrows went up. "You're making fifty dollars a week as a night manager. Cooks, to start with, only get thirty-six."

"I don't feel right at a cash register," I said. "I feel right cooking."

The old gentleman studied me. "All right, George," he said with a smile, "start tomorrow."

At the end of the week my check was still fifty dollars. I worked harder than ever.

I began to have a different kind of wealth, a feeling of personal dignity. I attended plays, operas, and symphonies; it seemed a miracle that I, a cafeteria cook, could enjoy these pleasures along with people who lived on Nob Hill. In the restaurant, I talked with bankers and writers, politicians and policemen, and all sorts of people. They never made me feel that they were better than I. And this feeling of being rich in dignity grew deeper, because I knew that in the old country, in my station of life, I would not have been allowed to address them.

One of those who helped me the most in those early days was a young man who had attended the University of Chicago and the University of Wisconsin. In spite of the fact that he had degrees in journalism and education—I think he would have made the best professor in the world—he had left the academic life, at a great sacrifice of his desires and ambition, to become an editor of Armenian newspapers.

His name was Armen Bardizbanian. Here in America this name sounded too long; so he dropped the "ban" and became Armen Bardizian. At the universities, even this seemed too long, and he changed it to just plain "Bar." Then he became self-conscious because his name was so short and lengthened it again to Bardizian.

When I first knew him, he was between newspaper jobs, and was spending most of his time studying at the University of California in Berkeley. He wanted to know why I did not become a columnist. I thought he was joking.

73

"*Asbarez* is looking for a columnist. You could do it. You have it in you."

Asbarez was the Armenian-language newspaper in Fresno. It had a bigger circulation than any other Armenian newspaper in the United States.

"What is this all about?" I asked.

"They had a columnist," Armen said, "but he left to open a tailor shop in Modesto. They're looking for someone to take his place."

I thought it over. Armen was right. It would give me something to do besides my work at Compton's. It would keep me alive to world affairs. And perhaps somehow it would be a way of helping my fellow Armenian-Americans.

It was Arshag who really made up my mind. "If you were a columnist," he said, "anyone'd think twice before they called you just 'a nice boy from the old country.'"

The following week, with Armen's influence, I got the job. In my column I mentioned current news items from the San Francisco and San Joaquin Valley papers and then went on to make comments on these events. I called the column *"Azgay Angay"*—"Here and There."

Armen and I had many things in common. We talked for hours about Armenia's glorious literature. But there were times, too, when we were silent. He had a way of making things seem important by surrounding them with silence. I remember days when I would go down to the ferry building and meet the boat that brought him from Berkeley. Then, slowly, we would walk all the way up Market Street to Civic Center—Armen with two or three books under his arm, because he never walked without books, and walking very straight, head thrown proudly back, and never saying a word. Then from Civic Center we would walk to my hotel. Turning to leave me at the hotel door, he would smile and say, "Well, we had a wonderful time, didn't we— just walking, and not saying a word."

Victoria slipped away, and I wrapped myself in my work at Compton's and in my column for *Asbarez* and in my

74

walks and talks with Armen and our other friends. Things have a way of being quiet before an earthquake.

Late in 1926 one of my brother-in-law's relatives came to San Francisco to visit Aram and Baidzar. She was Aram's second or third cousin from Fresno, and her name was Armine Galashian. We all called her Minnie.

One day, three months after her arrival, Arshag walked into Compton's and bought a cup of coffee. He seemed excited. We talked for a few minutes. Then he said, "George, I want you to get off work and come with me. You have to be there."

"What are you talking about? Where do I have to be?"

"At our wedding. Minnie and I are going to get married. Vahan Guleserian has talked with Doctor Gordon at the First Congregational Church, and he'll marry us for five dollars. Vahan is going to be best man. But we want you there, too."

In fairness to Minnie and Arshag, they always swore that Doctor Gordon's bargain rate had nothing to do with their hasty decision. It was a case of love that couldn't wait. I got my coat and hat, and we ran down Powell Street to the Flood Building, found a jewelry store, and bought the wedding ring. A few hours later, they were married.

When we went back to the house of Baidzar and Aram to celebrate the wedding, a terrible thing happened. Aram would not let us in. He was white-faced with anger.

"Armine," he said to the bride, "you were a guest in our house. And you married Baidzar's brother without our knowledge or consent. It was an insult, in return for our hospitality. Baidzar and I will never forgive you." With these words he shut the door in our faces.

From that night on, the situation in my family was a very painful one, because the two couples—my brother and his wife and my sister and her husband—did not speak to each other for an entire year. They finally made up when Arshag and Minnie had their first child, Gregory.

It was a few weeks after the baby was born, when our

75

friend Hatchig got married at their house, that our next family trouble began. Hatchig was still another florist. He tried very hard to marry several nice Armenian girls who lived in Fresno. But every time he went down there to ask the girl's parents for their consent, they would get him alone in the sitting room and ask, "How many acres have you got?"

Hatchig would have to reply, "Acres! How can I have any acres when I'm a florist in San Francisco?"

The mother and father would shake their heads. "No acres, no girl."

Finally Hatchig fell in love with a girl from Long Beach, and the miracle about it was that her parents didn't care at all about acres. They thought Hatchig was a fine, up-and-coming fellow with a brilliant future in the business world.

When we saw that nothing was going to stop him this time, we thought that at least we could see that our old friend had a suitable place for the wedding and the finest priest we knew. The place we picked was Arshag and Minnie's new home on Sutter Street; it was out near Presidio Avenue, across the street from Aram and Baidzar's, where they had moved right after baby Gregory brought back peace to the family. The priest was the favorite of us all, Father Markarian of Fowler.

In 1909 and 1910, when I was a choirboy in Scutari, the primate of our Armenian Gregorian Church of the Holy Cross was Markarian Vartabed, which means, simply, Father Markarian. He was a graduate of Armash Seminary, which is on the shore of the Sea of Marmora, about a day's drive from Scutari. On his graduation he had become secretary to the patriarch. Later he became the head of our church.

When we saw him coming up the street in Scutari, we used to run to him and bow and kiss his hand. To us children this was an honor and a privilege. Father Markarian did not bore us with drawn-out tales from the Old Testament; instead he told bloodcurdling stories of Armenian revolutionaries and how, back in the mountains, they were avenging the misdeeds of our enemies, the Turks and the Kurds.

76

In 1912, Father Markarian was given some other parish. No one seemed to know where he had been sent. Hong Kong, some said. My mother thought he had gone to Africa. We children missed him very much and never understood why they took our hero away and gave us instead a priest who told long-winded Bible stories.

In the year of Arshag's marriage I went on a visit to Fresno. Someone mentioned a Father Markarian.

"Could that be the Father Markarian who used to be the primate at Holy Cross Church in Scutari?" I asked.

"Primate!" The man laughed. "No—this is a priest who was hurt in an automobile accident a year or two ago. They say he is still light in the head because of it."

The next day, a friend drove me to Fowler, a tiny farming community not far from Fresno. We stopped in front of the parochial school next to the Armenian church. I told a pupil I would like to speak with Father Markarian. He ran into the wooden schoolhouse. A moment later, the teacher, a lady, left the school by the side door and hurried across the dusty, sun-baked playground to the parsonage.

A little old man appeared on the parsonage porch. His priest's robe flowed to his heels. His hands were folded together on his chest, giving him a simple, childish look. He stood on the top step and peered this way and that through the oddly shaped spectacles that sat on the end of his nose. Then he saw me, and with short, skipping little steps ran across the yard.

"*Americatsi? Americatsi?*—Are you the American?" He looked up at me with round, questioning eyes. It was the priest who had been our hero so long ago in Scutari.

He stepped back. "Georgie! Aren't you my Georgie? My Holy Cross student?"

"Yes, Father, I am."

He took my hand in both of his. Suddenly it was as if all those years since I had last seen him had never been. I bent down and touched his fingers with my lips.

"How big!—how big you've grown!"

He pulled me across the yard, up the steps and into the

77

school. He had read my column in *Asbarez*. Oh, yes, he said, laughing happily, he had been following my career. He was very proud of me. He knew I wouldn't forget him, and would come to see him some day . . .

It was a one-room schoolhouse. He led me to the teacher's platform. The pupils stared. They didn't know what to expect.

Father Markarian turned on them angrily. "Why are you sitting there like dummies? Are these the manners you have been taught? Stand up! Stand up!"

The pupils leaped to their feet. Father Markarian moved to the back of the platform, pushing the teacher aside. He pulled me after him. Then he faced the children again. "What are you standing there for? Sit down!"

Obediently, they sat down.

He turned me so that they could get a good look at me. "You see this man? Take a look at him. That's the kind of student I have brought up in this world. Look at his size!"

Years ago, of course, I had had to stand on tiptoe to kiss his hand. Now I towered over him. He couldn't have been much more than 5 feet tall. But he was bursting with importance. It made him seem much taller.

He went on. "I want you to remember, this is the kind of student I have brought up. Just because I have come from the biggest institutes and churches in Scutari and Istanbul to this flyspeck of a town, you think I'm a failure—a small man. I may be small in stature, but in brains I am a very big man. Look at this boy—one of my pupils—"

He pulled on my sleeve. "You, George—you tell them."

I told the children how delighted I was to see my old teacher. He had been an inspiration to me because of his wonderful understanding of religion, history, and many other subjects. He stood aside throughout my flowery little speech, nodding and smiling with satisfaction.

"Now," he said when I had finished, "go home and tell your fathers and mothers what kind of man your parish priest is, what caliber of man you have for a school principal.

78

Tell them what kind of men I have brought up in the world as students. School is over! Go home and tell them!"

He turned suddenly to the astonished teacher. "You may go, too!"

We were alone in the room. We heard the shouts and running footsteps of the children outside. They had expected some terrible punishment from the Father, the way he had started out. Instead, school was over, and they were free for the day.

But the freest of them all, I thought, was little Father Markarian. He had carried that bitterness in his heart for a long time. He pulled me to a chair. "Tell me, Georgie, all about yourself—"

We took him back to Fresno for the afternoon, and after that had many delightful and amusing hours in his company. So it seemed appropriate that Father Markarian should marry our close friend Hatchig. He made a special trip all the way from Fowler to perform the ceremony.

There were thirty or forty guests at Arshag and Minnie's home for the wedding, mostly Armenian-American girls and young men from the YMCA and our church in San Francisco.

I hardly knew some of them; others I had even forgotten. I wasn't taking part much in the plays and other activities any more. I seemed to have grown away from them. There was Betty Nolan, an American girl who had moved to San Francisco from Providence, Rhode Island, that I was seeing, and it didn't leave much time for these affairs. Even now, as I nodded and forced a smile, I was sorry I had come. If I couldn't be with her, I didn't want to be with anybody.

I had known Betty for two years. During the last six or eight months, we had been together almost constantly. Every moment that we could steal from our working and sleeping hours we were having dinner together, or going to the moving pictures or a concert, or walking in the park, or climbing the hills and exploring the picturesque streets of the foreign colonies. Sometimes I thought that her lovely blue

79

eyes, her laughter, her low, melodious voice, and her hand in mine were the only things that kept me alive.

The only one I ever talked with about Betty was Armen Bardizian. Armen loved beautiful girls. But he was very shy about taking them out: nearly every penny he earned in newspaper work went for tuition bills at the university, and he never thought he had money enough to entertain them as he would like.

Once in a while I invited him out to dinner with Betty and me. We would go to a little Armenian restaurant called the Ararat—it was up a flight of stairs on Fourth Street—and there we would eat *shish kebab,* pilaff, *dolma,* and delicacies that you could find no place except in an Armenian home or restaurant.

One night we left the Ararat—the three of us—and crossed Market Street to the Powell Street turntable, which I had seen from the taxi window my first evening in San Francisco. There we got on a cable car and rode over the hills to the apartment house where Betty lived with her mother.

It was a warm, clear evening. The bay was so calm it looked like a huge lake. We were sitting on the outside seats, and could see the riding lights of the ships anchored across the water and the far-off lights of the cities on the other shore of the bay, which were like shining gold dust scattered on the hills. At the intersections the gripman jangled his bell happily. Once in a while we heard an answering tinkle from another cable car in the distance. Betty's hand was in mine, and the three of us sang all the way out Jackson Street.

It was such a lovely night that Armen and I decided to walk back downtown. For a long time we walked in silence. Once more we heard far-off cable-car bells. I could have sworn that they were answering the bells ringing in my heart. I was very happy.

At length, I could keep still no longer.

"Armen—"

We were on Nob Hill, passing an old brownstone mansion that had survived the earthquake and fire of 1906. Armen

80

put out his hand as we strolled along, and ran his fingers along the mansion's bronze fence. "Yes, George."

"I'm going to marry Betty."

There, on the other side of the street, stood the Fairmont Hotel. If I climbed to its roof and shouted the words out over the bay, would the whole world hear them? That is what I felt like doing. We crossed Mason Street and started down California Street.

"She's a very lovely girl," he said. His voice sounded far-away. Or was it the sadness in it that made it seem so?

"Is that all you can say, Armen?"

Armen laughed. It was a short, uncomfortable laugh of embarrassment. I put my hand on his arm and stopped him in the middle of the sidewalk. "But this is not like you, Armen."

For the first time that I could remember, there was some kind of barrier between us.

"Anybody can see that you two are very much in love—"

"Then what is the trouble?"

He hesitated. "She's an American girl, George."

In my relief I almost burst out laughing. I shook his arm. "Armen, that's just what is so wonderful! I'll work my head off for her. I'll make her the happiest girl in the United States."

But Armen shook his head. There was a troubled look in his eyes. "I didn't mean it that way."

I couldn't get through my head what he was driving at. "What's so terrible? What're you worried about?"

Again Armen hesitated. Then he said, "You."

I was annoyed. I must have shown it. Armen held up his hand.

"George, before you say anything—wait. I'm not going to argue with you. You can rationalize your affair with Betty all you want. You can patch it all together so that it looks just the way you want it to look. But I know, and you know, that down here"—his finger tapped his chest, over his heart—"it goes against the grain."

81

"I don't know what you're talking about. We're not in the old country now." I was almost shouting. "Next year I'll be an American citizen. That gives me the right to marry anyone I please."

"Does it?" Armen asked softly. He took me by the arm. "Come on, George. Let's walk it off. Let's walk down the hill to Union Square and sit down. I'll say what I have to say—it won't take long—and then you can go ahead and do what you want to do." He stopped and turned me around to face him. "If you promise me one thing—"

"What's that?"

"That we'll still be friends."

We started down the Powell Street hill. When we came to Union Square, we walked under the palms toward the Victory monument in the center of the square. Armen stopped in front of a bench and sat down and lighted a cigarette. He seemed to know exactly what he was going to say.

"We all go through this, George—all of us immigrants, whether we are Armenians, Italians, Germans, Chinese, Jews —no matter what we are. I don't say that it never works, but in many, many cases, mixed marriages have meant real tragedy for the alien, or the native-born, or both. Marriage, even in its simplest form, is difficult enough, without complicating it with religious and cultural issues."

I didn't see it that way. "That's just what has made America great. That's the secret of her vitality—that she is such a mixture of all nations, all races, all religions."

"But George"—Armen held up his hand—"is America great because she is such a mixture? Is 'mixture' the right word? Isn't it rather that she is strong because she has taken all the nationalities, in all their integrity, and wound them together like strands, and out of them has made a rope with the combined strength of them all?"

He smoked for a moment in silence. "In any event, I believe America's real gift to civilization is a certain freedom —the greatest freedom of them all. And that is the freedom of any heritage under the sun to express itself and offer itself to the American way of life, the American culture. The

82

freedom of the wise, and the young, and the beautiful from any land to offer their most precious and shining gifts. The freedom—to give—"

His voice died away. For a moment the square was completely still. Then a streetcar clattered past on Geary Street.

"An immigrant, George, is a bridge between the Old World and the New. He carries centuries of Europe or Asia on his back. When he marries an American girl, either she has to renounce her world and live in his, as represented by his background and family, or he has to renounce his world and live in hers. It's too much to ask of either one. They spend their lives trying to comprehend and understand things that a husband and wife should take for granted."

"You are talking like a professor," I said bitterly. "Do you think a man can pick and choose the girl he's going to fall in love with—the girl he wants to marry—like he picks out a suit of clothes, or an automobile? Next, I suppose you're going to tell me immigrants shouldn't get married."

"No, George." Armen shook his head. "It's an immigrant's duty to get married. But it's also his duty to marry someone who, like him, is *becoming* an American—someone who has as much to learn, or almost as much to learn about it as he does—someone who can face the problem together with him, and share it, and live through it, and help him with his children."

He dropped his cigarette on the pavement and slowly crushed it out with his foot.

"Do you know what will happen if you marry Betty? She won't give up her world, so you will give up yours. You will waste your life proving that you are an American. You will do that, instead of enjoying the most precious thing America has for you—the freedom to add something that is pure Armenia, that expresses *your* Armenia, the best and the essence of the Armenia you know and love—to add that, to give it to this wonderful and beautiful land of liberty."

My elbows were resting on the back of the bench. As Armen talked, I looked up at the windows of the Hotel St. Francis. Some were lighted and some were dark. I heard waltz music coming from a ballroom on the street floor. What high-sounding theories Armen is talking, I thought. What ideals! What do they have to do with real life?

Perhaps Armen read my thoughts. He leaned over and tapped my knee.

"George, picture this: You come home from work some evening, all fagged out. You forget about playing the American husband to your American wife. She is working hard in the kitchen. Perhaps something is burning. Anyway, you're all fagged out and you want attention. Like any real Armenian, you pull down your tie, kick off your shoes, flop down on the living-room couch, and let out a big, weary *'Eof!'*"

Armen sat back and folded his arms.

"Would your Betty know what you meant? Could any woman really respond to that *'Eof!'* unless she was an Armenian and had been brought up among an Armenian father and brothers and uncles and cousins?"

Again his words faded away, and the square was quiet. In the distance the waltz music went on and on.

Armen rose. "Time to go, George. Tomorrow's a work day."

I stood up beside him, and we started slowly along the walk, toward Powell Street. He put his arm through mine. I let it stay there. I knew he was trying to help me, and we were still friends.

Many a sleepless night I had after that. I would try to see Betty as my wife, who would put up with or try to get along with Baidzar and Arshag, and perhaps someday my mother and little sister Alene.

Would she approve of them? Would they approve of her? I had introduced her to Baidzar and Arshag, and they seemed to like and admire her. But from one or two things Baidzar said afterward, I knew they did not think she was serious enough. She liked to dance too much. She cared too much for expensive clothes.

And I thought about what Armen said about *"Eof!"* This is pronounced almost as if it were spelled "Erf." What does

84

it mean? Well, it's an exclamation that means, "I'm tired and disgusted and I've had a hard day. Don't bother me. Leave me alone. If you have to do anything at all, pamper me. Wait on me hand and foot. Show me I am a king in my own house."

It says all that in one word, and Armen was right: it would be very hard for an American girl to comprehend it. I had to admit that if I said *"Eof!"* to Betty when she wasn't feeling well, I wouldn't stand much of a chance of getting attention. She would expect me to hug her, and tell her how sorry I was, and cook the dinner.

Already I knew one thing about Betty: she certainly wouldn't enjoy Armenian plays or socials given by Armenian-American societies or lectures by visiting Armenian intellectuals. The Armenian intellectual is very long-winded. What an American lecturer will say in 15 or 20 minutes, he will take three hours to say. And not only will he say *that,* he will throw in the history of Armenia for good measure. Armenians loved this, but no American girl would stand for it, no matter how much she loved her husband. I had taken Betty to two or three of these lectures. She might as well have been in the dentist's chair.

I knew these things, and yet—I couldn't help it. We saw each other more and more often. It seemed as though I had become part of Betty, and she had become part of me. It was because she couldn't be at Hatchig's wedding that I couldn't really enjoy myself there.

But the wedding went off beautifully. When the ceremony was over, some of the fellows wanted to kiss the bride. "No you don't! No you don't!" said Hatchig, laughing. And he pushed them all away and kissed her himself.

It was time for the Armenian wedding dinner that Minnie and Baidzar and their friends had prepared. Father Markarian pushed into the dining room. It was very crowded.

"Now," he said in a businesslike way, "I must have two chairs at the table."

He took off his robe. "As all of you who knew me in Scutari remember, I was Yervant Markarian before I went into the seminary. When I came out, I was Father Markarian. The trouble is, a Father can eat only enough to keep a sparrow alive. Our religion says so."

He draped the robe over one of the chairs. Off came his turned-around collar. He placed it carefully on the seat of the chair. He patted the robe. "Now, Father," he said with a twinkle in his eye, "are you comfortable? Are you all right?"

While the rest of us were sitting down, with Hatchig and his bride at the head of the table, and Minnie and her friends were bringing in the food, the priest put one little slice of roast lamb and one piece of *lavash* upon a plate and set it down in front of the chair where he had put his robe.

"That," he said, bowing, "is for you, Father Markarian. It will keep you alive until tomorrow."

Then he got another plate and heaped it high with lamb, roast chicken, steaming pilaff, stuffed grape and cabbage leaves, *pasturma*, Armenian cheese and olives, and a dozen other delicacies. He filled a glass brimful with wine. It was a meal for a longshoreman after a hard day's work on the docks. All this he put down in front of the other chair.

"And this," he said, beaming with delight, "is for you— Yervant Markarian."

Then he sat down in his shirt sleeves with the rest of us, ate every bite from the overflowing plate, drank until his eyes were bright and his cheeks rosy, and came back for more.

"Well, Father," he would say, turning to the empty chair beside him and the untouched plate, "you don't seem very hungry this evening."

Of all of us there at the wedding at Minnie and Arshag's house, the little priest was the gayest and the happiest.

The trouble between Arshag and me came as I was leaving to go to my room in the Fairfax Hotel. We had taken a long while over dinner, and now it was too late for the girls who had come alone to leave without escorts. Armen was going home with two of them. Arshag wanted me to walk home with Minnie's friend, Mariam Hagopian.

We stood in the little hall. The other guests were in the

86

living room and dining room, laughing and saying good-by and all talking at once. I put on my coat.

"Please don't ask me to do that, Arshag."

He looked at me queerly. "But it's right on your way."

"Mariam is a nice girl. But I don't want to take her home. Or any of these girls," I said. I opened the front door. I knew that trouble was coming. I wanted to leave before anything happened.

"George—!"

I turned back. I didn't like the look on my brother's face. "Don't say it, Arshag. Don't say anything you'll be sorry for. We've had enough hard feelings in our family."

"We've had enough of your American girl, too."

Arshag had hit me hard, and he knew it.

"What business is it of yours?"

We were both raising our voices. But there was so much noise in the other room no one heard us.

"I'm your brother. That makes it my business. You're out of your head. Everybody's talking about it. I've written to Uncle Krikor—"

The people in the other room were coming. I could hear Minnie's voice, and Armen's. I was sick inside.

"He'll tell you what a fool you're making of yourself."

I looked into his eyes for some sign of sympathy, of understanding. But they remained angry and stern. I shut the door and went down the steps to the street. Behind me I heard the others crowding into the hall where Arshag stood. "Good night— Good night— Thank you— Good-by."

The night mist was blowing in from the sea. The street was black and deserted. Down on the bay the foghorns were blowing. I started the long, lonesome walk to my hotel.

CHAPTER SEVEN

That is where you fight the battles with yourself—in the night, in the mist, in the lonely street or the dark, quiet room. The words of Arshag had not surprised me. His bitterness did not come as a shock. My conscience had been whispering to me for months. It had spoken to me as if it were my father, or an ancestor who had died long ago. I even think I half expected Arshag to say them and had been waiting.

Arshag had had high hopes for me. I was the one, he believed, who would raise the honor of the family. But now that I was seeing more and more of Betty Nolan as the weeks and months passed by, he thought I was wasting my life and my opportunity, that I was throwing it all away. That is why he had been so angry the night of the wedding. He was ashamed of me.

88

But I was angry, too. If Arshag were a real brother and had a real brother's love for me, he would understand. Instead of trying to stop me from getting what I wanted, he would help me. As it was, he was being selfish; he wanted to pick the girl for me to marry, and run my life. We grew farther and farther apart.

One evening after work I returned to the Fairfax to change my clothes for dinner with Betty. The desk clerk handed me a letter. It was addressed in Uncle Krikor's handwriting and was from Pleosti, Rumania, where he had moved with my mother and Alene. I took the letter to my room and lay down on the bed and tore it open.

I knew almost at once what it was. "My sister, your mother Haiganoush, gave me to read the letter recently received from dear Arshag. . . . I can assure you I write after long meditation, with a heavy heart and unwillingly. . . ."

I closed my eyes. Something told me to tear it up without reading it. But I had always loved Uncle Krikor. I remembered how happy he had been to see me, how excited he had been, the night I returned home from the Caucasus, how he had brought the dagger and proudly hung it on my *kinto* belt. As my mother's brother, he had been the patriarch of our family, ever since father died. Part of me was afraid of that flimsy, foreign paper and those stamps and the sharp, precise European handwriting of my uncle. But part of me longed to read it, longed to have it tell me what to do, what would be the best thing, the most honorable thing . . .

"You must understand, dear George, I have attached great hopes to you, and rightly so. If others have sent rude, rough, ignorant, and vulgar youths away, with the hope that in the course of time they would bake in the oven of life and become useful men, I have sent you off as a youth who already had the necessary education, refinement, and healthy judgment. You were full of vitality and ambition. You had a Spartan body. You were handsome in features and presentable in personality. Everything good could have been expected of you.

"If you do not believe me, I ask you to stand in front of

89

a large mirror and look yourself full in the face, with my eyes. Admire yourself as I admired you. Say if you can, 'Uncle, you are wrong!'

"And so, at the very thought of disappointment, my heart aches. Spare me this, George, for I tremble at the thought.

"But I still have hopes that you will pause, and realize the dream I have cherished—and we all have cherished—deep in our hearts for you.

"Without being you, without having tasted the good and the bad that America may have offered you, I can visualize the atmosphere and environment with which you—handsome, presentable, and manly—find yourself encircled.

"If you let yourself go with the current, you will only float to and fro with the ebb and flow of life.

"But I trust that you will look about you with the eye of an eagle, and see the truth.

"Enjoy the pleasures of life, but only as much as a true knight is entitled to.

"You are barely twenty-five. Stop for a moment, and think, and see how much time you have left in which to enjoy the pleasures of life, which, as they had no beginning, have no end. Do not hurry. You have many years ahead of you. Be temperate. Control and subjugate your passions in a masterly manner. Do not try to seize and possess in a few years what is yours for a lifetime to enjoy.

"I can write no more. This is what your father would write, were he here, in my place. These are the truths your mother would speak, if she could look into your eyes. . . ."

There were a few more sentences, telling how Alene had become a wonderful dressmaker, and how much my mother appreciated the money that I was sending her each month. Then he said that they were all well—he and his wife and their son, Sebouh, and Mother and Alene—and were living for the happy day when we would be together again.

The letter was signed, "Your Uncle Krikor, who loves you and prays for you, and asks God to bless you, guide you, and keep you."

So many things flooded back to me—so many voices, so

90

many memories from the Scutari days and my childhood—
and I felt such a homesickness and loneliness for my mother
and my home and my dead father as I read the letter, I was
crying when I came to the end.

There is a time for crying, and that time had come. I
switched off the lamp. The light from a flashing electric sign
across O'Farrell Street came through my window. I lay there
on the bed. I thought of who I was and where I came from.
I thought of my country and my family and my grandparents
in Xanta. I thought of how and why my father had died.
I thought of the words that came whispering to me that daybreak on the deck of the *Meghali Ellas:* "Believe in me, as I
believe in you—" Over and over I heard those words, *"As I
believe in you."* And I thought of the wise things Armen
said, on the bench in Union Square, and I remembered
Uncle Krikor.

The telephone bell rang. It rang again and again. It
couldn't have been anyone but Betty. More than anything
in the world I wanted to hear her voice. But how could I,
now? They were right. All of them—Armen and Arshag and
Uncle Krikor and all my wise ancestors who were speaking
through them—they all were right. I wasn't meant for her;
she wasn't meant for me. The differences were too big.
They'd destroy us both.

I fought against the bell with all my will and strength.
My hands knotted into fists. Sweat broke out on my forehead. I thrashed on the bed. The ringing jangled and
hammered into my head. It went on and on. I reached
out to grab the phone and smash it on the floor to make it
stop. At that very instant it went dead.

I lay there breathing hard, as though I had run a long
way.

I didn't go to work the next day, or the day after that.
Instead, I stayed in my room. I looked back over the years
—the Scutari years, the years in the Caucasus, the years in
America. What had I done with them? Especially the years
in America? I had saved a few dollars. I had eaten well and
worn good clothes and had good times. What else—?

91

And I listened. The stillness in my room and in my heart filled with the sound of my mother's farewell, and the grinding engines of the *Meghali Ellas,* and the songs of the Greek playing his *oud* in the evening. I heard the long-drawn whistle of the train that carried me through the country of the pioneers, and the beautiful, joyful Song of America that I heard that Monday morning in Sutter Street.

What gladness had filled my heart! With my arms around my sister I had cried, "All I want is to be another happy American!"

I listened to Uncle Krikor. I pretended that he was there in the room with me, saying the things he had written. And I listened to Armen again. I remembered every word he said about giving, and the immigrant's wonderful privilege—the freedom to give the best of his heritage to America.

As I remembered all this I looked back, and I looked ahead. I cannot tell you the millions of things I thought of, but at last I fell asleep, and when I awoke, I knew what I wanted to do.

It was clear and simple. It must have been meant this way from the days when I used to burn my fingers lifting the lids of my mother's pots and kettles and when I used to cook shrimps and mussels in the beach fires by the Sea of Marmora, when everybody called me *Shishko* and I was always tasting everything.

I wanted to help Americans learn to eat better. I wanted to prepare the finest dishes and serve them to Americans. I wanted Americans to appreciate and enjoy these dishes. They had been so busy building this great country they had forgotten all about the art of living.

I would try to give America the best of Armenian and Near Eastern cooking, as I knew it and remembered it, as it came down to me in my bones and wherever it is that a man keeps the stored-up instinct and wisdom of his race.

This is what I was privileged to offer America. I would waste no more months, no more years. I would begin immediately. I would start out by learning and collecting for Americans the finest recipes of the finest chefs in the world.

Wherever they were—in luxurious hotel dining rooms or in tiny side-street hideaways—I would track them down. And I would visit the monastery of San Lazzaro at Venice, that wonderful treasure house of Armenian lore and culture. The wise Mechitarist monks there would help me. I would learn what these people and places could teach me, then leave the rest to the genius of my Armenian heritage.

The next morning I went down to Pier 48. One of my regular customers at Compton's had often told me that if I ever wanted to go around the world, I should call on him at that pier. He was in charge of port employment for the Dollar liners.

He recognized me right away. I told him I wanted a job. He frowned. "Too bad you didn't come in before. You just missed a sailing." He looked through some papers on his desk. My heart sank. Then he found the one he wanted.

"Well, let's see." He puffed his cigar and studied the paper carefully. "Yes, I believe we can get you on." He studied some more. "The *Wilson* sails next week—August 10. I can ship you as a steward. Can you make it?"

Could I make it? Could a bird fly?

There were unhappy duties to face—two of them.

The day before the *President Wilson* was to sail, I said good-by to Betty. She knew by then that everything was over. We had talked and talked and talked, until both of us were more tired than we had ever been in our lives. There was nothing more to say. We had never thought that it would end like this. But there we were, saying good-by. Our dreams were dying, and a part of us, a part of youth, was dying. We tried to smile. At last we turned away.

That night I went to Arshag's house.

"I am going away," I said. "I'll be gone for four months."

He wanted to know what had happened, where I was going, and why and how. But it was too long a story to tell him now; I had come too far to tell where I had been.

"I wanted you to know that I was going away. I didn't want you to worry when you didn't see or hear from me."

That was all I could say. I went back to the Fairfax and

93

finished packing. Then there was nothing left to do. I had already given notice to Mr. Compton. He had wished me luck and told me to call on him if I needed work when I came back. I turned off my light. For the last time in that room, I tried to go to sleep. But in a little while, I was praying. I prayed for strength to do my best with the gifts that God and my fathers had given me, and then I prayed for us all.

At noon the next day, the decks of the *President Wilson* were crowded with people—passengers and friends, relatives and well-wishers there to see them off. In less than an hour the *Wilson* would cast off and back into the stream, with people shouting and crying and waving and laughing, whistles blowing, and paper twirling through the air like snakes.

I stood in the chief steward's office, waiting for instructions. I glanced through the porthole. Outside on the deck was Arshag.

I excused myself and stepped outside. I led him quickly down the deck to an empty stateroom and shut the door.

"What's happened?" I asked. "What are you doing here?"

Arshag's face was filled with reproach. I shook him by the arm. "How did you find me?"

"The room clerk at the hotel. I made him tell me."

Happy crowds pushed by outside, their footsteps shuffling along the deck. Members of *bon-voyage* parties were blowing horns.

"Why are you doing this to us, George? Why aren't you telling us where you are going or what you are going to do?"

I thought back to the long walk home from his house the night of Hatchig's wedding party. Angry, sarcastic words crowded to the tip of my tongue. I could fairly ask what made him think he deserved my trust and confidence. But it wouldn't be right. It would start everything out all wrong.

"Don't you see, Arshag? Don't you understand that this is best? Can't you trust me and help me? It isn't easy to go—"

94

"Then stay, George. They will get somebody to take your place. We need you here with us."

On one of the lower decks a bugle began to play. It was the warning for the guests to go ashore.

"No, Arshag. My mind is made up."

He looked deep into my eyes for almost a minute. He saw that he could not sway me, that no one could. Then he held out his hand.

We kissed each other, the way Armenian brothers do, and he left.

Out on the deck the bugle blew again. A band started to play. People laughed and sang. I left the stateroom, shut the door behind me, and joined them. I was carried along with the crowd on the deck. I felt the warm sun on my face, and somehow I knew that the day would come when I would be happy again.

CHAPTER EIGHT

The Pacific was blue and sparkling. The skies were bright and clear. The *President Wilson* steamed west to Diamond Head, then west again. She had several hundred passengers on board and a mixed cargo that included millions of dollars in gold and silver bullion.

My work as steward was pleasant. But I was happy when Rudolfi, our chief steward, gave me the additional job of ship's storekeeper. It gave me valuable experience in dealing with meats and other foodstuffs in quantity.

Some of the chefs were artists who had worked with Victor Hirtzler at the St. Francis or had been in the kitchens of the Palace or the big hotels in New York and were now seeing the world on a Dollar liner. In my off hours I watched

96

and helped them. If you win the respect of a fine chef, he will gladly teach you what he knows about cooking. Only those who are second-rate hoard their secrets and cling to what they have learned.

I looked forward to our ports of call. Not only were there strange new dishes to be tasted and studied, but in every country in the world you will find Armenians. It had been more than six years since I had seen or talked with any who lived outside the United States. I wanted to see how they lived and thought and how they adapted themselves to their new homes. Wherever our big white ship stopped, going ashore was an adventure.

The ship sailed to China, and at a Kowloon bazaar I bought a pretty roller canary for Arshag's wife, Minnie, who loved birds, animals, and pets of all kinds. I named the canary Ragsdale, in honor of my friend George Ragsdale, the *Wilson*'s concessionaire.

I found Armenians in Shanghai. Day and night I haunted the kitchen at Tchakalian's. Tchakalian had been the cook for the French consul in Erzerum. The consul was transferred to China. He took Tchakalian with him. Then, when the consul was ordered back to France, Tchakalian refused to go. Instead, he stayed in Shanghai and opened a restaurant, and a bakery and grocery store as well. They were among the finest in the city.

But I think that the most wonderful Armenian dinner I ever had in the Far East was in Singapore, in the rectory of the Armenian church.

When the *Wilson* was in port, we used to leave her for a day or two, to give our "sea legs" a change. At Singapore, Ragsdale, Leon Barbeau (the second steward), and I went to the Raffles Hotel. I asked the bellboys and desk clerks where the Singapore Armenians lived.

They couldn't help me. "We know Parsees, but no Armenians," they said.

Parsees were fine citizens. They were Persian Zoroastrians —fire worshipers—who had fled to the Orient from the persecutions of the Mohammedan Persians. But I was more in-

97

terested in Armenians. I said to Ragsdale and Barbeau, "Let's go for a ride. I'm sure there are some Armenians around here somewhere. Maybe we'll bump into them."

We got in a carriage and gaped like any American tourist at the traffic policemen in their white shorts, with the peculiar wings on their shoulders that showed which way the traffic was supposed to go. We passed through crowded side streets and alleys and came at last to a broad, busy thoroughfare. At the first intersection I leaned over and tapped our driver on the shoulder.

"Stop here. I want to get out."

"Well, Leon," Ragsdale said, "George has seen his Armenian."

"No, I haven't. But I've seen something almost as good." I pointed over our heads to the street sign. It read, "Armenia Boulevard."

I crossed the street to a dry-goods shop and found the manager in the rear of the store surrounded by bolts of many-colored cloth. "Would you mind telling me, sir, why this street is called 'Armenia Boulevard'?" I asked.

He looked at me with surprise. "Why, we have many Armenians in Singapore. Some of them are very prominent. Armenians own, for instance, the best hotel in Singapore."

It was my turn to be surprised. "Is that so? What hotel is that?"

"The Raffles. It is owned by the Sarkis brothers and their brother-in-law, Haroutun."

For a moment I didn't say anything. I was too busy thinking of what I was going to say to my bellboys and room clerk.

"If you drive down the boulevard three more blocks," the store manager said, "you will come to a big church. That is the Armenian church."

A few minutes later our driver halted the carriage opposite a high, narrow door in a vine-covered wall. The wall was built all around the block of property on which stood the Armenian church and rectory. I lifted the heavy knocker and rapped. In a few moments I heard footsteps, the jingle of

98

keys, then the turning of the lock. The door opened, and before me stood a scholarly looking church attendant. I bowed, and he bowed.

"Greetings," I said in Armenian. "My name is George Mardikian. I'm from America."

He immediately looked interested. "America? You've come from America?" He stepped back. "Come in. Please come in."

I told Ragsdale and Leon to go on without me. Then I returned to the church. The attendant led me to the rectory and introduced me to a plump, handsome, red-cheeked priest.

He smiled at me. "Do I have the pleasure of meeting the famous columnist—the author of *Azgay Angay?*"

I was amazed. "How do you know?"

"Several times a month the steamers bring us newspapers from America. We subscribe to *Asbarez* of Fresno and read every word in it."

I told him about my new assignment from *Asbarez,* how I was to send back stories signed *Sherchig Mardik*—Mardikian the Rover—giving my impressions of the foreign lands and cities that the *Wilson* visited. I had already submitted three—on Japan, on Manila, and on Shanghai—but not enough time had gone by for them to be printed and sent back to the Orient.

"We will give you something to write about in your paper," the priest said with a smile.

And he was right. Two nights later—the night before the *Wilson* sailed for Penang—the parish gave a dinner. There were twenty-two of us there, including the Sarkis brothers and their mother, the matriarch of the Armenian colony, who gave me a large ruby ring as a souvenir of Singapore.

The priest told me during dinner that the people who were there included almost everyone in his congregation.

"But your church will seat a thousand!" I exclaimed.

"It was built for Armenians who migrated to the Orient and settled here in Singapore in the eighteenth century," he said. "They came by the hundreds and amassed great fortunes. Then, as time went on, they integrated themselves

99

into the British colonial life. In marriages with the British and the natives they gradually lost their racial identity. Out of all those hundreds and thousands, there are left today in Singapore only twenty-eight Armenian families."

"Do you like having such a small parish?" I asked.

He sipped his wine. "At least," he said, "there are no financial worries."

As for the meal itself, we were served whole roast lamb. It was accompanied by an exotic and most delicious dish made of sautéed apricots, and by the whitest, fluffiest pilaw, which is a Persian pilaff, or rice with chopped almonds, that I had ever seen or tasted. When it was over, I spent more time talking with the lady members of the parish than I had at the dinner table. They hadn't trusted their own cooks and chefs; they had told them to take the evening off and then had prepared the meal with their own hands. Word for word I took down their recipes and filed them in my notebook.

The next day, under a blazing sun, we came down to the docks with an hour to spare before sailing, and a fakir approached me with a coin trick. He held out his hand. A silver coin jumped and leaped across the back of it, as if it were alive. He saw that I was fascinated and did the trick again. I pointed to the coin and then to the back of my own hand.

"You teach me?"

He wore only a loin cloth and was dark-skinned and thin. Black, stringy hair hung to his shoulders. He felt my white duck uniform.

"Give me suit, I teach."

Stewards bought their own uniforms. I had an extra one in my suitcase. I got it from the bag and held it up. The fakir reached for it. I held it back. "Teach me trick."

He showed me how it was done—with a long hair and a tiny piece of chewing gum. A child could have figured it out. I was angrier with myself for falling for it than I was with him, but I held on to the uniform. He saw that I wasn't satisfied and said, "I tell fortune."

100

"Make it better than the trick," I said.

He studied my right palm.

"You come back to Singapore. Not work on ship. You come back passenger—first class." He traced out a line. "You get married."

"When?"

"One year. Maybe two."

"Who is the girl?"

He raised his head and frowned. His eyes closed. He seemed to be trying to hear something. "Her friends call her—" I bent closer. A look of pain crossed his face. He motioned with his finger, as if he were trying to write in the air. "It has three letters—"

Three letters? It didn't mean a thing. But he obviously believed what he had told me. I handed him the uniform.

"I don't know whether you earned it or not, but take it," I said. He snatched it and backed away, bowing. Then he turned and lost himself in the crowd.

The *Wilson* steamed to Penang, and finally crossed the Indian Ocean to the Red Sea. I had written ahead to some of my friends who had been with me in the Armenian boy scouts and who had fled to Egypt at about the same time that I had gone to America. I told them to expect me on the *President Wilson,* and the evening she docked in Alexandria they took me to a tiny side-street café for a reunion dinner.

There we had another wonderful Armenian meal. It was as good as you could find in Istanbul, or anywhere in the Near East. I asked my friends, "Who cooked this masterpiece of a meal?"

"Don't you recognize the touch of the genius?" they asked, laughing. "Ashji! Come meet an old friend from America!"

Out of the kitchen shuffled an old man with white hair. He wore a white chef's apron and cap, and glasses that magnified his eyes strangely. I had never met this famous man, but from his name I knew who it must be.

"Are you Ashji Mugurdich?"

He put out his hand. I felt the way an unknown student

101

artist would feel shaking the hand of a world-famous painter. "Yes, my boy, I am Ashji."

For many years, Ashji Mugurdich had been the best-known chef in Turkey. He had been head chef at the luxurious Tocatlian Hotel in Istanbul. His name was familiar to everyone. When husbands wanted to please their wives after a good meal, they kissed them on the cheek and said, "Ashji Magurdich himself could not have cooked such a meal."

But changing times had made him, like other Armenians, a refugee. Now, instead of preparing meals for the great Tocatlian dining room, with its glittering chandeliers, he was cooking them for this little hidden-away café. Instead of entertaining royalty, he was faithfully serving compatriots who were also refugees.

I could not have asked to meet a man who, in his day, had been a greater chef than Mugurdich. I told him this and asked him for his favorite recipes. He studied me from behind his heavy glasses.

"No," he said. "Ashji Mugurdich keeps his recipes to himself." With a solemn wave to my friends, he shuffled back into the kitchen.

He was such a genius in my eyes that I returned the next day. I took one of my boy-scout friends with me, and he told the chef about my background in Armenia and about my family. I offered to leave the *President Wilson* and go to work for him, if he would make me his protégé.

"Why are you so anxious to work for me?" he asked. "Why do you want my recipes?"

I told him that I wanted to learn how to make his immortal dishes and present them to Americans as the creations that he, Ashji Mugurdich, had given the world in the name of the Armenian cuisine.

I could see that he was beginning to soften. The more I talked, the broader he smiled.

"Well, so you want to cook my dishes for the American people! Why didn't you say so? When is your boat leaving?"

It was sailing the next day for Naples.

"No matter," said Ashji Mugurdich. "I'll write them out

102

for you and mail them to you. You shall have them all. The delicacies that delighted crowned heads at the Tocatlian in Istanbul will draw the praises of American connoisseurs in San Francisco."

We had a cup of Armenian coffee to close the bargain and then said good-by. Ashji Mugurdich did keep his promise. For several years after I returned home to California, I received letters from him every once in a while. They contained page after page of his priceless recipes. But his handwriting was like the tracks of a chicken. I could never make it out.

Chief Steward Rudolfi, who had been maître d'hôtel at the Palace in San Francisco, was a very lenient superior. He allowed us stewards to leave the ship at certain ports and rejoin it later on.

All through the Orient I had saved my turn, so that I could leave the *Wilson* at Naples, take the fastest train north to Venice, stay there ten days, then meet the ship at Genoa. At Venice was the storehouse of treasures that I had been impatient to see and study since that long night and those days in my hotel room when it became clear to me why I was alive—what I wanted to do and what I had to do.

I found it just as my father and Uncle Krikor and my teachers had always told me it would be, amid the groves of cypress trees and the sweet-smelling gardens of a little island in the Lagoon of Venice. It was the Armenian monastery on the island of San Lazzaro, run by the Mechitarist Fathers, and founded almost 250 years ago by the Armenian Abbot Mechitar, the "Comforter."

It was a strange and beautiful thing to find there in that ancient Italian city a kind of complete and independent Armenia. Armenians all over the world have no country they can call their own, but they do have this tiny island. It is a treasury of the heritage and history of the Armenian nation.

In the library of San Lazzaro, for instance, are more than 35,000 volumes in every language under the sun. There are also more than 2,000 manuscripts in Armenian dating back to the fifth century A.D. There are copies of all the books,

103

magazines, reviews, and journals ever published in Armenian, copies of every book written about Armenia or the Armenian people in any language, and copies of the more than 1,500 books printed in the last two centuries by the San Lazzaro press of the Mechitarist Fathers.

I learned that the outstanding father of San Lazzaro since Mechitar himself was Father Alishan, who wrote many classics on the history and struggles of the Armenian people. I never knew until my visit to the monastery, however, that Father Alishan had never set foot on Armenian soil. He sat under the olive trees of San Lazzaro and dreamed and wrote, and inspired Armenians everywhere to love and cherish their heritage. Another author who wrote at San Lazzaro was the British poet Lord Byron. He spent six months at the monastery studying Armenian. The fathers will show you the terrace where, according to the tradition, Byron sat with his dog and watched the Venetian sunsets.

Among the collection of manuscripts, I found some that weighed hundreds of pounds. It took two or three monks to move them. The illumination of their borders had the same richness of color and design as ancient Armenian rugs. I pored over Father Hatzouni's long book on Armenian food and eating customs down through the centuries. *Djacotz Purotz,* he called it—*Meals for the Many.*

Here, and in the dry, precious parchments, were the treasures I had been trying to find, gems that had come down through the centuries, bits of the heritage of my mother country that I could interpret for all Americans, and give to them. They were what I had crossed the world to find.

Every morning I left my hotel on the Grand Canal and took the little *vapore* from the pier at the Riva degli Schiavoni, near the monument to Victor Emmanuel II. The fathers greeted all of us who were arriving at the island. Then I walked down the cloisters to the vestibule, up the six stone steps into the library, and into the past.

Ragsdale thought of himself with pride as a connoisseur of the beer of the various countries we stopped at. He always said that the best beer was made by those who invented it—

the Germans. I found something for him in those old manuscripts: Armenians drank beer 3,000 years ago, when the Germans, if there were any, were living with the wolves and the bears. I discovered that Xenophon, the great Greek general, had drunk beer on his way through Armenia. He and his foot soldiers sipped it through straws from earthenware mugs.

These same manuscripts told of the first Armenian gourmet—King Shara, who lived more than 3,500 years ago. Archaeologists opening the tombs of Egyptian rulers were no more thrilled than I was, when I stumbled upon the story of King Shara. My notes covered page after page in my notebook.

King Shara moved his capital from one part of the country to the other, according to where he found the best barley for his beer, the best grapes for his wine, the sweetest fruits for his table. One capital that he built was Shirag—the present-day Alexandropol, that I knew so well.

High in the Caucasian mountains, in remote villages, the legend of King Shara lives even today. As I read, I remembered traveling through Kharakelesa during the war. I came to a very small village where there was no hotel or inn. I was the guest of the mayor, who was also the police chief, fireman, judge, and every other official they had. That evening, in the kitchen of his mountain cottage, his grandmother sat to one side as we feasted. According to the custom of that region, she was the head of the family. I was very hungry from the long day's journey. She watched me as I thoughtlessly reached for more than my share. At last, she tapped me on the shoulder.

"My son," she said, "you may have the appetite of King Shara, but remember—our warehouses are not as full as his."

In other words, "We know you are our guest, but please leave some for the others."

In the history of King Shara I read, too, about *Arkayagan Abour,* or "royal soup." Every Armenian knows how royal soup is served on special family occasions, like the birth of a

105

baby boy, or the homecoming of an eldest son who has been away to war. It is also prepared when townspeople are honoring a distinguished national leader or foreign visitor.

But 1,500 years ago, an Armenian monk had written down on parchment that in "the ancient time of King Shara" it was an Armenian monarch's solemn duty, when he returned victorious from the wars, to go into the deep forests and bring back wild birds and gazelles. He would bring the game to the palace steps, where an immense *gatsa*, or kettle, had been placed by the coppersmiths. After his servants had cleaned the birds and gazelles, the king with his own hands would prepare royal soup and serve it to the nobles of his court. Then they in turn would serve the commoners who had come from every village in Armenia to celebrate the victory.

Generations passed. Wild fowl and game became scarce. Instead of pheasant breasts and huge chunks of gazelle, the kings had to substitute chicken and deer meat. In spite of this, the monk wrote, the soup kept improving. In King Shara's day, they had put young grapes into it for flavoring. "The modern way," he wrote in the fifth century A.D., "is to add lemon juice and eggs that are beaten together. The resulting flavor is truly delightful."

Hour after hour I worked in the library of San Lazzaro, writing these things in my notebook. Someday I would make royal soup for Americans, and when they looked up at me with pleased and happy expressions and asked, "What is this wonderful soup? Where did the recipe come from?" then I would be able to tell them that it came from the archives of San Lazzaro and the ancient, conquering kings of Armenia. I looked ahead to that day. I worked long and hard over these books and manuscripts that had been gathering dust on their shelves for many, many years.

When, in the late afternoon, my eyes were tired with reading and my fingers were tired with writing, it was one of the pleasantest things I have ever known to walk down the long valley of cypress trees and sit by the lagoon, where Lord Byron must have sat, and sip the delicate cordial that the

106

Mechitarist Fathers made, and look across the water and the lovely city to the hills of Padua.

That was really the climax of my trip around the world. The ten days at San Lazzaro had made it much more than worthwhile. The legends, the lore, and the knowledge I had found there would pass through me to many thousands, and through them to many millions. Whether they knew whose it was or where it came from did not matter; all that was important was that it was passed along to them to give them pleasure and to make them see how good life could be.

A dancer who has learned the basic forms and steps gains the courage and confidence to go beyond the fundamentals, to improvise and create. In the same way I, as a chef, was now eager to put into practice what I had learned and to experiment with ideas of my own. Already I was thinking up variations of the old recipes and planning menus that would be a new experience to Americans.

Where was I going to serve these menus? Why, in a restaurant of my own. I pictured how it would look—rich wood paneling and a thick carpet on the floor and soft lights, gleaming silverware on white tablecloths, tables crowded with happy, fashionably dressed patrons, waiters leaving the kitchen with trays of Armenian and Near Eastern dishes prepared with the love and tenderness that only I, George Mardikian, was capable of; and me, in spotless white from shoes to the peak of my high chef's cap, watching over the ranges and sometimes, when I had a spare moment or two, going out into the lovely dining room, smiling at all the people, and asking them how they liked their dinners, like a real host—as if I had welcomed them into my home and they were not only my guests but my very dear friends as well.

I even had a name chosen for my restaurant: Omar Khayyam's. While to some it might be a wine-women-and-song kind of name, to me it was something else, something that called to mind the deeper spirit of the *Rubaiyat*. It would mean that here was a place where you could live solely for this happy hour; here, in this pleasant atmosphere, you could forget your cares and worries and do both your body and

107

mind a good turn by ordering a meal that was a little different, even a little exciting, and still healthy and nourishing. Someday, I thought, as I sat there on the terrace at San Lazzaro, I would have a place like that—a beautiful place called Omar Khayyam's.

I met the *Wilson* in Genoa as I had planned. Ragsdale took me to a restaurant that he had discovered where they catered to gourmets. Ragsdale felt like celebrating.

"Waiter," he said, "to go with our dinner I want champagne—the finest and most expensive in the house."

When the proper time came, the waiter popped the cork high in the air and, as if he were performing an important ceremony, filled our glasses from the bottle, which was wrapped in a napkin. Then he stepped back and looked from Ragsdale to me and back to Ragsdale again, to see if we were pleased.

"Delicious!" exclaimed Ragsdale. And it was.

Later, as I poured more into our glasses, the napkin fell back from the label.

"Ragsdale," I said, "look. See where the finest, most expensive champagne in the house comes from."

It had been grown, bottled, and aged at St. Helena in the Napa Valley, 50 miles north of San Francisco. Then and there I realized that it is the same all over the world: anything that comes from far away tastes better—and costs more.

There are four and maybe five more things that happened. Perhaps there were even more that I should remember, but by then I was anxious to get home and thought of little else. I felt as though my whole life were ahead of me, and I was eager to begin. Ragsdale and Leon Barbeau said I had "channel fever." That was true, but not in the sense that sailors mean it. I didn't want to have a good time; I wanted to get down to work—my real life's work.

One November morning the *President Wilson* steamed up New York Harbor, and there again was the Statue of Liberty. As I stood on the deck and saw her once more, welcoming us, a lump rose in my throat. I was apart from the others, thinking back to a summer morning six years before.

108

A few steps down the deck one of the passengers, a father, stood holding his little boy up in his arms.

"Look, son. See the statue?"

"What a beautiful lady!" exclaimed the boy.

All of us—the little boy, the father, and we who stood against the rail—were all so proud of her, as she held her torch high above the harbor, it was hard to keep back the tears. The little boy said what we were all thinking. She was a beautiful lady—the most beautiful lady in the world.

After the *President Wilson* left New York, she sailed to Boston, then steamed south to Havana, and crossed the Caribbean to Panama.

If New York had been a lovely sight, so was San Pedro, the harbor city for Los Angeles, because it was so close to home. Here while the *Wilson* was in port, I went to see some of my old friends.

The evening I liked best was a quiet one at the home of an Armenian newspaperman and his family. There was a very fine, home-cooked Armenian dinner, with lots of informal conversation and traveler's tales afterward. Among the half dozen or so who sat listening very quietly were Lucie and Nazenig Ruzvanian, who were going to school in Los Angeles, and their mother. It was almost time to go before I realized that Nazenig was the leader of Proff Calfayan's choral group, the girl who had been so haughty and superior at the concert in San Francisco.

As we were preparing to leave, she said, "It's too bad you have to go on to San Francisco so soon. My mother and sister and I would like to hear more about your experiences in the Orient, and especially at San Lazzaro."

What a difference a little trip around the world makes, I thought. But I didn't say it. Instead, I said, "Well, I could write about them to you—if you don't mind hearing from 'a nice boy from the old country.'"

She smiled. "That wasn't very gracious of me, was it?"

I felt that she was saying she was sorry, but I had forgiven her even before she spoke.

"What shall I call you?"

109

"My mother and sister call me Naz," she replied.

"Very well then, Naz. I'll write to you."

The *Wilson* steamed through the Golden Gate. There once more, after four months on faraway seas and in faraway places, was the beautiful city that I called home.

I guess our arrival in New York was still fresh in my mind, for as wonderful a sight as the bay and city made, something was wrong. I looked up the stream toward Alcatraz, and I knew what it was.

What a thrill it had been to enter New York Harbor and be welcomed by the Statue of Liberty. Now, what a shame it was to enter the bay of San Francisco, world-famous for its size and loveliness, and be welcomed by a prison, the home of the nation's worst criminals.

A hope filled my heart that has never left it—the hope that some day the prison will be torn down and in its place will rise a twin, an exact duplicate of New York's Statue of Liberty, facing west. Calmly and proudly she would stand there through the rains and the mists, through the sunny days and the soft, starry nights.

Millions of Americans would see her every year and be inspired by her, and many travelers from foreign lands would wonder at her and what she stood for, and see that she belonged there. She would raise her torch high over America's western gateway and welcome those who had crossed the Pacific to find her. And in San Francisco, the birthplace of the United Nations, what could be more fitting than that?

CHAPTER NINE

In San Francisco I took Ragsdale—the canary—and all my things to Minnie and Arshag's new house on Thirty-first Avenue, and I knew that no matter what lay ahead, there was one thing I had to do, one thing I had to be, and it had to come first, before everything else.

Inside of me, in my heart, I felt that I had come home. America was my home. I had been homesick for it. I had longed for it the way a hungry man would long for food. Yet what right, what legal right, did I have to call it my home, my country? None—none at all.

Wherever I had traveled, people had looked at my steward's uniform from the *President Wilson* and had taken it for granted that I was an American. But sometimes, because of my accent, I was asked about it. "No," I had to reply, "I'm not a citizen. But some day I will be."

How I yearned to throw out my chest and say to all the world—to shout it from the housetops if I could—"Yes! I am an American. I have the privilege and honor of being a citizen of the greatest nation on earth. She has given me this treasure, this precious gift."

As I looked around me in San Francisco in these first months back home, I saw friends and acquaintances—men and women alike—going through all their lives without becoming citizens. Why? Mostly because of a funny, childish pride.

Maybe they had won a reputation in their neighborhood as wise men; yet in their hearts lay the fear that they couldn't answer the questions of the naturalization examiner. Or their friends had always taken it for granted that they were already citizens, and they were ashamed to admit that they weren't. You must remember that in those days a person's citizenship status was seldom questioned. No one had to carry draft cards, or alien or identification cards. And you must remember, too, that there were no social security benefits for citizens that would make aliens eager for their naturalization papers. Uncle Sam was not so generous in passing out money as he is today.

As I talked with them and studied them, I realized that although they lived in an American city and under an American sky, they were still foreigners, and perhaps always would be. There was even something dishonest about it. Here they were accepting all the advantages of America, without assuming any of the responsibilities of citizenship or loyalty.

Then, on the other hand, there were the others, those who really cut the ties between themselves and their mother countries and who became Americans in every sense of the word. They walked with firm, strong strides, like men and women who knew where they were going, and they wore their citizenship like a bright badge, like a decoration, like a medal on their chests.

That is what I wanted. How wonderful it was that my

112

five years of waiting were over and that at last I could step forward and claim my own responsibilities as an American —and my own shining medal that I was burning to wear forever.

The way everyone suffers who has ever gone through the citizenship test, I suffered with doubts and fears that I would not pass. I had nightmares in which the examiner asked me questions in Chinese and Norwegian and other strange languages, and when I couldn't answer, he would frown terribly and shake his head and turn his thumbs down the way Romans did with their gladiators, and I would start awake in a cold sweat.

But I made up my mind that, pass or fail, I had to try, and so I filed my application, and one beautiful morning in June the miracle happened.

The day began with the *lodos*, the south wind, rippling all the bright, brave flags. I never remembered the *lodos* in San Francisco before. It blew just the way it used to blow in Scutari, when Father was alive, and we went down the hill together, to the beach and the Bosphorus. I could feel it on my face and close my eyes and be back there in the springtime, with the silvery *khamsi* running and the blue *manghal* smoke rising all over the city. Why was it blowing here in San Francisco at last, on this sunny morning, this June 3, 1929, that I would surely remember all the rest of my life?

I did not know, but it shook the beautiful flags out softly, and it made me feel my hand in my father's, as it used to be in those Scutari springtimes that were now so far away.

On this morning, it was Armen Bardizian who walked at my side—Armen and my two witnesses, Charles Janigian, a young lawyer, and Dr. John Shotigian, a dentist. All three were my very good friends. We walked up Market Street to Seventh Street, and turned down Seventh to the Main Post Office and Federal Court Building.

We climbed the stairs to the second floor and entered a courtroom of great dignity. The flag in here hung still from its staff, in rich, silky folds. My friends wished me luck.

113

I stepped forward, toward the man at the table. He wasted no time.

"George Mardikian?" His voice was crisp, like an Army officer's. "Candidate for citizenship?"

"Yes, sir."

"Sit down."

I sat in a chair across the table.

"You have been attending the citizenship classes in one of the public schools?"

"No, sir. I haven't had time. But I am ready for my examination."

He shot me a look from under raised eyebrows. I guess he thought I was a "smart guy."

"What is your real name, please?"

"George Mardikian."

"No," he said. "Your Armenian name."

"George Mardikian, sir."

I was irritating him, but I could not help it.

"Do you mean to tell me that your name in Armenian was George?"

"Yes, sir—pronounced *Gay-org*—G-e-o-r-g. No 'e' at the end of it. All my life I was called *Gay-org*. Except when I was a little boy."

"What did they call you then?" He leaned forward, like a prosecutor.

"Georgica. Little *Gay-org*."

I looked at my friends. They were trying hard not to smile. I showed the examiner the passport that had been issued to me by the Armenian Republic. I pointed to my official Armenian name: "George Mardikian."

His mouth made a thin line. "All right. We will get on with the examination."

Although I hadn't been able to go to school, I had worked hard for almost seven years at learning to speak English. I had read newspapers, and magazines like the *Literary Digest,* and I had taken time out from my sleep to study the columns of Arthur Brisbane and American history books.

114

My idols had been men who knew all about these things, like Captain Milton D. Brown and Dr. John Voris. In an examination room or anywhere else, I wasn't going to let them down, if I could help it.

So we went swiftly through the simple questions. Then he looked at me oddly, as if to say, "Here's one for you, smart guy."

"Who," he asked, "was the Secretary of Commerce during President Coolidge's administration?"

In justice to the examiner asking me this unfair question, I think he was just trying to take some wind from my sails, and would have passed me even if I couldn't answer it. He sat there sternly. I glanced at Armen and my two witnesses. They looked so unhappy I felt sorry for them. It was obvious they had no idea who was President Coolidge's Secretary of Commerce. I couldn't help smiling. My hero of heroes was coming to my rescue.

"Herbert Hoover," I said. I was very proud, just to say the name that became to me—and millions of other needy Europeans after World War I—a symbol of American generosity and mercy.

Suddenly, almost before I realized what was happening, the white-haired Federal judge was standing there in his black robes, and we had our right hands raised, and I was repeating after him the oath of allegiance to the United States.

We came to the end. My shoulders were thrown back. I was standing as straight and tall as I could. Before me was the beautiful silk flag. I loved it with my very life. The golden words rang through the courtroom.

"George Mardikian, now you are an American citizen!"

In the corridor, my friends shook hands with me. They patted me on the back. Shotig stopped me. "How did you know?"

"What?" I asked.

"About Herbert Hoover."

I smiled again. "I just happened to remember." I think

if the examiner had asked how many fish my hero had caught on his last vacation trip from the White House, I could have told him.

We walked down Market Street. There was still the *lodos* in the air, shaking all the flags out softly. The bluest of June skies was above us. We were on Powell Street again. They were all going back to their work. Armen was the last to say good-by.

He held out his hand once more. He knew how I felt.

"Isn't it a wonderful thing, George?"

I couldn't speak.

"There isn't any doubt about it now, is there?"

"No," I said. "Now I am really an American."

Armen nodded slowly. Then he said, "When we immigrants are granted our citizenship, we are ready to fall down on our knees with gratitude. And that is the way it should be. But we can always be very proud of this: We are American citizens by choice. Native-borns are indeed fortunate. But you can point to every one of them and say that somewhere in their past was a man or a woman like us, who left the only home he knew, and crossed the sea, and chose America."

I walked on up the street, past the St. Francis and Union Square. The usual thing to do was find some wine or bootleg whisky and give a celebration party and get drunk, like on New Year's Eve. But I wasn't much of a drinking fellow. I thought of going over and sitting in the square, where Armen and I had sat and talked that night that seemed a hundred years ago. But buildings fenced the square in. I was a giant, and there wasn't enough air for me. There wasn't enough space to hold me.

A block away I got on a Sutter Street car. It went west and crossed Van Ness Avenue. Soon we were out there where there was more sky and light.

This was Monday. By the time we reached the beach and the ocean I was the only one on the car. I got off as if I were a knight getting down from my white horse. I laughed aloud and waved to the conductor and the motorman and ran down the curving walk past the Cliff House to the beach.

116

The wind had shifted and blew gently off the sea. The beach was deserted. I walked along the sand to the south, filling my lungs with the fresh salt air. The sea shimmered and sparkled under the afternoon sun. Far down the beach I found a white, barkless log of driftwood and sat down with my back against it and looked west.

Since the world began, many men of many races have looked upon the sea as a mother. I am one of them. I cannot live very long without seeing the sea. And so on this day, there was no sky big enough for me except my ocean sky. And no place was home, except here, where I could hear the waves breaking in and racing up the sand.

I thought for a moment that it was as if I had been given a beautiful jewel. I treasured it so highly that here, beside the ocean, I had to examine it with awe and wonder, and I had to look closely at every shining facet of it before I could share it with anyone else.

You who have been born in America, I wish I could make you understand what it is like not to be an American—not to have been an American all your life—and then suddenly, with the words of a man in flowing robes, to be one, for that moment, and forever after. Think of it. One moment you are a citizen of Armenia, a brave and tiny state out of sight beneath the red tide of Russia. The next, you are an American! One moment, you belong with your fathers to a million dead yesterdays. The next, you belong with America to a million unborn tomorrows.

Oh, the honor of it! And the thrilling pride, and yet the humility, with which you wear that honor!

I could remember feeling something like this twice before; once, when I was a flag-bearer with the Armenian Legion, and I held high the tricolor, the red, blue, and orange of Hayastan; and again, the morning we all stood on the deck of the *Meghali Ellas* and saw in the dawn that beautiful lady of hope and trust and liberty.

Hours passed, and my thoughts turned the day into Thanksgiving Day. No one stands alone. That morning, in my proudest hour, the courtroom was filled with people. I could not see them, but somehow they were all there with me. And now I gave thanks to them. I thanked my dead father and my mother and my Uncle Krikor for their love and their patience and the beautiful childhood they had given me. I thanked Mr. Hoover and Dr. Voris, and other wonderful Americans whom I had never met, for their inspiration. I thanked Mr. Compton and the other men who had given me work for their belief in me. I thanked my brother and sister for a thousand acts of unselfish kindness. I thanked my friends everywhere for all their help. I thanked Armen especially, for being wise enough to see the truth, and honest and brave enough one night in Union Square, to tell me what it was.

The wind died down. A freighter came through the Golden Gate and steered for the setting sun. She pitched and tossed and then buckled down to business as she met the offshore rollers. I watched her grow small and lonely and become a smoking speck upon the sea. How fortunate she was that the world was round! No matter where she went, if she just kept sailing she would find her way back home to some safe, friendly harbor, in this beautiful land of the free.

I was still inside and quietly happy—happier than I had ever been. Now my own footsteps belonged in the Song of America. My own footsteps, and the beat of my heart, as long as I lived.

CHAPTER TEN

But the thick notebooks in which I had stored all my treasures of the world's cuisine for quite a while lay neglected in my suitcase. Every time I thought of them or noticed the suitcase on the closet floor, they reproached me.

It was strange, and hard to understand. I had so much to do and accomplish, I didn't know where or how to begin. The task ahead was so big, how could I ever hope to do it, and do it right? It had to be on a large scale, and it had to be perfect. Now that I was a citizen, it was more than ever necessary that I make America and Americans proud of me. I could not make one mistake. But, facing all this, I couldn't get started. The thought paralyzed me.

I began writing long letters to the Ruzvanian girl, in Los

119

Angeles. "Dear Naz—" they began. I covered page after page, telling her about the places I had been and the things I had seen and learned on my trip around the world. And I told her how thrilling it was and how proud I was to be an American citizen. I shared my precious jewel with her. Her replies were warm, yet graceful and restrained, just as she was.

Finally my confusion and my disappointment with myself found their way into my letters. What was wrong? I had such high hopes and ambitions, such plans and dreams; what was holding me back? Time was passing. The money that I had saved on the ship was gradually disappearing.

"Perhaps you want to do too much, all at once," she replied. "Perhaps you want to climb Big Masis in one afternoon. But it takes many steps, one after the other. It takes a long time. You have many wonderful years ahead of you."

I read her words over and over again. It was as though she had somehow reached out across all the miles that separated us and placed her cool hand on my forehead.

One afternoon I put my precious notebooks on the back of the closet shelf at Arshag's. Then I packed my suitcase and took the train to Los Angeles.

The name of Naz's mother was Anitza. She was a large woman, and very gentle. Her hair was silver gray. Her beauty and dignity were like a queen's. And always, when I was with her, I thought of the Armenian proverb, centuries old and centuries wise, "First look at the tree, then pluck the fruit." Someday her daughters would have the same queen-like beauty, the same dignity, the same gracious poise.

Anitza's people came from Tokat, a countryside below the Black Sea known for its rich Turkish tobacco and its miles of orchards. Her father had died when she was a baby, and she had been brought to America by her mother, Prapion Chalikian, and her older brother, Yeghia.

I was also very fond of Naz's father. We hit it off from the start. Hagop was his name, Hagop Ruzvanian, and he had come from Cilicia. Now he was a businessman and real-estate investor of Fresno. While Anitza—or Mother, as we

120

all called her—was living with the daughters in Los Angeles so that they could go to school there, he was as unhappy as they about the divided household. Every moment he could spare from business he spent in Los Angeles with them.

There was something dashing and Continental about Hagop. He loved good food and fine liqueurs, and an expensive Havana after dinner. But, there was another side to his nature: he was known everywhere in Fresno for his generosity to the needy. I liked him from the beginning too for his easy, hearty laughter. Many times I have seen him so carried away by his own funny story or someone else's that he would laugh until the tears streamed down his face. I have a good feeling for anyone who can laugh like that.

The warmth of this family, its friendship, its sympathy and understanding became tremendously important to me. We spent many happy hours together over the dinner table in the evenings. And every afternoon Naz and I went for walks, up and down the long Los Angeles streets in the summer sunshine. Our walks always ended not far from their home, in little Westlake Park. There we would sit, with the big city all around us, and watch the swans gliding across the lake, and smile at the children at play. When the shadows grew long and it got cool, we would leave the park and walk slowly down the street to where they lived.

So the days went by. Our relationship deepened. Gradually my thoughts and desires turned again to the months and years ahead. Naz was right: you could not get on top of Big Masis in one afternoon. You started out and took step after step and began to climb. Then, in God's own time, not yours, you reached the summit. Sometimes, as we talked, I felt as though part of me were studying the maps and planning the way up the mountainside. Soon this part of me would say, "We are ready." And we would start the long climb.

This moment came, and I said good-by to Mother and Father Ruzvanian, Lucie, and dark-haired Naz. There was no need to try to tell them how grateful I was for everything; I felt we would all know each other for a long time. I returned to San Francisco refreshed and confident.

121

I went back to work at Compton's, and early in 1930 Mr. Compton made me manager of his new restaurant at Twelfth Street and Broadway, in Oakland. I moved to an apartment on Third Avenue. Its windows overlooked Lake Merritt, which is in the middle of downtown Oakland.

There lived in Oakland a family named Adoor—Mr. and Mrs. Paul Adoor, and their little daughter Elizabeth, who was thirteen. They had moved to Oakland from Fresno. We became very friendly. I went there frequently for dinner and a relaxing evening in the pleasant atmosphere of their home.

One night, as I left to go to my apartment, Mrs. Adoor said, "I understand you have good friends in Los Angeles."

That was true, I said.

"Perhaps one of these evenings you will have a nice surprise." And that was all she would tell me.

Sure enough, the next week Mr. Adoor invited me to visit them. The Adoor family met me in the hall. We shook hands. I said, "Good evening, Miss Adoor," and smiled down at Elizabeth. She looked flushed and excited, as though she were holding back a big secret.

"Well, Elizabeth," I said, "what is the matter?"

Her eyes were dancing.

"Evidently the cat has got your tongue."

Still she said nothing. We left the hall and entered the living room. There, on the couch, sat Mother Ruzvanian and Naz.

It was the first time I had seen them since the spring before, when I had left Los Angeles. I looked at Naz and she looked at me. My heart stood still. I felt a sinking feeling inside. That was the moment, the very first moment, that I knew we were in love.

It is strange that at the most significant times of our lives we usually say or do something very simple, even commonplace. While my heart sang, I stepped forward and took their outstretched hands in mine.

"What a surprise!" I said. "What a beautiful surprise!"

Naz and I decided to go ahead in the old-fashioned way.

122

We had been brought up to respect our elders and the traditions that they believed in. So, almost as if we were in the old country, we had our family go-betweens, the Adoors representing the Ruzvanians and a friend of mine, Haigan Shotigian of Oakland, representing the Mardikians.

At a dinner at the Adoors', it was understood that I had the blessing of Mother Ruzvanian, the absent Hagop, and Mr. and Mrs. Adoor. That evening little Elizabeth went around in a dream. I am sure that she looked on Naz and me as a lovely princess and her prince. This was all something in a fairy tale.

Then, of course, it was necessary for my brother and sister to approve of Naz. The following night we all met again for dinner, this time at Haigan's house. The evening was not half over before I knew by looking at Baidzar, and especially at Arshag, that Naz had won their hearts, as she had won mine.

"She is the girl for you, George," they both told me. "You are very lucky, and we are very happy for you both."

The Armenian custom is that the engagement shall be announced at a big party given by the parents of the bride-to-be. The day Naz and her mother left for home, we decided to waste no time. We would have our engagement party in Los Angeles on March 15, the day after Naz's birthday.

On March 13, Baidzar and Arshag and I set out for Los Angeles. Baidzar's husband, Aram, couldn't go because of his work, and Minnie, Arshag's wife, couldn't go because someone had to stay behind and take care of Ragsdale, the canary, and Gregory, their little boy. We were driving and we reached Fresno late that afternoon and went directly to the house of Naz's grandmother, Prapion Chalikian.

Grandma, which is what I always called her, although it made her look sharply at me many times, was at this time about eighty years old. She was a large lady like her daughter, Anitza, and had much of the same dignity, so that some of the Fresnans who had known her a long while called her "the duchess."

123

She had been about forty when she lost her husband, and when she had gone to America with her two sons and the little girl who became Naz's mother. As I said, they came from the tobacco country of Tokat; so it was natural for them to go into the tobacco-growing business in Fresno. They had a small plantation that grew filler tobacco. So did other Armenians south of Fresno, and her son Yeghia was the agent who represented them all and arranged for the sale of their crops to the American Tobacco Company.

They say in Fresno that, although Yeghia was the brains and the manager of the enterprise, it was Grandma's push and gumption that made the business a success. Both Naz and Lucie could remember how, as children, they used to hear Grandma using some very strong language about the Hindus that they employed to irrigate the delicate tobacco plants. If she had reason to believe they were not hard at work, she would tie her skirts out of the way, grab a pair of binoculars, and climb nimbly up the ladder to the top of the plantation's lookout tower. There, 90 or 100 feet above the ground, she would spy on the Hindus through her glasses. If they were working, that was fine, and she came down grumbling about having to watch them so closely. But if they were lying around smoking by the irrigation ditches, as they sometimes were, Grandma was flying in a fury across the fields, giving them a tongue-lashing even before she was close enough to make them hear what she was saying.

Yeghia died about 1910 or 1912, right in the middle of the tobacco harvest, which was the most important time of the year for all the tobacco growers. It was Grandma who stepped in and completed the business arrangements with the big executives from the East, and haggled and bickered with them for months, and finally sold out her interests, and the interests of Yeghia's estate, for enough money to buy three handsome houses in Fresno that would support her well for the rest of her life.

As with many of the older Armenians, the "Evil Eye" was very much a part of Grandma's daily life. She wore blue beads to ward it off, and was always careful to put her

124

hand around and touch her bottom, whenever anyone said anything nice to her.

If you told her what a pretty dress she was wearing or what good jam she had made, or how nice she looked, she would study you with steely eyes, as if to say, "What is in back of that remark? What are you after?" Then, to protect herself against the evils hidden behind this flattery, her hand would steal around in back of her, and she would touch her bottom.

The wonderful thing about Grandma was her magnificent, unyielding pride. Most of the women of her generation were living with their married sons or daughters, or even their grandchildren, and were sometimes quite a burden. But our Grandma was independent. She lived in her own house. When her daughter or her grandchildren or other relatives wanted to see her, they called on her, at her house. This made her a proud matriarch among the Armenian colony of Fresno. And it was a special sign or symbol of Grandma's pride that she never wore a shawl. You would see other Armenian grandmothers downtown, or shopping at their neighborhood groceries, with old-country shawls covering their heads and shoulders. But never Grandma. On her head she wore Alice Chase hats, the most fashionable that anybody could buy in the city of Fresno. Even in those days, they cost twenty-five or thirty dollars each.

In her home in Fresno that night Grandma served us a wonderful dinner of *bott*. This is a Lenten dish, and she must have worked hard over it all afternoon.

To give you an idea of what it is like, *bott* in Armenian means "to dip," or "dunk." The home of every Armenian from Tokat has in its basement or storage room large barrels or earthenware jugs of grape leaves preserved in a salt-water solution. Some of this water is drained off—it isn't a brine, because it isn't that strong, and it has a light, fresh flavoring from the grape leaves—and with it is mixed a large assortment of ingredients: chopped onions sautéed in olive oil, chopped raw onions, sliced broiled green peppers, sliced and sautéed whole-pack tomatoes, crushed walnuts, tomato

125

paste, fresh dill, black-pepper seasoning, and a few fresh mint leaves.

Grandma, as was the custom, served it cold, and we sat around the table and ate it with big spoons. Golden-crusted *peda* dunked in it made a delicious variation. We even wrapped the mixture in the grape leaves themselves, and ate it that way.

Not only did Grandma outdo herself preparing *bott,* she also arranged what Armenians call "a regular Father Abraham's table," that is, a table spread out with all sorts of good things to eat—roast chicken, steaming pilaff, ivory-white roasted almonds, *gatahs* (or cakes), *paklava,* and other delicacies.

Then, as if this weren't enough, she made us eat some *media dolma*—mussels stuffed with rice, currants, onions, pine nuts, and parsley—and some delicate, flaky hot cheese *beurek*—tiny triangles of pastry, like small apple turnovers, only filled with a light Armenian cheese. I say "made us eat," but I guess I shouldn't. Grandma didn't exactly have to hit us on the head to get us to eat her wonderful dinner.

Long after dark, we resumed the drive to Los Angeles.

The next evening, at the Mayfair Hotel in Los Angeles, Father and Mother Ruzvanian took over an entire ballroom. There Naz and I exchanged our betrothal vows, gave each other rings, and received the blessing of the Armenian priest. Now we were really engaged.

After the banquet and the speeches that Armenians are always making whenever they have an excuse, the orchestra started playing Armenian songs, and many guests danced native dances on the wide ballroom floor. When this orchestra stopped, there was another one to play American tunes, so that the younger ones could fox-trot.

Arshag pulled me aside. "You see this, brother? Two orchestras? We have to do even better."

"What do you mean?" I knew that when the time came for the wedding I would have to pay the bill, as was the Armenian custom. But I couldn't believe what I was hearing from my thrifty brother.

126

"Family pride," he said. "We can't let these in-laws put one over on us. We have to give the biggest wedding they have ever seen—even if it takes you two years to pay for it."

The next day I left for Oakland to return to work. I held Naz in my arms for a long time. It didn't seem as though anything in my world could ever be wrong again.

March and April are beautiful months on the San Francisco Bay, and the skies stayed like blue cashmere week after week. Every morning I went to work with singing in my heart. We hadn't set the date for our marriage. It would probably be early in the fall.

Armen gave us his blessing. He told me one afternoon, when he came into the restaurant for a cup of coffee, that he was very happy for us both.

"Naz has lived in two worlds. She grew up with Armenian parents and Armenian ideas in the air around her. In Fresno, her mother has taken her down the street to the Turkish baths, just as she would if she lived in Istanbul, or Scutari. She knows the Armenian mind and heart. Then, too, she has many American friends and has gone to American schools. She is an American, and you, too, are now an American. You both have the Armenian heritage in back of you to give to your new country. I'm sure this will make you better and happier Americans."

In a little while Naz came again to visit the Adoors. On my days off we rode the ferryboat to San Francisco and went for walks in Golden Gate Park to see the rhododendrons in bloom. In the evenings, when I was through work, we would go for rides in the Berkeley hills. We never got tired of talking about the wonderful years ahead of us.

When we received invitations to an engagement party in Sanger, a town in the San Joaquin Valley not far from Fresno, Naz was delighted.

"It will be a wonderful party," she said. "We have to go."

"How?" I asked.

"We'll drive down in your car."

This is something I cannot explain, but I have always had a premonition deep down in my heart whenever something unpleasant is going to happen. This feeling warned me against the trip to Sanger.

"Let's stay in Oakland and send a telegram," I said.

"But why shouldn't we go?"

I told her about my feeling.

She laughed. "You're as superstitious as Grandma," she said, "believing in these funny feelings of yours."

We left shortly after noon the day of the party—Naz and I, Haig and Esther Kapigian, and Peggy Terzian, who was going to meet her escort in Fresno. We got on Highway 99. Outside of Merced it started raining hard. It was difficult to see through the windshield. The road was wet and slippery.

As we went around a curve, I thought Naz, in the front seat beside me, was thrown against the door. I looked over. The door was swinging open.

"Naz!" I said, and reached for the collar of her fur coat.

The car slid into a long skid. I couldn't steer it. It skidded off the road, struck the shoulder, and shot high into the air and turned over and over. Something exploded in my head.

I came to as they were lifting the car so they could pull me out from under it. I was covered with blood. I felt blood all over my face. I staggered to my feet. On the ground nearby lay Haig and Esther and Peggy. Peggy was groaning.

"The other girl," I said. "Where is she?"

A crowd was gathering. Someone said the ambulance was on the way.

"Naz! Naz!" I shouted. I stumbled through the crowd and the rain looking everywhere for her.

A little man came up to me. "I think I saw her."

I shook him. "Where is she?"

"I was right behind you. I saw a body fly out of the car, just as you went off the road."

Young wheat grew in the next field. He and I ran to the fence and climbed over and trampled through the wheat. Others followed us. The ground was soft and black with the rain. In this field, a few yards off the road, I found Naz. She was lying on her back. I went down on my knees beside her. I must have been a terrible sight.

128

She couldn't speak because of the pain. She gasped and tried to smile. Her leg was twisted under her in a funny way, and I was sure it was broken. I picked her up and carried her out to the road and put her in the ambulance. The others were already inside. It turned around and started toward Merced. I never heard anything so filled with agony as its siren, screaming almost the way a tortured human being would scream.

It seemed as though a thousand cars were parked along the road now in the rain, and as though five times that many people were staring at me, or at my wrecked machine in the middle of the field. I answered all the questions of the police; then a bystander and his wife drove me to the emergency hospital in Merced. My bleeding had stopped, but I felt as though I had been clubbed from head to foot.

"Where is Miss Ruzvanian?" I said.

An interne tried to pull me into a first-aid room. I pushed him away. "Take care of me later. Where is she?"

The interne looked at the register. "Ruzvanian?—No one here by that name."

I gave him Haig's name, and Esther's, and Peggy's. He shook his head. I thought they were all dead. There hadn't been any use to take them to a hospital. I was on the point of breaking down. I could feel myself going.

One of the nurses said, "You're getting excited for nothing. Maybe they were taken to the other hospital."

They telephoned. She was right. The man and wife who had taken me to the emergency hospital drove me across the city to the other hospital. It was a terrible ride, because I hadn't had the courage to ask how Naz was. I didn't know what was waiting for me.

Haig, Esther, and Peggy were sitting in chairs in the lobby. Their cuts were bandaged. Haig's wrist was wrapped in tape. They all looked shaken and pale.

"We're all right," Haig said.

I scarcely heard him. There, on a guerney, lay Naz. I went to her. She gave me a little grin. "You look pretty," she said.

"How do you feel?"

129

"My back hurts. And my leg hurts."

"Are they taking care of you?"

"I want to go home to Fresno," she said.

I went to the telephone and called a friend in Turlock. He came and got us and drove us to Naz's house in Fresno. We had telephoned Father Ruzvanian, too. He had two doctors waiting for us. One of them patched me up. My cuts were nothing serious. All I needed was rest because of the shock.

The other doctor examined Naz. As he came out of her room, Father and I met him at the door. Neither of us said a word.

"She's very lucky," he said. "Nothing broken, but she has a badly sprained ankle. Her back is bruised and wrenched. That heavy fur coat she was wearing probably saved her from a broken spine."

Downstairs, Grandma gave me a disgusted stare. "What are you trying to do—see how strong our little girl is? Why aren't you more careful?"

I tried to explain about my premonition.

"You forgot to touch your bottom, to ward off the Evil Eye," said the old lady. As long as she lived, that remained in her mind as the cause of our unfortunate accident.

I had to be at the restaurant the next day. I caught the valley milk train back to Oakland. After opening the manager's office for the day's business, I called Mr. Compton and told him what happened. He came down, took one look at me, and said, "Go home and go to bed and don't move for three days." I didn't argue. I did just what he told me to do.

The way Italians go into debt over their funerals and their tombstones is the way Armenians go into debt over their weddings. There is no such thing as you can't afford it. You afford it.

I was thinking of this, and getting up my nerve, because now, after the accident, Naz and I were seeing each other more than ever before. I took the long train ride to Fresno every chance I got. She had almost recovered, but it seemed

130

as though the accident, the experience, the terrible hour we had gone through, had brought us closer together than ever before. And not only that, but I had realized, in those nightmarish moments when I was afraid she was dead, how much she meant to me. She was my world and my life. If she was lost, then they were lost, too.

Toward the end of April, there didn't seem to be any point to our waiting until fall for the wedding. On my next trip to Fresno, I said, "Naz, let's get married right away. The sooner the better. After what we've been through, we know, don't we? We're sure—we don't have to wait—"

She put her hand over mine and bent her head close. "No, darling—we don't have to wait—"

The wedding took place June 1, 1930, at the Little Church Around the Corner, on Fulton Street in San Francisco. More than 1,200 relatives and friends were there. We had sixteen ushers and sixteen bridesmaids; little Gregory was the ring bearer; and Mary, Baidzar and Aram's daughter, was flower girl.

In Los Angeles, Lucie had studied costume designing with Howard Greer, and she made Naz's elaborate wedding dress—an exact copy of the dress that Bessie Love, the film star, had worn in her recent wedding.

Both of us wanted Father Markarian of Fowler to perform the ceremony. But the Armenian Gregorian Church in San Francisco had a pastor, and the prelate, Archbishop Karekin of Trebizond, didn't want to ask another, outside priest to marry us.

So, uniting us in the long and very complicated ceremony was this white-haired pastor, with a snowy beard and flowing robes. The way it turned out, he had been given a new parish in Rio de Janeiro and was soon to leave San Francisco. And so he used our wedding as an excuse to preach an endless sermon on the joys and responsibilities of married life.

Naz and I, kneeling before him, still were stiff and sore from the accident. We were in agony as he went on and on.

Finally, Naz and I looked at each other. We looked up at

131

him. His rich voice filled the church. He was having a wonderful time.

I reached up and tugged his robe. *"Derhair,"* I whispered. "Cut it short. Cut it short."

The only effect was to make him even more eloquent. Some of the older women in the church were sobbing softly.

I tugged again. *"Derhair.* That's enough."

He stopped and looked down at me. "My son," he said gently, "I'll never talk to this many people again."

(As it turned out, he spoke the truth. He died in Brazil, before the end of the year.)

At last he finished, and Naz and I were really married, and we turned and walked back down the aisle. There were sixteen rows of pews. At each row stood an usher and a bridesmaid, each holding an old-fashioned bouquet above our heads, so that we walked down between them the way the bride and bridegroom do in a military wedding, only we walked beneath flowers instead of swords.

No hall in San Francisco was big enough for the reception; so I hired the Scottish Rite Auditorium. A twelve-piece band played for dancing. Long tables sagged under food enough to feed a regiment. In the center of the table, where Naz and I and our families sat, rose an immense wedding cake made by the bakers of Compton's restaurant. It was like a cake at an international exposition. It weighed 150 pounds and turned slowly on a moving platform that was run by a concealed electric motor. It was so big, the ordinary doll figures of the bride and bridegroom had looked like ridiculous pygmies on top of it. We went and bought large kewpie dolls and dressed them up in wedding clothes, so that the figures would be in proportion to the cake.

Thanks to one of Arshag's friends, we had plenty of gin for our reception guests. He was a Shriner who had recently returned from a convention in Canada. He had smuggled several cases of gin across the border in the bass drum of the Shriner band.

John Hagopian, a lawyer and one of my most intellectual friends, was the *tamada,* the master of ceremonies. When

132

everybody had finished eating, he introduced those who wanted to make speeches. The various Armenian toasts took a long time. The flowery speeches took even longer. Then the band played, and everybody started to dance.

I'm sure that the noise and the happiness and laughter made Arshag very happy, and Naz's family, too, but you can imagine that by that time Naz and I were very tired. Finally we were able to say good-by. In a snowstorm of rice on that beautiful June evening, we got in our borrowed car and drove out of San Francisco and headed for a cottage at Capitola-by-the-Sea. This was a resort near Santa Cruz, on the blue Bay of Monterey. I wanted to go there to fish and to eat the wonderful Monterey sea food.

Arshag told me later that the reception rolled merrily on long after we left. Then he took our close friends and the Ruzvanians out to his house to continue the festivities. Some Italians who lived next door joined the party with jugs of wine.

It was getting to be a real neighborhood affair, when all at once the doorbell rang. Arshag peered out the window, expecting to see more wedding guests. Instead, he saw two policemen.

He ran to the kitchen. "Get rid of this stuff," he said, and began pouring all the wine and liquor down the sink. Others pitched in and helped. As the last quart gurgled down the drain, Minnie opened the door.

"Good evening," the policeman said with a smile. "You are making a good deal of noise."

Minnie smiled sweetly back. "Yes, we're celebrating. You see, my husband's brother got married this afternoon. We all came here after the reception."

"Well," said the policeman, "in San Francisco we never let prohibition stand in the way of a wedding party." He and his fellow stepped into the living room. "Mind if we join the fun and drink a toast to the newlyweds?"

Arshag almost had to catch Minnie to hold her up.

"Toast!" she gasped. "We just threw all the wine down the sink!"

133

And so ended the biggest wedding party in the history of the San Francisco Armenian colony. The Mardikian family honor had not been disgraced. It took me two years to pay the bills.

Our little cottage at Capitola-by-the-Sea still stands on the brink of a high cliff. Down below was a private beach, where I fished every day and hunted for mussels. I cooked the mussels over open beach fires, the way I used to cook them on the shore near Scutari, in the days of my childhood.

There are things you never forget about a honeymoon. If you are happily married, the things that Naz and I remember are probably not much different from those that have remained with you through the years.

But one morning, late in the second week, when I put a wonderful slice of broiled sea bass on the breakfast table, buttered and salted and right out of the oven, I noted a strange expression on my bride's face.

"Sweetheart, what is the matter?" I asked.

Naz shook her head. "Nothing, dearest. Everything is beautiful."

I put some of the fish on her plate. Weakly she picked at it with her fork. I thought back. As we had agreed before our marriage, I had cooked every meal we ate at our cottage. In the daytime I caught fish, and we had it for dinner—unless we went over to Monterey for a sea-food dinner at Fisherman's Wharf—and for breakfast the next morning.

Naz hadn't eaten very much, not nearly as much as she used to eat at home. My explanation for this was that she was on her honeymoon. She was actually living on love.

But on this morning, as I looked at her across the breakfast table, I wondered if a diet of love would leave her quite so pale. Wouldn't her cheeks be rosy and blooming?

"Please eat some more, honey," I said. "You don't look very well."

All at once, she picked up her napkin and began to cry. "I can't keep it up any longer. I'm sorry, darling—I just can't—"

I was at her side in an instant. "Naz, what is it?"

"When I was young, Mother used to make me take cod-liver oil—"

I wiped her tears away. "But—what's wrong now, sweetheart—?"

Muffled through the napkin, out it came at last. "George—I hate—fish—"

I went down to the store and came back with a sirloin steak. By the time I was through cooking it, Naz was very hungry. She ate like a foot soldier after a day's march. With that steak breakfast she started regaining her color. In another day, she was her blooming self again.

The last day of our honeymoon ended, and we watched the sunset for the last time from our happy cottage.

The next morning, we returned to real life and its cares. There was a telegram from Fresno, saying that Father Ruzvanian had had a stroke. Mother Ruzvanian and Lucie had waited to send us this unhappy news until our honeymoon was over, and it was waiting for us when we reached Oakland. We got in the car again and drove down through the valley. Neither one of us said more than ten words during the long, hot drive. Our hearts were too filled with anxiety to speak.

When we saw him the next day at the hospital, it was clear that this man, who had so brightened the lives of all those around him, was not going to live much longer.

I telephoned Mr. Compton. He said to remain in Fresno as long as I was needed. We stayed with Mother Ruzvanian and Lucie. The days dragged by.

Father Ruzvanian died on the afternoon of June 30. He was buried two days later in Ararat Cemetery, Fresno, under the valley trees that he loved so well.

All of us—Naz and Lucie and Mother Ruzvanian and I— were stunned. Just a month ago, he had been so happy at our wedding party. Now the house seemed empty, and quiet. We all felt somehow left behind, deserted. We wondered what we were going to do without him.

CHAPTER ELEVEN

Father Ruzvanian had a partner. His name was Hagop also
—Hagop Terzian. But they had adopted nicknames, to make
identification easier for their friends and customers. Hagop
in Armenian means "Jacob," so Hagop Ruzvanian was Jake.
Hagop Terzian was Jack.

Between them they owned a little one-story building on
Van Ness Avenue across from the Fresno County Courthouse
and Courthouse Square, and they operated in this building
the City Pool Hall, City Barber Shop, City Shoeshine Parlor,
and the cigar and lunch counter called the City Café. If any
one came in while Jake Ruzvanian was there, and said, "Is
Jack here?" Jake would shrug and say, "My name is Jake, not
Jack." And the person would have to look elsewhere for

Mr. Terzian. Sometimes we all wondered if it wouldn't have been less confusing for them to have kept their real names.

It was a strange partnership. On the whole, they got along together very well. To the outsider they seemed to have an ideal business relationship. Other sets of partners formed, quarreled, and split up, but these two went on and on, for thirty years. Whenever someone doubted whether two Armenian businessmen could get along together, there was always someone else to speak up, "Look at the two Hagops. Look at how *they* get along together." And the doubter would yield, and everyone would nod, "Yes, that is true. The two Hagops are proof that we Armenians can get along together in business affairs."

No Ruzvanian or Terzian, who knew better, ever disagreed. But the truth was, for weeks on end Jake and Jack were so disgusted and angry with each other, they weren't on speaking terms. Relatives acted as go-betweens and carried messages from one to the other. Yet they would work side by side in the City Café, and the public would never know about their quarrel.

Jack and I had trouble from the beginning. Out by Roeding Park, the Armenians made a beautiful cemetery called Ararat. Its wide green lawns were shaded by shrubs and mulberry trees from Erzyrum and Trebizond and the real valley of the Ararat. All the Armenians in America, when they die, want to be buried there.

A gravel road wound through the cemetery. Beside this road, toward the western boundary of the cemetery, was the Ruzvanian family plot. Directly across the road was the Terzian family plot. Jack had planted there, at the head of the space reserved for him, two needlelike cypress trees.

A few days after Father Ruzvanian's funeral, Jack called on me. I was the head of the Ruzvanian family now, since Father's will had named me executor of his estate.

Jack said, "George, I think you should plant two cypress trees above Jake's grave, so that it will be just like mine. Then people will see his trees and mine and remember that we were partners."

137

But I had already formed my opinion of Jack's cypress trees. "We are going to do no such thing. They remind me too much of the trees in Turkish cemeteries."

Jack's face got red. "Are you telling me I have Turkish trees over my grave?"

"Never mind." I said. "You will not plant any trees like that over my dead body—or his either."

Between Jack and me it was like that, from then on.

I struggled with the affairs of Father's estate. In his safe I had found a little black book. It listed his most private accounts—how much he had given certain families in Fresno to bring their relatives from Armenia, how much he had given a farmer for his wife's operation, how much he had given an editor to meet his bills, so that he could keep printing his Armenian-language newspaper, how much he had spent on sheet music for the church choir, how much he had given one of the *derders,* or married priests, to help him with the grocery bill for his large family.

He had been a kind man. I began to understand that he had given me not only a title as his executor but a position in the community. One day toward the end of July, Naz and I returned to Oakland. I handed Mr. Compton the keys to my office. I thanked him for everything he had done for me and told him that I was resigning and that Naz and I were going to live in Fresno. A few days after that, the movers took everything out of the apartment. We looked out the window at Lake Merritt for the last time, and then, for the last time, shut that door behind us.

I wish, somehow, that I could take you back to that Fresno of the summer of 1930. Then maybe you would understand why Naz and I decided to start out there. It was like beginning at the beginning.

Traveling *badvelis,* Protestant ministers of Armenia, saw the San Joaquin Valley many years ago. It was flat and very hot, but they could stand in the dusty streets of Fresno, then a little farming community and railroad town, and look to the east, and see snow-capped mountains.

In the summer evenings, the trees stood still in Courthouse

138

Square. Footsteps echoed down the quiet streets. Sometimes a train whistled. On the outskirts of town, farmers, scrubbed clean and in their slippers and shirt sleeves, sat on their porches in the dark. Their wives finished up in the kitchen and joined them.

They sat there and rocked. Sometimes they worked chilled pomegranates in their fingers, crushing down the pulp until they could break the skin and suck the cold, tart juice. They looked out across the hot, flat, dark, sweet-smelling country. It was theirs. It was their life.

The *badvelis* were in love with this land. "My dear friends," they wrote their parishioners back in Armenia, "you should see this valley. It is like the country around Van. Or it is like the valley of Ararat. There are many vineyards and fine orchards. Far away are the mountains. Even now, in the heat of the summer, they are white with snow, just like Little Masis and Big Masis. The farmers here are free. Their land belongs to them and their sons. No sultan or czar can hit them on the head and say, 'Give your land to me.' "

There were those back in Armenia whom these letters filled with hope and dreams. The day came when they left their homes and took their families across the sea. They brought with them melon seeds from Dikranaguerd and Kharpert. They brought cuttings from the vineyards of Ararat and young fig trees from Izmir. They took them to the country around Fresno and dug their irrigation ditches and planted their acres. And so they helped to make an Eden in that part of America.

But there were others, too. I think that Fresno in 1930 must have been like San Francisco in the Gold Rush. Down its streets walked people of all nations. They had come to Fresno almost a century later for treasure of another kind— the kind that grew in the black earth of the melon ranches, in the Muscat vineyards, on the trees of the peach and fig orchards.

Many of the Armenians lived out along Van Ness Avenue, but you could leave Mother Ruzvanian's house and walk past the Arax Grocery and in a few blocks be surrounded by

139

the homes of German and Swiss people. Nearby was an Italian settlement, and across the Southern Pacific tracks were Chinatown and the shanties and *cantinas* of the Mexican field hands. They shook whenever the big valley freights rolled through Fresno.

You know how they refer to sections of cities as "Little Tokyo" or "Little Italy"? Well, in 1930, Fresno was "Little America."

The four of us were living in the big, four-bedroom Ruzvanian home on Van Ness Avenue near the Emerson School, about six blocks south of Courthouse Square. Entering the front door I didn't even have to say, *"Eof!"* Naz smothered and pampered me with attention, and Lucie and Mother gave to me all the devotion that they could no longer give to Father. Grandma stayed sharp-tongued and critical and suspicious. But that's the way she was toward those closest to her, and especially toward me, because I was always kidding her and saying that when I married Naz I helped her get rid of her *dunmena* granddaughter.

All this love and attention in one way made our first Christmas a rather unhappy one for me. I wanted them to have so much; yet I couldn't afford even the smallest presents.

On Christmas Eve it was misty, and the Christmas singers looked cold outside in the streets. But their voices rang with warmth and happiness as they chanted the traditional Armenian Christmas Eve song:

> *Melkon, Kaspar yev Baghdassar!*
> *Avedis! Avedis!*

> (We are Melchior, Gaspar, and Balthazar!
> Tidings we bring! Glad tidings!)

Then they rang the doorbell. *"Schnoravor dzenount!—* Christ is born!"* they shouted, and crowded inside, fifteen or twenty of them, for refreshments of cakes, dried fruits, Armenian coffee, and liqueurs.

Many guests called on us that evening, many more than usual. Some came to wish Naz and me happiness. Others

140

were old-timers who missed Father Ruzvanian and wanted to pay their respects to his widow and his memory.

When they had all left, I remained downstairs to turn off the lights and lock the doors. I had something else to do as well. On the dining-room table, where they would be seen the first thing in the morning, I placed four Christmas cards, addressed to Naz, Lucie, Mother, and Grandma. In each envelope I put a check. These were my Christmas presents. It was the best I could do.

Altogether the checks came to $14,500. I couldn't really write checks for that much. I couldn't write a check for $140. But I believed in myself. I believed in our future and the country's future. In spite of the terrible depression times, something told me that everything was going to be all right. Maybe this was a childish way of showing it, but that's how I felt.

Grandma, of course, came for Christmas breakfast. After we had finished, I said, "Now Grandma, open up the Christmas card." As she pulled the card from the envelope, out fell her check. She picked it up and studied it through her glasses. "What's this?"

"Put it away and save it," I said. "Someday it will be good."

Lucie leaned over. "Grandma! A check for five hundred dollars!"

"Well," Grandma said, "that's very nice. Thank you, George." She put the card and the check back in the envelope. "But I would have preferred something smaller," she said, "—and more tangible."

In Lucie's envelope was a check for two thousand dollars. She smiled. "You didn't have to do that, George. Just the card would have been enough."

Mother Ruzvanian's check was also for two thousand dollars. She kissed me on the cheek. "Thank you, son. I know it will be as good as gold. And we won't have long to wait, either."

Then Naz opened her Christmas card and took out the Christmas check I had written for her. It was the biggest of all, for ten thousand dollars. She ran to me and hugged

141

me. "I have everything I want or need," she said. "You've made every day a Christmas Day for me."

"That's for a trip to Europe—someday," I said.

That very night, before she went home, Grandma tore up her check and threw it into the wood stove on the back porch. Lucie kept hers for a few days, then dropped it into the fireplace. Mother Ruzvanian said again and again she was afraid she'd lose hers, and finally one day she destroyed it, so that it would never fall into someone else's possession. Naz hid her check in her bureau drawer. What I had said was bound to come true. Someday it would take us on a second honeymoon, to Europe.

For some time after our arrival in Fresno, I did nothing but arrange Father's affairs. Finally I told Jack Terzian that we would keep our interest in the building across from Courthouse Square and that I would be down every day to help out, just as Father Ruzvanian had when he was alive. Every morning I walked the six blocks down Van Ness Avenue and went to work in the City Café.

The winter rains came to an end, and all the world burst into bloom. Spring in the San Joaquin Valley is like the birth of the world. The soft green leaves are unfurling, the orchards are covered for miles in white, sweet-smelling blossoms, flowers are blooming in the grazing meadows, and the wide sky is a misty blue. The world seems so new and beautiful, it takes your breath away.

Fresno Street, along the north side of Courthouse Square, was jammed three days a week with the rigs, wagons, and trucks of the farmers' free market. The stalls were set up along that side of the square, and on market days they were stacked high with all the San Joaquin Valley gold—melons, and other fruits, and vegetables of all kinds. In the evenings there were band concerts in the square. Couples strolled arm-in-arm beneath the elms, just as they did in the *Frenginler* of Scutari.

On all these days and evenings, Jack Terzian and I did a heavy business. It wasn't just the pool hall in back. But in the daytime all those farmers and their customers, and in

142

the evening all the strollers, crossed the street to our windows for cigars and cigarettes, or the biggest treat of all, a root-beer float.

In the center of the street floor was a doorway. It led back to the pool hall. On the left of this doorway was the cigar counter. On the right was the lunch counter we called the City Café. At the front of this café was a window that in summertime was wide open to the street, and right there by the window was the huge Hires Root Beer barrel with the silver hoops and the spigot at the bottom. For ten cents you got a root-beer mug, white with frost from the ice chest, with two scoops of ice cream in it and then filled to the brim with sparkling, ice-cold root beer from the barrel.

The summer sun blazes over Fresno. It blinds you. Walk four or five blocks without protection, and you feel as though you have been struck on the head. Your shirt is wringing wet. Your mouth is dry. You almost taste the heat. The world is slowly baking. Fresnans used to say that only two things brought relief: the cold, crystal-clear Fresno water from the High Sierra and our root-beer floats at the City Café.

The stand had some famous customers. Paul Mosesian, the wealthy grower and shipper, used to stop at the window. Jake and Jack knew without looking that it was Paul; before he said a word, they would hear his coin on the counter—always the same, a twenty-dollar gold piece. To look at his overalls and roughhewn face and big peasant shoulders, you would take him for an Armenian field hand.

One Sunday afternoon Arshag and I went to his luxurious ranch house for a barbecue. Paul greeted us in a new eighty-five-dollar suit with the cut of Fresno's most fashionable tailor, Chet George. He wore a white shirt with collar and tie. His face was flushed, and you could tell that he was hot and uncomfortable.

Just as we were about to sit down at the outdoor tables, a ranch hand ran to Mosesian. "Boss!" he cried. "The wall of our ditch has broken! We're going to lose all our water!"

Paul ran across a narrow field in back of the house. I ran behind him, to see if I could help. He didn't hesitate a second.

143

He threw himself into the muddy ditch and blocked the break with his body.

"Shovel it over me, boys!" he yelled. The ranch hands worked frantically. Wet earth and muck showered on Paul's expensive suit. His body held the first spadefuls in place. The precious water that his trees and melons needed stopped spilling through the break and began flowing once more down the irrigation ditch and across the fields. They got some heavy logs and sandbags, and the emergency was over.

Black mud covered Paul from head to foot. He went into the house, and when he came back, he was in his workshirt, collar open at the throat, and in a clean, comfortable pair of overalls. Until the last guest left for home, he was relaxed and completely at ease, in a way that he could never be in his necktie and his Chet George suit.

From that day on, I never thought of Paul Mosesian as anything, from the bottom of his heart, but an American. To me, the spirit he showed that day was the spirit of the plains crossers.

Another root-beer float customer of ours was also a successful grower and shipper, Tom Mouradick. What first interested me about Tom was his crate label, "Locomotive Brand." Most of the shippers' labels showed glamorous bathing beauties and had names like "Ruby" or "Cinderella" or "Princess Fatima." Why was Tom Mouradick glorifying a steam engine?

Jack Terzian told me the story. Tom Mouradick was the first Armenian locomotive engineer in American railroad history. He took fast passenger trains of the Southern Pacific on the Los Angeles–San Francisco run. Sometimes he was even at the throttle of the big engines that pulled the transcontinental express trains. The Fresno Armenians, and the native-borns, too, looked upon Tom as a hero who had lived a valuable and exciting life. Now he had retired. To keep busy, he raised fruit and vegetable crops and marketed them all over the East as Tom Mouradick's "Locomotive Brand."

There were furniture stores on each side of our café, and their salesmen came in once or twice a day. Mr. Arioto came in from his fish market two doors down, and Mr. Homan, who later was mayor of Fresno, from his sporting-goods store on the corner. The big brick post office was a block and a half south, at the corner of the square and across the street from the Fresno Republican office, and the postal clerks had root-beer floats after work.

The famous Saghatelian brothers were also customers. We were all very proud of them, because of what happened when the Union Pacific Railroad tried to buy their lot.

The Saghatelians were bakers (as their sons are today), and were proud, stubborn people from the Armenian region of Moush, also known as Daron. Daron produced the fiercest warriors and the most gifted literary figures in Armenian history. It was the home country of the warlike Mamigonians. It was the birthplace of Vartan the Great, whose armies won from the Persian Zoroastrians the right for Armenians to worship as Christians. Also, the hills of Daron were the home of Mesrob Mashdotz and Sahag Gatoghigos, who had invented the thirty-six-letter Armenian alphabet.

All *Darontsis* are conscious of this heritage. So when the big man in the stiff white collar and the expensive overcoat came from the Union Pacific and asked them if they would sell their lot, Jezahir, the eldest brother, was ready. He dusted the bakery flour from his hands with poise and dignity, like a nobleman taking off his gloves. The rich smell of baking *peda* filled the little shop.

"Yes," he said slowly, "we will sell our lot."

"Ah-h," said the railroad official. "I thought so." With a confident smile he took out his checkbook. "Have you and your brothers decided on a price?"

Jezahir folded his big arms and leaned on the bakery showcase. He nodded. "Two bucketfuls of gold."

The visitor's smile vanished. He stared at the muscular baker. "Two bucketfuls of gold!"

Again Jezahir nodded. "Maybe you want to give us one thousand or five thousand dollars. How much money is that? My brothers and I do not know. We have never seen that many dollars all at one time. But if we see and lift a

145

bucket filled with gold, we will know how much it is. And that is what we want for our lot—two of them."

The railroad man said he would take it up with his superiors and let Jezahir know. But he never came back, and the Saghatelian bakery still stood on that lot, filling the air every morning with delicious smells.

Sometimes a thin, hungry-looking farmer in patched jeans and ragged straw hat would come down from the free-market stalls and ask for a root beer in a soft drawl—one of the thousands of Oakies that had traveled into the valley from the Dust Bowl.

It seemed to me that many times these people were treated with misunderstanding. When someone didn't like another person, he would call that person an "Oakie," in the same spirit of intolerance as we were sometimes called "damned Armenians," or Italians were called "Dagos."

But my experience with the Oakies was that most of them were good men and women who had lost everything through no faults of theirs, but through a freak of nature. Somehow, in their broken-down cars with mattresses tied to the top, they had struggled across the deserts to the San Joaquin Valley, to try to earn an honest living. Wasn't that better than begging?

They reminded me of the refugees who came to the Caucasus after the first World War. The Oakie mothers on the streets of Fresno made me think of my own mother, of all the mothers everywhere who have tried to keep their brood of children together and alive, when food was scarce and work hard to get.

What I am trying to say is that the streets of Fresno were filled and moving with life in those days of the early 1930s. The streets were not those of the big city, where you could lose yourself in an apartment high above the crowds, with a dog or a canary to keep you company. The streets of Fresno were like Main Street in all the towns of the U.S.A.

We had all this different trade, and we had plenty of other Armenian customers as well. Upstairs, over the furniture,

146

store next door to the south, was a small hall known as the Armenian Coffee House. It was run by a little fellow named Hadji. The older Armenians gathered here to drink Armenian coffee and play *tavloo*, which is backgammon, and read *Asbarez* and other Armenian-language newspapers. I never realized until I spent some time in the Armenian Coffee House that each copy of *Asbarez* was read by at least a hundred Armenians. The copies in the coffee house, anyway, were worn thin by the time the next semiweekly issue came out. One customer of the coffee house would sit reading the paper, with two or three friends peering at it over his shoulder. He would finish the article and start to turn the page.

One of the others would tap him on the shoulder. "Just a minute, please. I haven't finished on this page yet."

"Who asked you to read over my shoulder and breathe down my neck?" the other would demand. "Who was here first?" And the argument would be on.

It was Father Ruzvanian, though, who fought the most famous battle of the Armenian Coffee House. Four or five years before I arrived in Fresno, Mother Ruzvanian once told me, there was an Armenian couple whom everybody called *Sev Hokys*, or "the Black Souls."

The Black Souls were always saying unkind and untrue things about their neighbors and causing trouble by starting nasty rumors. One day the husband of this couple passed a remark, in a leering way, about Naz. It was something no Armenian father could hear without coming to his daughter's defense; such a remark, in an Armenian community, could ruin a young girl's life.

That very night, Father Ruzvanian marched down to the Armenian Coffee House. He found Black Soul sitting at a table over his coffee.

"I've had enough of the lies you and your wife are spreading," growled Father Ruzvanian. "Get up and fight."

Everybody looked up from his *Asbarez*, his coffee, or his *tavloo* board. No one had ever seen Father Ruzvanian like this. The room was very still.

147

Black Soul cringed. "But you can't strike me. I have glasses on."

"Maybe I can't strike you, if you're too cowardly to stand up," said Father. "But there's no law against this." And he slapped Black Soul as hard as he could on the cheek.

This was the famous "Battle of the Armenian Coffee House." It stopped for a long time the wicked gossip of Mr. and Mrs. Black Soul.

I cannot tell you how beautiful it seemed to me—all this life, this movement and color, that I found in Fresno in those years. Naz and I were very happy. Mother Ruzvanian was still a queen, and Lucie was like another sister to me. And besides that, I felt that this was my home. I was among friends, among people I understood and who understood me. We weren't out to cut one another's throat in business competition or any other way. We all wished each other well. We enjoyed each other's good days and successes, and we all tried to comfort each other when something went wrong.

The life that went by on Van Ness Avenue and across the street in Courthouse Square was like a beautiful pageant, the pageant of an American town. The evenings I liked best were those you have seen pictured by artists a hundred times, in summer towns from Cape Cod to the West Coast. The painting shows the town or village square on a warm summer evening. The band is playing a concert. Moths flutter in the bandstand lights. Tall, leafy trees grow in the square—elms, perhaps, like in Courthouse Square—and the street lights throw the shadows of the leaves and branches across the grass and the walks. People stroll down the broad walks beneath the trees or lie on the grass, fanning themselves, smoking in the dark, listening to the music. All of you who have ever lived in a small American town or city know what I mean. There is a friendship and peace about it, a feeling of being home. It is a part of American summer nights, all the way across the continent.

Jack Terzian and I were both interested in the affairs of Holy Trinity Church—the basilica on Ventura modeled after the cathedral at Etchmiadzin—but that is about all

148

we had in common. He and Father Ruzvanian had served only sandwiches at the little counter of the City Café. It seemed to me that we should serve food that was stronger, more nourishing. Many workers in that neighborhood needed substantial lunches. Jack did not think much of my idea.

"Sandwiches have been fine up until now," he said. "Why should we do any different? Besides, it's a depression. People don't have money."

The more stubborn he became, the more I argued. I told him he didn't have to do anything. I would do all the extra work. And, in the end, I did. I even built a makeshift kitchen in the basement, where I could cook the things I wanted to serve, mainly my pot-roast special and chile con carne and clam chowder.

You may think that this was not right, or was a compromise with the ambitions and dreams of San Lazzaro— the ambitions and dreams for a paneled Omar Khayyam's restaurant, with all the foods made from the ancient, legendary recipes, and with all the famous people there. But I disagree. I had come to believe in the beginning where God put you, in starting from there. Naz had made me see that you must climb the foothills before you scale the mountain. Not only must you get the actual physical distance behind you, but you must also pass the test of the foothills, to be fitted for the harder, more complicated tasks ahead.

So I felt happy, and sure in my heart that this little lunch counter, with the simple, plain foods, was the right beginning. And I tried hard to satisfy all the different kinds of customers that came through our door and to give them something unusual.

For instance, so that our pot roast wouldn't be like the pot roast at Hart's or some other restaurant down the street, I roasted potatoes right along with the beef. This gave them a fine rich flavor. I served these to the customers instead of the usual spaghetti. Also, I added vegetables, such as peas or string beans.

Perhaps it was because we were close to the Southwest and

149

Mexico, but the people in the valley, I learned, were very fond of chile con carne. I experimented, and finally created a heavy, spicy chile, a large bowl of which sold for twenty cents. The clam chowder you may think strange for a place like Fresno, but I can tell you as an authority that the favorite food of Fresnans was fish and all kinds of sea foods.

Mr. Arioto, the fish dealer, and I talked about this many times. We agreed that it was because they were far away from salt air and salt water. Their systems had that longing of all mankind for the sea, and this was one way—through eating fresh fish from the ocean—that they could satisfy it. Whether this is the true explanation or not, my clam chowder became very popular. I added thick tuna-fish sandwiches to our menu. They were very popular, too.

Soon, to Jack Terzian's surprise, we faced a seating problem. All we had were stools down the outside of the counter. And now that my new policy of heavier foods was a success, Jack wanted to do something about it right away.

"We have to move into the pool room," he said, "so we can serve more customers. We'll take out two or three pool tables."

"Jack," I said, "we are going to disagree again. I think we should leave things the way they are."

I didn't like the thought of customers crowding into a pool room to eat my food. Besides, if the food is really good, people do not mind a reasonable wait.

We had it out one night after we closed up for the evening. In the end, he stamped off grumbling to the coffee house next door. I had my way.

CHAPTER TWELVE

In the autumn, when the leaves began to fall in Courthouse Square, something told me that it was time to move along. At the City Café I had proved my point. Every noon the customers were crowding in for steaming dishes of chile, clam chowder, and pot roast. I had a wonderful time making it for them and serving them. Still, it was time to start climbing again.

Joseph Dale was one of the members of Dale Brothers, a wholesale coffee firm. Every week he went from one restaurant to another with his coffee deliveries. One morning in December I asked him to find me a good location.

"Don't tell me you want to start a restaurant!"

"Yes," I said. "I do."

"Now? In the middle of this depression? With everybody out of work?"

I had thought about this a great deal. His questions were all logical. But I had my answer ready.

"Maybe I'm crazy, but I think this is the best time, when everybody is crying and everything is sad. Maybe I'll be able to show people that our country isn't going to the dogs. Instead of crabbing and crying, now is the time people should get out and work. Now is the time for them to show they really believe in themselves and their country."

Two weeks later Joe came back with a location. It was two blocks away, at 1918 Mariposa, between Fulton Street and Broadway.

"But I'm afraid it's jinxed," he said. "Three different restaurants have gone broke there in the last two years."

"I'd like to have a look at it," I said.

I got my hat and coat and went down Mariposa to 1918, a block and a half west of Courthouse Square. It was a small, old-fashioned two-story building next door to Doc Corcoran's optometrist shop. On the other side was a dry cleaner's. Up and down the block were stores that had gone bankrupt. Their windows were rain-streaked and empty.

The place was smaller than I had expected. It was long and narrow, with the kitchen far in the back. There was a front window, to the left of the door. I stood in the center of the cold, gloomy restaurant, trying to picture what I could do there. Outside, in Mariposa Street, it was raining.

Down one side of the room ran a long counter with stools, like at the City Café, only longer. Tables and chairs were crowded against the wall. That was all that was left of three restaurants. Restaurant men, or hotel men, will know what it was like—like standing in a graveyard.

But I had to begin sometime, somewhere. I closed the door behind me and locked it, and went back to Van Ness Avenue and found Joe Dale. "I think that's the place," I said. "I'll take it."

It wouldn't have been good to start out with any money except my own. I had a $1,000 note from Jack Terzian, but it wasn't due for another six months. A friend of the Ruz-

152

vanians gave me $780 for it. Six months later, when Jack paid up, the friend made $220 in interest. Nevertheless, I was happy to have the money ahead of time, so that I could go to San Francisco and talk with the supply houses.

In my enthusiasm and confidence and my happiness over the way my dreams seemed to be coming true at last, I was bubbling with excitement as I prepared for opening day, which Naz and I decided would be February 12, 1932, Lincoln's Birthday. I had agreed to stay with Jack Terzian and help him with the City Café until the first of the year; right after New Year's we wished each other good luck and parted friends.

The first thing I did was order chinaware with five different colors on it—the most expensive pattern made by the Syracuse people. Then, between the front door and the side counter, I had the carpenters install some booths, which were very popular in the California restaurants of those days. There were eight or nine, curtained off, and three for families, seating five or six, and one large one, near the kitchen, which sat at least twelve. Altogether, when the carpenters were finished, the restaurant would seat between sixty and sixty-five. I had them put my office under the stairway that ran from the street to the second floor. It was just wide enough for a small desk, and so low that I couldn't stand up in it without bumping my head.

Over the front door electricians put up a sign that would not have been out of place in Times Square. It cost almost as much as my five-colored china. Every few seconds, it lighted up and showed a turbaned man lifting a ladle out of a big pot of soup. It was a reproduction, in lights, of a design that Lucie, our artist, had drawn for the cover of the menus.

On the front window and on the sign and the menus themselves was the name that I had chosen years before—Omar Khayyam's. Underneath was the motto, "The Food of Quality." Also on the menus were two verses from the *Rubaiyat of Omar Khayyam*. I arranged with the printers to change these every day; that is, to use two new verses every day until

153

we had gone through the entire poem, and then to start over again.

One of the delicacies I thought of that might contribute to our atmosphere was rose-petal preserves. "You're dreaming," Naz said. "This is the first week in February."

I smiled. "Have you seen the side of the house of Mukhtar Khatchig? Near the Arax Grocery? It's covered with rambler roses in bloom. They came out yesterday."

"He'll never let you pick them."

Mukhtar Khatchig was a retired grocer. "Wait and see," I said. "I'll offer him forty-five cents a pound for his rose petals."

But when I called on him, Mukhtar Khatchig narrowed his eyes and thrust out his lower lip. "Just the petals?"

"That's all I can use," I said.

"You would take all my roses, and I would only have ninety cents."

Even when I offered sixty cents a pound, he refused. I gave up the idea of rose-petal preserves. When more roses were in bloom, I would think about it again.

Several evenings later, two boys who were pupils in the Emerson School knocked on our back door. They had two big paper bags filled with rose blossoms. I looked closer. I was sure they were Mukhtar Khatchig's roses.

One of the lads said, "We heard you would pay forty-five cents a pound for rose blossoms."

Yes, I said, that was right. "But where," I asked, "did you get them?"

They looked at me with big innocent eyes. "Why, they came from our own back yard."

The blossoms weighed 3 pounds. I gave them $1.50 and took the bags to Naz. "See, honey? Now we can serve rose-petal preserves!" That very night we started crushing them, and getting ready to jell them with orange honey, to make the delicious preserves.

Mukhtar Khatchig pounded on our door the next morning. "My roses are all gone!" he cried. "You have stolen them!"

154

"No, Mukhtar Khatchig," I said, "we have not stolen them. I bought them from some schoolboys."

"They're robbers! They picked them while I was asleep!"

Mother Ruzvanian came to the door. "And they must have needed the money more than you do," she said quietly. Grumbling, the old man went away.

I posted signs all over Fresno: "Watch for It—The Opening of Omar Khayyam's." The carpenters had set up a small display area in the front window of the restaurant, and as the opening drew nearer, I arranged objects there that attracted the attention of passers-by—a gleaming samovar, a necklace, a *narghile,* which is like the Turkish water pipe, and the pages of an ancient Armenian manuscript. Outside in Mariposa Street I put up a sign saying that the restaurant would open at noon on Lincoln's Birthday, which was a Friday.

The days flew by. The carpenters were still hammering away at the booths. The beautiful plates and saucers arrived, and the silverware. The electric sign flashed on and off over the front door.

"Now," Naz said, "you have everything but food." We were standing in the kitchen. I looked at the empty cupboards, at the long row of shining pots and pans and waiting ranges.

"That's just the trouble, honey," I said. "We've run out of money."

It was the truth. The three-year lease, the costly china, the booths, the signs, and everything else had taken all the money I had. The only food on the shelves was our homemade rose-petal preserves.

The next morning, a friend of Lucie's took me to the Better Buy Wholesale Grocers and introduced me to a Mr. Morgan and told him my problem. Mr. Morgan introduced me to his partner, Harry Markowitz.

"Times are hard," said Mr. Markowitz. "We will advance you $250 in credit for groceries, providing you agree to pay in one month. Any additional buying will have to be settled at the end of every week."

155

I remembered my conversation with Joe Dale. Maybe I really *was* crazy.

Mother Ruzvanian and two housewives who were pastry specialists started baking *paklava*, the fifty-six-layer cake, for the opening luncheon and dinner. I got my little group of helpers together: Hiram Sadoyan and Bart Rustigian, whose father had built the first bus station in Fresno; Bart's fiancée, Alice, who was going to be our cashier; Little Jeff, whose real name was Sarkis Yeretzian, who had been a minister; Vahan Bodourian, and Shishman Simon, which means "Fat Simon," who was an excellent Armenian chef and who could help me with the Armenian and Near Eastern food that I was going to offer as specialties.

February is generally a rainy month in Fresno, but Lincoln's Birthday was a clear, beautiful day. The sun had hardly risen before we were down in Mariposa Street, getting ready for our first customer.

Mother Ruzvanian was still baking. Naz and Lucie arranged flowers. I was trying to be in twenty places at once, but spending most of my time in the kitchen with Shishman Simon. We were going to serve a "blue plate" for forty cents and a complete luncheon for sixty cents. The big five- and six-course dinners would start at eighty-five cents.

In the middle of the morning the telephone rang. It was Father Markarian.

The good father had been growing a little eccentric. Not long before this, a ten-year-old boy had died in Fowler. Father Markarian came with the funeral procession and all the mourners to give the sermon at the graveside in Ararat Cemetery.

As they gathered around him, he solemnly placed his hand on the boy's casket, and peered at the large crowd over the spectacles that sat on the end of his sharp nose.

"My dear people and fellow mourners," he began in a dreary, nasal voice, "the world has recently suffered the terrible loss of three great men."

He paused and looked out at the people. The relatives in the front row frowned. What kind of funeral sermon was this

going to be? they wondered. In the back rows, the schoolmates of the deceased listened respectfully.

"The first of these great men," continued the little priest,
"was that outstanding apostle of revolution—Lenin. We
did not believe in his doctrines, but we must admit that he
was a great man.

"And after that, we lost that wonderful humanitarian,
that great personality who actually gave all of Armenia back
to the Armenians, with the famous Wilsonian boundaries. I
am referring, of course, to that remarkable American, President Woodrow Wilson.

"And now"—Father Markarian struck the boy's casket
with his hand—"we are entrusting to the cold earth the
third great man—"

The mourners looked at each other in amazement. The
schoolmates tittered. Father Markarian drew himself up and
glared at them angrily. "What are you laughing at?" he exclaimed in a loud voice. "How do you know? If this boy
had lived, maybe he would have grown up to be greater than
they were!"

Later, when they were telling this story down at the
Armenian Coffee House, it caused a bitter argument and
much shouting. Half the old men were shocked. But the
other half thought that the little priest might have been
telling the truth.

"Is this my George?" asked the priest when I went to the
telephone. He said that he was at the City Café and that he
had come to Fresno to bless the restaurant on its opening
day.

He arrived a few minutes later. He was all warmth and
smiles and good nature. With great dignity he blessed every
booth, every seat, every part of the counter. Then he went
into the kitchen and blessed the range and all the pots and
pans and Shishman Simon and all the others. Then, standing
in the center of the restaurant, he led us in a prayer for the
success of our undertaking. We all knew that it came from
the bottom of his heart.

The first customers came through the front door a few

minutes after twelve. Naz helped to seat them. They were curious and very friendly and wished us well. Soon the place was humming.

Side by side Shishman Simon and I worked over the range, filling the orders for *shish kebab, kouzou kzartma,* and other Armenian dishes. My heart was very happy. Sometimes I couldn't keep the happiness in, and I would burst out singing. I'm sure the customers out front could hear me, but I didn't care.

This was one of those moments when America keeps her promises. What an opportunity she was giving me! And how eager I was, and how hard I would work, to give her in return my loyalty, my gratitude, and the best of my own heritage. At last I was really beginning. With all these feelings inside of me, I sang even louder, and soon Shishman Simon, with his sad face, was singing, too.

Grandma came down in a special limousine that we sent for her. They told me later that when one of the lawyers from the courthouse greeted her and said what a beautiful place her granddaughter's husband had just opened, Grandma smiled and bowed and thanked him. Then, all at once, she frowned, and her right hand stole around and touched her bottom.

At one o'clock Naz's head appeared in the round window of the swinging door to the kitchen. She motioned to me. Her face wore a big smile.

"Look, George," she said proudly, and held the door open.

Every seat in the restaurant was filled. Behind the counter stools stood a line of patrons, waiting for an empty seat. The people in the line had happy expressions on their faces. The line extended down past the counter, past the booths, through the front door and out into the sunlight of the beautiful February afternoon.

❖❖

CHAPTER THIRTEEN

All of us worked hard, as though our lives depended on the restaurant's success. In a sense, mine did. This went far back— to the days of my childhood on the beaches of Marmora, to a glimpse of the Statue of Liberty at daybreak, to a train ride west with an immigrant's badge on my lapel, to the happy medley of the Song of America, to an evening on a bench in Union Square, and a June afternoon by the sea with the priceless jewel of my citizenship. It went back also to San Lazzaro, to mornings and nights of hard work at the City Café, over by Courthouse Square. This was where I began my labor of love, to repay the debt I owed to America. I was on the slopes of Big Masis at last.

The success of the opening day kept up. It seemed as

159

though every citizen of Fresno came in for lunch or dinner. To my surprise, one of those who came during the very first week was Mukhtar Khatchig. We treated him like royalty. We served him *bott* and cheese *beurek* and *shish kebab* and lots of warm *peda,* with a large dish of preserves made from his rose petals to spread on it. When it came time for him to leave, I wouldn't let him pay his bill.

"It was a pleasure to prepare and serve you this meal—in memory of two enterprising little schoolboys," I said. Mukhtar Khatchig smiled and held out his hand, and I felt much better about the 3 pounds of rose petals.

I felt that I should tell the story of Omar Khayyam's on the radio. Once a week, I took $18.50 from the cash register, walked down the street to KMJ, handed over the money, and talked for fifteen minutes about the foods of Armenia and the Near East.

Half-forgotten sights and sounds and landscapes came back to me, legends and ceremonies I knew about from my father, or that I had read about in the manuscripts of San Lazzaro, or that I had heard, perhaps from Uncle Krikor long ago. As I stood at the microphone in the little studio, I made believe my voice was going all over America, telling the whole nation about ancient Hayastan and its customs.

Many of our customers, for example, asked why we made such important items of *shish kebab, kouzou kzartma,* and other lamb dishes. On my radio program I tried to give the reasons.

I explained how lamb in Armenia is a traditional ceremonial food, like turkey in America. I told them about my first impression of the mountain people of the Caucasus, when, years before, I had marched over the rocky highland roads to Karabagh. There were no inns. If you were a person of importance, you were a guest of the *melik,* or mayor, and the entire village. You stood in the evening in front of the *melik*'s house, and the villagers came up one after the other to shake your hand. You heard the tinkling bells of the sheep flocks coming over the meadows. As they passed, the *melik* and the elders selected the fattest horned ram.

160

The ram was slaughtered and cleaned, stuffed with seasoned pilaff, and baked in a firepit all night long. While the logs crackled in the pit, the people danced and sang to the music of the village minstrels.

The following evening at sunset, the ram was lifted from the pit and placed upon a ceremonial table. The village priest blessed it. The carver stood by, holding his blade ready, until everyone held a beeswax candle made by the priest himself. The *melik* took a light from the priest and carried it to the guest of honor, the only one permitted to light more than one candle. The guest lighted the candles of his neighbors to his right and left. The light passed around, until every candle glowed. Then the carving began.

Expertly the carver pulled back the crisp, flaky skin and laid bare the steaming meat that flowed with juices. The hungry villagers came forward and dipped *peda* in the juices and ate it. Then they stood back and waited in the candlelight for their meat and pilaff. In the tradition of their forefathers before Christ, they ate with their hands.

Since a whole sheep could not be spared for every important occasion, the mountain people sometimes feasted on sections of lamb that they speared on their swords and roasted over their campfires. When lamb was cooked in this way, it came to be called *shish kebab*, which means, literally, "skewer-broiled."

Following this tradition, we featured *shish kebab* at Omar Khayyam's from the beginning. But before we cooked it, we seasoned the lamb in sherry wine (which, during prohibition, we got from the homemade stocks of our farmer friends), and with onion and oregano, a Mediterranean herb. The combination gave the lamb a delicate, garliclike flavor. And, as they did in the Caucasus, we always served it with pilaff.

"Have you tried *shish kebab?*" I would say into the microphone. "Have you eaten delicious *kouzou kzartma* at Omar Khayyam's? Or *haigagan sourj?* Or *paklava*, the fifty-six-layer Armenian honey cake?" Then Mr. Gladwin, one of the announcers, who was also a poet, would read some of the

161

stanzas of the *Rubaiyat,* or we would play a few bars of exotic Armenian music, and sign off.

As amateurish as it was, the program seemed quite popular. Wealthy Armenian farmers, who had always boasted about their native food, now had a place to take their skeptical American friends. Other listeners—traveling men with car radios, for instance—were naturally curious to see and taste for themselves the romantic foods that I talked about.

We would be waiting for them, Naz or I, or sometimes, if I was busy, Oscar would be standing there, twirling his handlebar mustache and smiling as if all the people who came through the door were royalty, and he was ready to serve them as they had never been served in their lives.

Oscar was a talented chef and Shishman Simon's bitter rival. When I hired him, no one thought he would last a month, for he was a tremendous drinker. The year before, with ten thousand dollars in life insurance left him by his brother, Oscar had opened his own restaurant. He invited all his friends to an opening night party which continued, without stopping, for four weeks. When the party finally broke up, Oscar's money was all gone, his restaurant was in bankruptcy, several of his friends were in the alcoholic ward of the hospital with *delirium tremens,* and Oscar himself, shaky but still on his feet, was in the kitchen of Omar Khayyam's, asking for a job.

He didn't seem too worried about what had happened. He shrugged and smiled. "Well, we had a good time, while the money lasted."

So I hired him. Drunk as he would be when he went home, he always came to work on time the next morning and, even better than Shishman Simon, cooked the meals that were making our little restaurant famous.

The summer days came and went, and the hot summer nights, when we could hear the band music drifting down Mariposa Street from Courthouse Square. It was like the summer before, when the people were strolling down the walks or lying on the grass, and coming to the City Café after the concert for their root-beer floats.

162

It seemed to me that a great deal had happened since then, but it was on a Sunday in October that one of the saddest changes took place. The telephone jangled in my office under the stairs. It was Naz. "Have you heard the terrible news?" she asked. "About Father Markarian?"

My throat tightened. "What is it?"

Naz was so upset she gave the telephone to Mother Ruzvanian, and Mother Ruzvanian told me what had happened.

The little priest had celebrated mass that morning at St. Gregory's Church in Fowler, and then had gone to the home of some neighbors, the Googooians, for Sunday dinner. At about two o'clock, Mr. Googooian said that he was driving his son to Yetem, which is Armenian for "paradise." Yetem is a small community near Visalia. Its setting is very much like the country near Yozghad, in Armenia, and no one lives in Yetem but Armenians. Father Markarian said that he would love to go with them. Autumn afternoons in the valley are sometimes very soft and tender, and the landscape is still and hazy, as if it were dreaming. This was such a day, and everyone expected a lovely outing.

Near Dinuba a car raced toward them from a crossroad. Father Markarian, in the back seat, saw it coming. He clapped his little hands together in distress.

"*Lementsank! Lementsank!*" he cried. "We are finished! We are finished!"

The cars crashed. Somehow the driver of the other car and the two Googooians escaped with minor injuries. But the priest was thrown out of the car into the ditch. Flying glass had cut his face and throat. He was bleeding to death.

"Father Markarian! Speak to us!" Mr. Googooian pleaded.

Father Markarian's fingers scratched the ground, as if he were reaching for something. Mr. Googooian took the priest's jeweled cross from around his neck and put it in his right hand. The hand grew still, and then Father Markarian stopped breathing.

Armenians everywhere mourned. A few days later the long funeral caravan moved through the streets to Ararat Cemetery. Thousands were at the graveside. Many must have

163

been remembering the sermons the little priest had delivered there, particularly the one beside the casket of the boy from Fowler.

Several of us were asked to make speeches. With a heavy heart I said good-by to Father Markarian in behalf of the newspapers *Mushag* and *Asbarez,* and all of us who had known and loved him back in the Scutari days, when he thrilled us with tales of the Armenian heros.

As the service closed, we heard the sound of planes. There were two, flown by young men who had been pupils in the Fowler school the first time I had visited it in the borrowed car. They swooped low. Down from the sky on the casket, the open grave and the bareheaded mourners rained hundreds of California roses. Some of them fell into the grave and were buried with him.

I cannot remember much of that winter, except that we seemed to spend all of our waking hours at the restaurant. Naz was a wonderful dancer, and we had loved to go dancing together. These days and months we never went.

Naz had one wonderful consolation: morning, noon, and night we ate at the restaurant. In her family it was Mother Ruzvanian who did most of the cooking. She was always trying the new and unusual and was always succeeding. She was so expert and all the neighborhood housewives praised her so loudly, her daughters seldom went near the kitchen. What was the use in learning? they said. No matter how hard they tried, they could never cook as well as their mother. When, on top of this, Naz married me, a professional chef, it finished her interest in cooking for life. Maybe once a month, she made a cheese sandwich, or halfheartedly cooked an omelet with parsley in it. What woman would blame her?

I began to feel, just as I had back in the City Café, that it was time to start climbing again. To climb was the American way. So, when I found a place for a bigger restaurant— on the street floor of the Hotel Sequoia, two blocks north on Van Ness—I decided to take it. There was still enough time for remodeling, and two things more: to open on
164

February 12, the third anniversary of the opening of the first restaurant, and to see that on that evening a very special person would be there that I hadn't seen in a long time— my mother.

I thought that, if we spent twenty-five thousand, we would have the best and most beautiful restaurant in Central California. In Hollywood, we found a wonderful Russian artist, Alexander Ignatieff. For three months he stayed with us, stenciling the walls of the new place, and painting over the bar a Persian mural that illustrated the lines from the *Rubaiyat:*

> A book of Verses underneath the Bough,
> A Jug of Wine, a Loaf of Bread—and Thou

In the middle of the night, Naz or I would wake up with an idea—a new type of upholstery for the booths, a different tint for the walls. We would rush down the next day and tell the contractors. "Fine!" they would say. "We'll go ahead with it." They never told us, and we never thought to ask, how much our midnight ideas were costing us.

The restaurant on the street floor wasn't enough. When the hotel owners offered us part of Anoush's Turkish Baths in the basement, we eagerly accepted and made plans for an elaborate "Persian Room"—a cocktail lounge and bar.

In all the confusion, we slowly came to recognize one strong influence of steadiness and stability. The owners of the Sequoia were the Kennedy sisters of Fresno. One of them was married to Ward Minturn. More and more, in all our hectic activity, I learned to appreciate Mr. Minturn, his wonderful character and his faith in people. He was and still is my idea of the highest type of American.

Later, someone told me a story that shows what he is made of. It is, somehow, a typically American story. When Mr. Minturn was a young man, a San Francisco bank placed him in charge of a great cattle ranch. A year or so later, it sent to the ranch an agent in disguise.

The agent, to test Mr. Minturn's honesty, said he was there to buy 500 head of cattle. If Mr. Minturn would make

165

him a special price, he, the agent, would split the profit. Thus, without anyone's being the wiser, Mr. Minturn could make two or three hundred dollars. Mr. Minturn looked down at the agent like an eagle looking at a snake. It was all he could do to keep from kicking the man bodily off the ranch.

Three or four months after that, when he was at a meeting at the bank in San Francisco, Mr. Minturn noticed the "agent" sitting behind a desk. "Who is that man?" he asked. When told that he had been an important employee of the bank for years, Mr. Minturn walked to the president's office and resigned as manager of the ranch. And he told the president his reason: no job at all was better than working for people who didn't trust him.

By the time the new restaurant was finished, we knew how naïve we had been. The bills came to fifty-two thousand, more than twice what we'd planned to spend. A dozen creditors stared at me coldly when we passed on the street. Five or six others demanded payment. Mr. Walter Shoemaker was a vice-president of the Security National Bank. He had been Hagop Ruzvanian's good friend and had known Naz all her life. So, I thought, this is simple. I'll just go down and see Mr. Shoemaker and everything will be all right. I was whistling a tune under my breath as I entered the bank.

I explained about all the expenses that we hadn't expected. Mr. Shoemaker nodded, I thought, sympathetically. "And so," I said, "I'm here to ask the bank for a loan of five thousand dollars, so I can hold off my creditors."

To my surprise, Mr. Shoemaker frowned. With his pencil he pushed an eraser around on the top of his desk. "George," he said at last, "I'm afraid the answer is no. You're biting off more than you can chew."

It was an awful blow. I went home that night ready to cry. I didn't sleep. The next morning, I took my pride and wrapped it up. It had shrunk so much during the night that it fit in my little vest pocket. I put it there and went back to Mr. Shoemaker.

"I'm sorry, Mr. Shoemaker, but you are right. Five thousand was too much to ask. I think two thousand is a more sensible figure. It'll carry me all right—"

He looked at me as coldly as only a banker can look. He shook his head. "It's a no-good risk. In a small city the size of Fresno you're opening a restaurant big enough for Wilshire Boulevard. You'll never make it."

I went to 1918 Mariposa Street and called Naz. "Come down to the restaurant," I said. "We have to have a talk."

She came right down. I told her what Mr. Shoemaker had said. We would need every penny. I was going to go back to taking care of most of the management and cooking myself. She would have to help again as cashier and receptionist. Naz took my hand and said the warm, encouraging things that she has always said when things go wrong and I need her help.

That night, I wrote to my mother in Bucharest. Already I had arranged for her to enter the United States on the quota and had sent steamer tickets for her and Alene's three-and-a-half-year-old son. Through the years, since my days at Compton's, I had been sending Mother a hundred dollars every month for her living expenses and comforts. Now, I wrote, there was an emergency and I couldn't send the money any more. For the remaining months before she left for America, she would have to depend on her brother, my Uncle Krikor, or Alene, who was dressmaking.

All of this made me very unhappy; yet it was a lesson to both Naz and me. It seemed to me that it was like when a champion boxer discovers halfway through the bout that the fellow he's fighting with is not so soft, after all. He has to get in there and really prove that he's a champion.

(Years later, Mr. Shoemaker came to my San Francisco restaurant with his daughter, son-in-law, and grandchildren. I told him something I had wanted to say for a long time. "I hope you've never felt bad because you turned me down on that loan. I admit my pride was hurt. But after a few days, I began to see that you had done me a favor. You made

167

Naz and me work more than ever, to prove to you we could do it the hard way, if we had to." And that was the truth. Sometimes the easiest way is not the best.)

The holidays came. We were so busy with our regular trade at the old restaurant and with getting our new one ready for the opening, we hardly had time for Christmas. In one of the last days of the year, we got a letter from Bucharest. All I could say, as I passed it to Naz for her to read, was, "Well, leave it to a mother—" and I turned away and swallowed very hard.

"It makes me very happy," she wrote, "that you are no longer sending me the money. I have been going to tell you that you have been generous, far more than you needed to be. Out of all that you have sent me, I have saved $2,720. I am bringing it with me to America, to help you in your trouble."

That was a bright spot in our lives, but an even brighter one was the moment when all the years of separation were over, and she and I were in each other's arms on the foggy February day that her ship arrived in San Francisco.

Naz and I had dock passes and stood at the end of the gangplank as it rattled ashore. I was looking up to the deck, and suddenly there she was at the railing, her beautiful blonde hair all gray, and Alene's little boy beside her. She came down the gangplank. I felt the tears on my cheeks, and I could see them on hers. She had been very brave to come all this way, so far from home.

"How little you have grown, Mother," I kept thinking—sons never realize that it is they who have changed—and then we were in each other's arms.

Of course, Arshag was there, and Baidzar and Aram and their three children, and Minnie and little Gregory; we must have petted and hugged Mother and all talked at once and laughed and cried for fifteen minutes before we moved through the customs and into our cars to drive to Arshag's house, where we were staying.

At the house, it began all over again. Mother told us of the long trip through the winter Atlantic storms. She had

168

brought three huge suitcases. After dinner she unpacked them and covered the floor with clothes and gifts and mementos. She was happier than I had ever seen her.

From the bottom of the last suitcase, she took something for which I had been waiting with great impatience: two hand-hammered Bible covers, very old and elaborately tooled, and covered with raised figures. My father had told me that they, and the Bible they protected, were more than a thousand years old. Generations of our family had kept precious records on the blank pages in the back.

Mother handed the metal plates to Naz. I waited. "Aren't they lovely?" Mother asked. Aram and Minnie and the children bent over them, exclaiming. Of course, they were old friends to my brother and sister and me. Finally I could wait no longer. "Mother—where is the Bible?"

Mother frowned. "The Bible?"

I pulled Naz's sleeve. "When you wrote Mother, didn't you tell her to be sure and bring the Bible?"

A smile of understanding spread across Mother's face. "George—remember the American Bible House in Istanbul, where they gave away Bibles?"

"Yes, Mother."

"I was going to bring the Bible, as Naz asked me to. But then I thought, why should I carry our old, handwritten Bible all the way to my son in America, which is the home of the Bible House that gives them away? He can get all the Bibles he wants over there—free."

"And what became of our old Bible, Mother?"

"After I took the covers off, I gave it to our neighbor in Bucharest."

I wrote letter after letter to the neighbor but never received an answer. In the end, Naz framed the lovely bronze covers and hung them on the wall as art objects. To this day I admire them very much, but I would much sooner have the Bible.

I don't think that anyone who was there will ever forget the opening of the second Omar Khayyam's. It was a beautiful restaurant that, with the accommodations downstairs

169

where Anoush's Baths had been, could seat more than five hundred patrons. There was lovely music, and many guests of honor headed by what the master of ceremonies called "the three M's"—Mother Mardikian, Mother Ruzvanian, and the Mayor of Fresno. From the time we opened at six o'clock until the last guest left at about three, the restaurant was filled with laughing, happy people.

The radio station, KMJ, had installed a direct line to the studio, and in their remarks over the air the mayor and all the other city officials gave us so much praise that I, for once in my life, was speechless. They made it seem that all my dreams had come true—not dreams of what I had wanted, but dreams of making the most of my opportunities, of repaying America for the wonderful life it had made possible for me, for my wife and brother and sister and fellow countrymen, and now for my own mother.

Mother sat at the table with all of us. In her big blue eyes were tears of pride and happiness as the speakers talked about Omar Khayyam's and how it proved that the American spirit of enterprise could conquer the despair and negative thinking of depression years.

When the broadcast and speaking were over, friends from the old Omar Khayyam's—many newspaper and radio people and home economists—asked for recipes for the Armenian and Near Eastern dishes that had been on the dinner. Mother, unable to understand English, was bewildered. What did they want? she asked in Armenian.

"These are cooking experts, Mother," I explained. "They are after some of my recipes, so they can pass them along to their readers and listeners."

"But George!" interrupted Baidzar in Armenian. "Your recipes are your stock in trade. You spent years gathering them. You can't give them away."

Mother smiled and turned to Baidzar and said something I'll never forget. "My darling daughter, remember our neighbor Makrouhi Hanum? Forty years ago I taught her how to cook *plaki,* and still she can't make it the way I can." She

170

turned back to me. "Son, give them the recipes they ask for. Even with the help of all the recipes in the world, they'll never be able to cook like you."

I agreed with Mother and, as I always have and always will, gave my recipes to all who were interested in Armenian cooking. Wasn't it one way of spreading the very thing I wanted to give this nation of ours? I thought so. And, besides, I believe in giving things away. I believe in giving your heart away, or your money, or the results of your talents, or even your life. Something never has more value than when you are giving it away.

CHAPTER FOURTEEN

Mother wanted to talk with me about something that night. I could tell from her manner. But I guess she didn't think that it was the time or the place for her own personal affairs. A whole month went by before I knew what it was. She telephoned to Fresno and said she wanted very much for Naz and me to visit her in San Francisco, at Arshag and Minnie's house. She had something important to ask me.

The evening we came, she and I went to her room. She hesitated so long that I had to ask her myself. "Well, what is it, Mother, that you wanted to see me about?"

I could see that she hated to begin, and so, for the first time, I knew that it was something for herself. If it had been for someone else, she would have spoken right out about it. That is the way Mother was.

172

But finally it came out. "Son, I've enjoyed the hospitality of your brother and his wife. And I've enjoyed the hospitality of your sister and her husband. But I would now really like to have a little room of my own somewhere, so that instead of being a burden to them, they could visit me. I don't need very much to live on, and so I am asking you, please do this for me. Please make it possible for me to have a place of my own."

For the first time I saw how thoughtless we had been. Our intentions had been good, but we just hadn't considered how Mother felt about living in someone else's house—even her own children's—after having a place of her own all her life. The next day, Naz found a little cottage almost next door to Baidzar's in the Sunset district of San Francisco. That became Mother's house, and we all went there and visited her.

She seemed very happy. When all of us were there, all except Alene, who would be coming to join us soon, I would catch a look of complete content on her face. It was almost just as it had been in Scutari, when Father was alive.

But Mother still had one or two things to do. Once more she called from San Francisco and said she would like to visit us in Fresno. By now Lucie had married and moved away, and Naz and Mother Ruzvanian and I were living in the Hotel Sequoia, where the restaurant was, and there was room for her in Mother Ruzvanian's apartment.

When we were alone, I waited again to hear what this beautiful, wise, simple woman would ask of her son. Whatever it was was hers already, even before she spoke, if I had the power to give her her wish. But I couldn't help wondering, what was it now that her mother's heart and wisdom desired.

"Son," she said in her low voice—I wish that those who say Armenian is a rough, harsh language could have heard my mother speak it—"I have not been in America very long, but I have been here long enough to learn a great deal about the ways of this wonderful country. Nevertheless, I'm a little worried. Even with the fast trains, and the telephone and

173

automobile, I cannot understand how you and your brother
Arshag can live so far apart."

Already I could see what was in her mind. But I knew she
would want to tell me in her own words. In a few minutes,
she went on.

"Now that you have this beautiful restaurant, with a
kitchen almost as big as our whole house in Scutari used to
be, and live in this huge hotel, I can call you my wealthy
son. But you, my wealthy son, don't think of your brother.
Arshag still makes shoes. He barely earns a living for himself and his family, but do you, my wealthy son and Arshag's
wealthy brother, invite him to come and help you with this
difficult job of yours?"

I had thought of this many times, but I had been putting
it off. Arshag was my older brother. I had done many things
that he had not approved of. If he came to work with me,
he would have to start at the bottom, just as I had—washing
dishes. Maybe it would all end in bitterness; it had before.
This was why I had never asked Arshag to Fresno.

But I knew that Mother had something else, something
bigger, in mind. It was important to her that we be together in every possible way.

"Mother," I asked, "would that make you happy?"

She looked down at her hands, which rested quietly in
her lap. "I cannot tell you how happy it would make me."

So that summer Arshag moved to Fresno with Minnie and
Gregory and even Ragsdale, the canary. His willingness to
learn and his desire to help pushed him along fast. In no
time at all, it seemed, he was able to be a manager. Once
more, Mother knew best.

I hired for the Persian Room a balalaika orchestra, with
balalaikas and violins that played Hungarian gypsy music.
Sometimes they would make me cry, and I would love it.
I began to notice that the crowds in the Persian Room became smaller and smaller, but night after night I still sat
listening to the gypsies.

One night a customer stopped on his way out. "Unless
you get rid of these tin-can balalaikas and these weeping

174

Willies and get a good dance band, I'm not coming back," he said.

Nobody could talk that way about my musicians. "Well," I replied, "I'm afraid you'll have to stay away. I'm not going to change them for any ragtime saxophone players."

A few nights later, Syd Ray, the master of ceremonies, said, "I hate to mention it, boss, but look around you." I looked around. Outside of two friends, Fenner Fuller and his music-loving wife, Esther, we were the only ones in the Persian Room. "What's the matter?" I asked.

"What's the matter!" Syd's eyes closed. His lips moved, as if he were counting to himself. "Look, boss. I know you're paying the bills. I know you love these gypsies. But isn't it time we got another band?"

I thought about it for a few days. More than one restaurant owner has gone broke running a place to suit himself rather than the public. It was heartbreaking, but we finally replaced the balalaikas and violins with a little band that played nice, quiet American dance music. And once more the Persian Room was crowded.

There was a special "Counselors' Room" at this restaurant. I had made sure of that, so I could take good care of my lawyer friends from the courthouse. It was just another quirk of the restaurant business that the Counselors' Room's biggest night was the night its guest of honor failed to appear.

One of the traveling men who came to Omar Khayyam's whenever he was in Fresno was the late Ellis Levy, who represented the Don Lee Broadcasting Company and several booking agents. One summer evening Ellis mentioned that Rudy Vallee and his orchestra were coming to Fresno to play at the Rainbow Ballroom.

Rudy then was at the very height of his popularity as the first of the crooners. Through Ed Fishman, Rudy's agent, I invited the famous band leader and his entire company to be my guests at Omar Khayyam's. Fishman promised faithfully that Rudy would be there.

Arshag and Little Jeff and Naz and I and all the others

175

worked hard all day. The Counselors' Room never looked more splendid. Never had we prepared and arranged more delicacies. The Shah of Persia himself would have been impressed.

Six o'clock came and passed. Then seven. The dance at the ballroom was to start at eight. Naz's corsage wilted. Arshag and I looked sadder and sadder. A little after seven, a young man with a Hollywood air burst into the restaurant. "Where's Rudy?"

I said, "You tell me. We've been waiting an hour for him. Who are you?"

"Sam Narvo. I handle Rudy's affairs. We were going to meet here."

"I'm happy to see you," I said, and took him back into the Counselors' Room. "This is what your boss and his boys are missing."

"Get me a knife, a fork, and a plate," Narvo said.

He ate a nine- or ten-course meal in about fifteen minutes. Then he said, "Please put on your hat and coat and ask Mrs. Mardikian to put on hers. If Rudy won't come here, we'll go to Rudy."

The Rainbow Ballroom was packed. Narvo pushed through the crowd, led us to the stage and at intermission time introduced us to the famous band leader. Rudy was very embarrassed. He had forgotten the arrangements Ed Fishman had made and had gone to another restaurant.

"But can we make up for it? Will you have us there after we're through here?"

I said that of course we would; he and his band would always be welcome. They came, and had a wonderful meal and a wonderful time. Rudy was the first great celebrity of the theatrical or musical world to be my guest at Omar Khayyam's, and for that reason he has always occupied a special place in Naz's heart and mine. Since that far-off summer evening, many world-famous men and women have dined at Omar Khayyam's in Fresno and in San Francisco. But the only portrait photograph I have ever put up in the restaurant is Rudy Vallee's. It is there to this day, on the

176

wall at the foot of the stairs, as you enter Omar Khayyam's.

Alene reached San Francisco at last, one January day in 1936. The night she came, we all sat together in Mother's little home. I looked at Mother and felt a strange pang in my heart. She was sitting back in the shadow, her soft face framed by her white, white hair, her eyes closed, as if she were with us, yet somehow far away, farther away than we could ever know. As I watched her, the voices in the room around me faded, and I was thinking of our father.

Father was a very warm, human person who loved people. His greatest pleasure—and Mother's, too—was having friends in the house. And I guess it was those long happy evenings back in our home in Scutari that Mother reminded me of, the night Alene arrived and we were all together again half-way around the world, in San Francisco. But back home, she had been with us all every moment; now, as she sat with her eyes closed, she seemed very far away.

Naz, Arshag, Minnie, and I went back to Fresno. Somehow it did not come as a surprise when, a few days later, Mother telephoned. "It doesn't seem right for us all to be so near, and yet not together," she said.

"Well, Mother," I said, "why don't you come down to Fresno and visit us. Then on week ends, Aram and Baidzar and the grandchildren can come down, and Alene and her little boy, too." It was February, the rainy season in San Francisco; in Fresno we would have some nice warm days, with spring in the air.

We were still living in the hotel. Arshag and Minnie were renting a nice home, and Mother stayed with them. It was only a week after she came that they took her to the hospital for an operation. Everything went well. We were all looking forward to bringing her home, when her doctor telephoned.

"I'm sorry," he said. "There is a complication. We can't let her leave the hospital. She has pneumonia."

Mother was in an oxygen tent for several days. We went to see her every day. She didn't seem to be recovering and said very little. The doctors did what they could. But she was slipping away. There was the look on her face that I had

177

noticed when Alene had come. I couldn't help remembering, then, the letters she had written from Bucharest, in the days when we were trying to arrange for her to come to America.

"I'm praying," she had written, "for the day when I can cross the sea to my children and my grandchildren. When that day comes, and we're all together again, I can die happy."

There had always been something childlike about her. It seemed to me that she had done her best to recover from her operation. But now that this illness had followed it, it was a sign for her to keep the promise she had made to the Lord. And it is true that she died peacefully, late one afternoon, with all of us around her hospital bed and with me sitting beside her, holding her hand.

She tried to speak.

"Father—" she said. That was all. She sank back with a happy smile on her face and closed her eyes, and that was the end. I kept holding her hand. The smile faded and left her face beautiful and still. It was like the falling of a leaf, or the setting of the sun.

A few days later, we laid her to rest beneath the mulberries of Ararat Cemetery. None of us thought she minded being buried so far from home, because now she was with Father once more.

By the spring of 1937, it seemed as though we had started to reap some of the harvest of all our efforts. The restaurant was beginning to be known all through the country. And it had won a solid position in the social and civic life of Fresno.

Yes, Naz and I could look forward to many happy years in this warmhearted community that both of us regarded as our home town, and that I loved in a way I could never love a big metropolis that didn't have vineyards and orchards at the end of its streets. But sometimes, in the restaurant or our hotel room high above the city, I caught myself looking out the window. From the restaurant window, I couldn't see the locomotives, but I could see their exhaust billowing and boiling up over the tracks and feel the floor tremble as they thundered through to Los Angeles, or north to San Fran-

178

cisco. And from the hotel window, toward the east, there were the faraway mountains. The sound of the engines and the trains, and the way they shook the building, and the sight of the distant mountains always made my heart beat faster. They made me think of the world beyond the valley.

On one of my proudest days I said to Naz, "I know that Grandma and Lucie and Mother Ruzvanian didn't save theirs, but what about you, finally—did you keep that check I gave you for Christmas our first year in Fresno?"

She smiled. "Yes, I think I have it around here somewhere."

"Bring it to me."

She looked through a bureau drawer, and then in a desk drawer, and handed me a small folded paper. It was the ten-thousand-dollar check.

"What did I tell you we'd use it for, when it was good?"

"You said that someday it would take us to Europe."

I took her hand. "Well, sweetheart, when would you like to sail?"

A week later—it was just after Thanksgiving, 1937, and the December rains had already begun—we were in San Francisco arranging a six-month vacation to Europe. There were clothes to buy, travel agents to see, hotel reservations to make.

One rainy afternoon, I left our hotel and walked down Powell Street. It hadn't changed at all. Union Square looked the same as it had when Armen and I talked there; the cable-car bells still rang out over the square and faded away as the cars climbed to the top of Nob Hill. Down toward Market Street, I saw the familiar stores and buildings that I used to see when I worked at Compton's. There was the Fairfax, where Vahram and I had lived and where I used to annoy the tenants shouting "Veel coot-lets!" and "Pasht ekks!" and on the building across the street was the same electric sign that flashed on and off all night long as I lay in bed.

I walked down the street and then slowly around the corner of O'Farrell, and I stood at the doorway of what used to be Coffee Dan's, where I had held my first job as an immigrant dishwasher.

179

Something seemed to be pulling me down the stairs and so I went, leaving behind the sounds of the street. It was dim in the restaurant. I looked around. The general outlines were the same. But it had been redecorated in a style different from the one I remembered. The bar was to the left. I walked over. Behind it was a bartender who had once worked for me in Fresno.

"Hello, boss," he said.

I had let him go, because he didn't believe in fifty-fifty, the way I did. He always managed to get two for himself and one for the boss. But there were no hard feelings.

He grinned at me. "Thinking of buying the joint?"

My early days there were coming back, days he never knew about, and I hardly heard him. Slowly I crossed the restaurant and pushed through the swinging kitchen doors to the dishwashing stand, where I had stood and worked over the live steam all those long, backbreaking hours. I remembered how my boss used to glance at me to see if the perspiration showed through my jacket. I looked around in a sort of daze. This was where it all began, fifteen years ago. This was where I started my American adventure.

I went back into the restaurant. The owner came over to me and held out his hand. We knew each other. He had been my guest at Omar Khayyam's. We shook hands. "I want to talk with you," I said.

An hour later I went back up the stairs, through the door, and into the rainy street. I walked up Powell Street to our hotel. We didn't have our ten thousand dollars any more, but Naz had always understood things. I knew that if she had been there herself, she wouldn't have hesitated.

Surrounded by packages from the stores, she was in our room resting on the bed. I closed the door and turned on the light. She pushed herself up on one elbow.

"Naz—"

"George! You look so carried away—what is it?"

"Honey"—I sat down on the edge of the bed and took her hand—"I've got to tell you something—"

A wife knows a man better than he knows himself. She

180

sat up. Suddenly I knew she knew. "Now, honey," I said, "don't be upset—"

"You've spent the ten thousand!"

I nodded.

"You've bought a restaurant—"

"It just made the down payment on Coffee Dan's—for an Omar Khayyam's in San Francisco."

For a long moment Naz looked at me, and I looked at her. For the first time I began to doubt what I had done. My heart was sinking. "Maybe it was a terrible thing to do," I said. "The money was yours." I couldn't sit still. I got up and paced the room.

"But maybe we'd never get another chance to buy the place where I got my first job in America—where I started working for twelve dollars a week—"

Naz caught my hand and drew me to her side. "I'm glad, George." She put her hands on my shoulders. "I'm glad—and very proud—"

"We'll have our trip to Europe. I promise—" All at once I felt the way I had the morning I became a citizen—like a giant. "Isn't it wonderful? Now we can shout the story to the whole world. We can say that America is the place where an immigrant youth could come from Armenia, and arrive poor, and unable to speak the language, and in fifteen years buy the restaurant where he started as a dishwasher. We can say to all the world that this is true. This is what America made possible—"

I looked carefully at Naz's face, to make sure that she understood, that she was with me.

"I've never seen you look so happy," she said.

She stood up, and took my hand again, and looked up at me. Slowly, a very happy smile lighted her face, and I knew that Naz, as always, understood.

CHAPTER FIFTEEN

The fog rolled in from the sea, and the fog-horns blew down on San Francisco Bay, those first weeks of 1938 as we rushed our preparations to open the new restaurant.

It was a disappointment that we could not open on Lincoln's Birthday, which had become our good-luck tradition with openings. Those thirteen days from Lincoln's Birthday to the twenty-fifth of February, the night we opened, seemed to go on forever. Bart Rustigian, Peter Gagoush, Aram Keosaian, and the others I had brought from Fresno were on edge every moment, all afraid that something would go wrong, because we had not been able to open on our good-luck day.

While I had known the place as Coffee Dan's, it had been

a long time since Coffee Dan's had been there. Recently, it had been a night club called the Greenwich Village, which had featured Jerry Lester, Martha Raye, and other comedians and singers. I had hired Ellis Levy, my Fresno patron, as my manager. He convinced me that in keeping with the policies of the location, we needed entertainment as well as food.

Even so, I was not going to serve my Armenian dishes in the atmosphere of an artists' dive or Bohemian hideaway. I sent to Fresno for the reproductions of the Dulac *Rubaiyat* illustrations that had hung on the walls of the Mariposa Street restaurant. I had not been able to part with them or destroy them, and had been paying storage on them for years. It was getting them out of the warehouse and to San Francisco, and getting them up on the wood-paneled walls of the Greenwich Village that held up our opening.

Ellis was against the entire idea. "This is going to be a night club, with fast-moving floor shows. Big-time acts! Big-time names! Who's going to look at pictures?" But I was boss, so up they went.

Bart and Peter and the others were almost able to say, "I told you so," about their premonition. The night of the opening the place was packed. Several hundred customers in a happy, expectant mood were waiting for the first-night five-dollar dinners and an extravaganza of a floor show called "Revue in Swingtime."

A long, shrill fanfare of trumpets opened the program. In the hubbub and confusion, our master of ceremonies was eventually pushed aside. In the struggle for the microphone, the winner was Tom Breneman, later famous for his radio show, *Breakfast in Hollywood*. Tom was in a lively mood and was turning the evening into a slapstick comedy when, out in the kitchen, smoke billowed from an overheated flue and Aram Keosaian rang in the fire alarm.

Bart somehow stopped the firemen before they could burst into the restaurant and led them helter-skelter down the back stairs from the Powell Street entrance. Meanwhile, I persuaded Tom to let go of the microphone. With my heart in my mouth, I began telling stories of the wonderful food

183

that was going to be served. All the while, I kept an anxious eye on the doors to the kitchen. If so much as one wisp of smoke drifted into the dining room, the crowd might panic. It seemed forever until Peter suddenly appeared and gave me a big smile and a wink, and I knew that everything was all right. A few minutes later the waiters came carrying great trays of *dolma,* or stuffed grape leaves, and we were serving our first meal at Omar Khayyam's in San Francisco.

All the people had a wonderful time that night, and the next night and the nights after that. But there were nights when I found myself looking around my restaurant and wondering what I was doing there. The time came when I knew we'd never make it. We just weren't bringing in enough customers for our wonderful food.

The entertainers were the very best. We were advertising as an "After-theater Rendezvous" with a "sparkling, intimate" floor show. Every night from nine o'clock on and every Saturday afternoon jitterbugs invaded our tiny dance floor for "swing sessions." They looked and acted very happy. But the sale of dinners fell off. The money we took in from our jitterbugging customers no more than paid for the entertainment. Omar Khayyam's was just another downtown night club.

I tried to think of ways to give it a name as a restaurant and the reputation that Omar Khayyam's had earned in Fresno.

One thing I did was start the Mavericks' Club. Robert O'Brien was a member, and Beniamino Bufano, the sculptor, and also Elizabeth Banning, the interior decorator and color consultant, and Julie Medlock, the newspaper girl, and others, workers in all fields of the arts. No dues were paid. It wasn't even important whether everyone could pay for his meal. Anyone who couldn't signed his check; when he made good, that was soon enough for him to settle up. Quite a few San Franciscans can look back to their struggling days and remember the big, warm, free luncheons of the Mavericks. We all had good times and long hours of talk and comradeship, and my files collected a rising stack of signed checks, but still Omar Khayyam's remained a night club.

184

San Francisco ever since Gold Rush days has been noted for its Chinese, French, and Italian cuisine, but what I was trying to give the city was new and strange and exotic. No Armenian or Near Eastern restaurant that I knew of had ever tried to cater to the American clientele. It was an idea that even some of the city's old-time chefs found hard to accept.

Once, at a dinner I gave for the San Francisco unit of the International Stewards and Caterers, an organization made up of the city's best chefs, I explained every item on the menu —how it was made and its history. Over the coffee and cognac, the pastry chef from the Hotel St. Francis said he would like to make a remark.

"We all recognize you as one of the finest pastry chefs in the world," I said. "We would love to hear your remark."

He stood up. He had a mustache and a goatee and looked every inch a great *cordon bleu*. "I am from Alsace-Lorraine," he said. "The art of great cooking is a tradition of my native land. It is all very well for us to sit here and eat grape leaves and cracked wheat and skewered lamb, but, after all, let us not forget that it has been *la cuisine de la belle France* that has made the world aware of food at its finest."

When the applause died down, I said, "As a guest, I respect you. As a chef, I admire you. But as a Frenchman, I must remind you that my Armenian ancestors were cooking dinners five thousand years ago, when yours were still living in the trees."

Once more I turned to the radio. I have never forgotten my first program for the two NBC stations in San Francisco, KPO and KGO. The moment the program went off the air, the door flew open, and Al Nelson, NBC's general manager, stormed into the studio. "Who the hell wrote that program?"

Producer Bob Dwan looked up in surprise. "I did. Something wrong?"

"That didn't sound like George Mardikian. That sounded like a member of a high-school debating society. From now on, I want him to sound like himself—the right word in the wrong place and the wrong word in the right place."

185

From that day to this I have never used a script. I stumble along and sound like myself. Most people, if they listen very hard, can make out what I am trying to say.

In spite of all these things that might have made an impression in Fresno or some other place, I was sick at heart. Every man has those times, I guess, when everything seems to go wrong, when all the world seems against him, when no matter how loving his wife or how kind his friends, he feels lonely and lost.

In Armenia, they say that some men wear a *voski abaranchan*—a golden bracelet. This means that they have a special ability, or a trade. A carpenter, for example, wears "a golden bracelet." My brother, Arshag, wore one, which was his craft at making shoes. The saying means that no matter what else a man loses, he always has this treasure, this golden bracelet, to keep him alive. This was my comfort, that, anyway, I had my own golden bracelet—my trade as a chef and my knowledge of cooking—to see me through anything that happened. If I couldn't face returning to Fresno, I could go back to sea.

How long could the restaurant last, how long could we hold out, the way things were going? This is what kept me tossing and turning in bed at night.

Once a week I left San Francisco at closing time and drove down to Gilroy and over the Pacheco Pass to Fresno, to spend a day there and help Arshag with his problems. "How is everything in San Francisco at the new restaurant?" he would ask. Or it might be Mother Ruzvanian.

"Fine," I would say with a smile. "Couldn't be better. We're a great success."

And I would say the same to all my old friends.

But during the long drive down, and then back, I would know differently. What was there to do? To have my restaurant in San Francisco, the city that all the world knew and loved, had really been the heart of my dream ever since I had ridden up Market Street in the taxicab from the Ferry Building to "Forty-eight Po-vell Street." I had worked hard, and I had studied hard. Then, in Fresno, I had tested my

186

gifts, my heritage, and they had been well received. But now that it was all within my grasp, something was going wrong.

I sat there late one night listening to the loud, brassy music. I looked around my restaurant. I could hardly see my beautiful Dulac illustrations through the cigarette smoke. The tables were tiny and crowded together. Dancers were packed together on the small dance floor. Around me sat a typical night-club crowd. You see them everywhere, in every night club in the world. The silent, bored ones. The noisy, boisterous drinkers. The artificial women. The tired men. And all of them looking as though they ought to be home in bed. On the tables of those who were dancing, *shish kebab* dinners that Aram had prepared with care sat untouched and grew cold.

Night clubs are all right, and the people who go to them are all right, too. Only then and there I made up my mind I didn't want to run one. Ellis Levy was sitting with the band leader and his party. When the number was over and the dancers were going back to their tables, I sent for Ellis.

"Ellis," I said, "is all the band here, and all the blues singers and comedians and other entertainers? Are they all here tonight?"

"Every one of them," Ellis said. "What's on your mind?"

"I'm sorry, Ellis, but this"—I waved at the dance floor and all around me—"is finished. I'm through running a night club. Give them two weeks' pay and tell them they're through."

Our talk lasted an hour. Ellis said I couldn't do it. He'd leave, too. I said his dance band and entertainment were competing with my food; they were making me my own competitor, and it was all wrong, anyway. I wanted to be in the restaurant business, not the night-club business. When we closed the doors that night, Ellis and I shook hands, and that was the end of that. I slept for the first time in months.

Sometimes I felt that, like Haig Patigian, the sculptor, I had to carve out a name for my Omar Khayyam's just the way he carved those big statues, chip by chip, out of solid marble. I can take you to restaurants in San Francisco where

187

you will find the same chairs and tables, the same faded murals, the same bent-over waiters that they had twenty or thirty years ago. But these restaurants will have their steady, faithful patrons who would stay at home and eat out of a can rather than go to another restaurant. Their mothers and fathers went there before them, and probably sat them up in high chairs for their first meal in public at these same tables. And the food is probably the same, too. In some of them, it is mediocre and always has been; in others, it is superb, and was superb back when the patrons drew up to its front door in hacks and silver-mounted carriages.

I started out to win this kind of loyalty for my restaurant. I gave more talks over the radio. I appeared before women's clubs. I sent out thousands of recipes. Ninety per cent of my former night-club customers drifted off into the night. But that was where they had come from and that was where they would always go, from one club to another, and I did not think that they would miss Omar Khayyam's very much.

How different a feeling there was immediately! The youngsters that I had brought from Fresno to help me had been bewildered and confused by the night-life atmosphere. Now that we were a restaurant again, like the famous Omar Khayyam's they had helped to build in Fresno, they were very proud.

We were ready now to serve all the world poetry in food, and that alone. Every man who came down those steps was a king, and every woman a queen. That was how we wanted them to feel. For the next hour or two at Omar Khayyam's, they would dine like kings and queens, and they would be treated like kings and queens. In our imaginations, the store clerk who sat at our table wore a crown, and his wife wore diamonds and sables. And we served them *arkayagan abour,* royal soup, and a meal fit for a palace table.

But still there were long lulls in the evenings. Sometimes I was thankful for my shipboard training in poker with Leon Barbeau and Ragsdale, because I could pay Bart, Michael Zaretsky, Jimmie the philosophic Greek, Peter, and the other help, and then, that same night, in their rooms at
188

the St. Marlow Hotel, win back from them their wages at poker. With this money I could pay the butchers and Dale Brothers, whom I still patronized for sentimental reasons, although they had to ship my orders from Fresno. Sometimes it was those poker games that kept us going, kept us in San Francisco, when any one of us would rather have died than admit defeat. I think, for this reason, they used to cheat a little and let me win. I was better at poker than they were— but not that much better.

You have to have faith in something, not just a faith that helps you accept whatever comes, but a faith that is alive and active and practical. One of those days I found it, or it found me, or a faith that I had always had was somehow re- born stronger than ever.

At nights, when it was hard to sleep, I would read Ameri- can books of all kinds to improve my understanding of the language and the country and the people. Sometimes I would read until the sun came up over the East Bay hills.

One book was a novel. I guess Naz brought it home from some lending library. Don't ask me who wrote it or what it was all about. All I know is that I shall never forget a line I read in that book. For weeks it ran through my head, like a bar of music you can't forget.

"Keep your face toward the sunshine, and the shadows will fall behind."

I thought about these words for a long time. What they seemed to bring to me was a message of help and hope. What they said was, "Turn your heart toward the radiance and warmth of God's love, and doubts, fears, and unhappiness will disappear. Walk in the light, and have faith."

The way so many inspirations arrive, it came when I needed it most. It took hold with such force, and inspired such trust, I had to obey. I turned my face "toward the sun- shine."

As I began to smile again, in spite of the struggle to keep the restaurant alive, I felt that now I had a real, enduring *voski abaranchan,* one that would last forever.

Julian Kursey was a wholesale dealer and an old friend.

189

For years I had been one of his best customers in the San Joaquin Valley. One evening, at dinner, Julian looked at me with concern. "How's it going, George?"

Every man has troubles. Julian must have his, although I didn't know what they were. He certainly didn't want to hear about mine.

I looked him in the eye. "Julian, it's terrific. It's never been better."

"Don't kid me."

"Really," I said, "it's wonderful."

I have always loved that word. No other one comes so close to expressing how I feel. I think America is wonderful. I think people are wonderful. I think life itself is wonderful.

"George, you are the biggest lying so-and-so I have ever seen." He nodded toward the bar. "I know, for instance, how much you're using over there. Our sales figures tell the story. With your payroll and overhead, what's wonderful about it?"

I told him I kept saying that anyway, and hoping. Besides, I didn't want to bore him with my troubles. When he left, he grinned. "I'll see what I can do."

Julian Kursey made himself a one-man committee to improve business at Omar Khayyam's. Everywhere he went he told people about our Armenian food. More and more people began to come in who had heard the radio programs. Clubwomen who heard my talks and cooking lectures before their organizations brought their husbands in for dinner.

Those whom Julian Kursey brought came back again, with businessmen and out-of-town customers and travelers. And what made me even happier, many San Francisco families began coming in steadily, Sunday after Sunday, week after week.

Pretty soon, it was almost as if there hadn't been a swing band and a dance floor and a night club at all, but only a bad dream. Or, maybe, no more than a shadow that had fallen behind.

◇◇◇

CHAPTER SIXTEEN

From the windows of our home on Nob Hill, Naz and I watched them build that remarkable 400-acre island in the middle of San Francisco Bay and then put up on it the fairy-tale city that became the Golden Gate International Exposition on Treasure Island. Night after night we watched the beautiful glowing lights come on around the Tower of the Sun, making a great, moving fan of colored rays that lit up half the sky. We marveled like children at the brilliant fireworks that burst high in the sky over the Port of Trade Winds.

The "fair," as everybody called it, was very much a part of the lives of all San Franciscans during those far-off days. We didn't know it then, but we were living the last days of an era. Hardships and sacrifices were ahead, and perhaps

191

most of us sensed it. Anyway, we were all glad to have this wonderful make-believe paradise of Treasure Island; it left us memories that would give us strength and faith in the darkness of the war years.

So, we lived in and for the fair in 1939 and 1940, and played host to all the world.

I stood at the foot of the steps one evening not long after the opening of the fair, and down the stairs came Mr. and Mrs. George W. White, who had saved my life with three cans of condensed milk on the Kars River bridge, on that bitter, zero-cold day twenty years in our past. Now he was manager of the American College at Salonika, Greece. He and Mrs. White were back home on leave from his duties there. They had gone to Fresno to find me. They had learned that I was in San Francisco, and so, when they came to the fair, they stopped to see me at Omar Khayyam's.

There was nothing that Naz and I would not have done for these two Americans, to whom I owed my life. One of the happiest memories of those years is having them as our guests for the three days they were in San Francisco.

That first night in the restaurant, I asked what they would like for dinner. As they hesitated, I had an inspiration. "Mr. and Mrs. White, you are both pilgrims to the fair and to San Francisco. I would love to make you the traditional Armenian dish for pilgrims—"

Mrs. White smiled with delight. *"Harissa—harissa kashgag?"*

I nodded and signaled to Bart.

I'm sure the Whites knew the meaning of this old, old dish. Armenians say it began in antiquity, when the mountain people were making a pilgrimage to their monastery for prayers and worship. It was a custom for them to bring offerings of food—roosters, or lamb, or goats. The monks would boil all this meat together in huge pots in the monastery courtyard. Then, when the religious duties were over, everyone would join in a happy feast.

The story goes that at one of these ceremonies the abbot-general was preaching his sermon, when the curtains parted

192

behind him and the monk in charge of the feast stuck his head through and whispered, "Father Superior, five hundred pilgrims have come, and we have only food enough for two hundred. What shall we do?"

The abbot thought for a moment. "You have the meat boiling in the pots?"

"Yes, Father Superior."

"Well, then, pour in a lot of wheat—"

"Yes, Father Superior."

"And, *Ez harestza!* [beat the devil out of it!]"

So that is what happened. They added more and more wheat and beat the devil out of it until it was a sort of oatmeal, with the shredded meat in it. Then they seasoned it with salt and pepper and melted some butter on it, and *harestza*, or *harissa*, as it came to be called, is today a dish that is served on every festive Armenian occasion. It takes much real labor to beat it. Much love goes into the making of *harissa*. That is really why I made it that night in San Francisco for my old friends the Whites.

On another day I received a telephone call from the Hotel St. Francis, saying that they had a guest who would like to talk with me. It was a Turkish ambassador from the Orient, on his way home with his wife and two children.

I went to the hotel and spoke to him in Turkish. He couldn't speak English and was delighted, although as we stood there, I'm sure we both were thinking that we represented two of history's outstanding enemy races. But still, I wanted to make his stay in San Francisco a pleasant one.

During her childhood in Fresno Naz had lived next door to Armenians from Yozghad who, in their youth, had learned to speak Turkish, because if they hadn't the Turks would cut out their tongues. They had taught Naz the language, and so she was able to speak with the ambassador's wife and their children. We offered to take them to Treasure Island.

As we drove down the long approach from Yerba Buena to Treasure Island, the ambassador's wife said, "Mardikian Bey, I cannot understand these Americans. We have driven through Texas. There they have millions of square miles of

193

empty land. But in order to have a site for a world's fair, they ignore all that ground, and all the other empty space in America, and instead manufacture an island in the middle of a bay. Why do they do that?"

It was a good question. I was wondering how to get out of it, when her husband saved the day. He turned around in the front seat, very annoyed. "Woman," he snapped in Turkish, "you keep quiet. That is progress. Your Turkish mentality would not understand it."

That night at Omar Khayyam's, Little Jeff brought us drinks before dinner. The diplomat glanced uneasily at me, at Little Jeff's Armenian smile, and at the innocent-looking cocktails. I knew what he was thinking.

"Take any one you like," I said, "and give me any one you like, and we'll drink."

He handed me a glass from the tray, then took one himself. We held them up. Our eyes met. We drank. He relaxed and sat back.

"A few years ago," I said, "you would have been wise to be careful. My greatest joy would have been to poison you, because you are a Turk. But now that I'm an American, I can look at you without hatred. Being an American is such a wonderful experience that I cannot be an American and hate any man, or any race. I look at you, not as a Turk, but as a fellow human being."

A puzzled look came into his face. He shook his head slowly, as if at something that he could not understand. "I know," he said. "I have a funny feeling over here in this country, too."

We had a juke box in those days. Tallulah Bankhead used to sit in the "Celebrity's Corner" in the restaurant late in the evening and play *A Pretty Girl Is Like a Melody* over and over again, and sing to it.

Her play hadn't opened at the Curran Theater yet, so one night I went to my office and unwrapped one of my good-luck spoons. They are large, unusual spoons. There are only two other persons that I have ever given them to. One is Rudy Vallee. I took it back to her table and said,

194

"Tallulah, I want you to have this spoon. It is over a hundred years old. It is handmade of rosewood that grew on the banks of the Arax River, in the shadow of Ararat. A few minutes before your play opens, pour some champagne into this spoon and drink from it. It will bring you luck."

I do not say that the rosewood spoon had anything to do with it, but the play Tallulah opened in was *The Little Foxes*, her most successful one, and it brought her into her own again.

In all of these times, when famous people were always coming and going in San Francisco, only once did any question of policy come up. That was one evening when a socialite telephoned and said that Miss Barbara Hutton wanted to take over Omar Khayyam's for herself and fourteen guests. Of course, I would have to close my doors to other customers, so that this party could dine in private. But Miss Hutton would see that I was well rewarded.

As I listened, I looked at my diners. They were schoolteachers, mothers and fathers with their children, businessmen, travelers, tourists, a few familiar faces—no millionaires this evening, or movie stars—just my kings and queens.

"I'm sorry," I said. "I would love to be of service to Miss Hutton. But I wouldn't think of closing Omar Khayyam's for her and her guests, or anybody else." And I hung up.

Thirty minutes later the same person called again. Miss Hutton and her party would come anyway.

I was very pleasantly surprised. I found in Miss Hutton a lovely sweetness and graciousness and a thoughtful consideration for others that convinced me she was, and still is, the most misunderstood woman in America.

One of the specialties that I served in those days was something that had been famous at Omar Khayyam's in Fresno, *lah majoun,* or "the food of the élite."

In an Armenian's life an essential food is paste. Little girls, before they are ten or twelve, learn to help their mothers roll fine layers of paste. It takes years of experience and practice to spread a layer 5 feet in diameter across a table, roll it over and over again, and do that with ten or twelve

195

layers, one on top of the other, without their sticking together. But no Armenian housewife is considered a good cook unless her pastry layers are thinner than the leaves of the mulberry tree.

Lah majoun is one of the most popular Armenian pastes. The recipe came from Babylon, and sometimes its ingredients are costly. Only sheiks of the desert can afford *lah majoun* as often as they want to.

Necessity was the mother of this invention, because sheiks traveling through the desert heat couldn't carry prepared food with them. They took their meat on the hoof; lambs and goats were herded along with the caravan. When they ran out of these animals, they killed their camels. They also carried their flour, and sometimes even whole wheat and pestles to grind it. With these ingredients they made *lah majoun*.

At the end of a day's travel, the men pitched the tents, and the women made the fires. Sometimes, at big oases, they would find ovens already built in the rocks. With a "starter" of bread dough they carried with them, the women made a new batch of paste. Butter was carried in earthenware jugs of rock salt. The men furnished them the meat, and they ground it finely with tomatoes and peppers and onions, and seasoned it with salt, pepper, and cayenne, and spread it on their paste shells and baked them over their campfires. I have never known a more beautiful smell than the aroma of *lah majoun* being cooked on the desert.

I served this to Miss Hutton the night that she came with her friends for the first time. It was her favorite dish. A few months later, she returned to Omar Khayyam's with her own personal cook from her home in Santa Monica, so that I could teach the cook to make *lah majoun* for her own dinner table.

Having a lot of money was not only Miss Hutton's problem. Mother Ruzvanian telephoned me one day from Fresno. A man named Kaftarian had died. He had a ranch near Visalia and a very big packing house. Mother Ruzvanian

196

said that in all the San Joaquin Valley, no one would be his pallbearer.

"But, Mother," I said, "Mr. Kaftarian was worth over a million dollars."

"I can't help it," she said. "No one will be his pallbearer. I think we have to help the family."

This was a curious thing. No Armenian ever refuses to be a pallbearer. In fact, if there is a funeral within a hundred miles—anybody's funeral at all—it takes a very big consideration to keep him from going and crying at the grave. In the Armenian colony of Fresno were some old folks who went to every funeral. No matter who was being buried, perhaps a complete stranger, they always sat in the first four rows of Holy Trinity Church and looked and acted as though they had lost their best friend. It was said that even these regular funeral-goers were staying away from Mr. Kaftarian's funeral. They were going to punish him for his thoughtless ways.

On the drive to Fresno, thinking it over, I decided that, while Kaftarian had made a fortune, he had failed to realize that with the possession of money goes responsibility, a social responsibility to use it wisely and well and to learn the art of spending and giving, as well as the art of getting. He had taken no interest at all in his community, his church or any other organization, or in the needy.

When I reached Fresno, I telephoned Dick Yezdan, a good friend and a shrewd businessman. He said that, as long as I had asked him, he would be a pallbearer. Not only that, but for ten dollars he would get another pallbearer. I promised him the ten dollars.

They had the funeral, and Mr. Kaftarian in a beautiful three-thousand-dollar casket was taken to Ararat Cemetery and buried not far from Father Ruzvanian and Paul Mosesian. During the services at the cemetery, I couldn't help wondering how those two were getting along. Before I knew it, Naz was poking me with her elbow and frowning, and I realized I had been standing there at that solemn moment,

197

almost ready to laugh out loud. For looking over at their graves, I had noticed the concrete wall between their plots, and it brought back the memory of an argument that had been a standing joke at Hadji's Coffee House for many months.

One day, Father Ruzvanian had reminded Paul Mosesian that their graves were going to be side by side. "And," threatened Jake, "if you don't behave yourself after we're dead, I'm going to get out of my casket in the night and go over and dirty your grave."

"Is that so?" said Paul, and hired a contractor to sink a concrete wall 6 feet into the ground between the plots. Not only that, he had the contractor fill in his plot, so that his grave would be 4 feet higher than Jake's.

He found Jake at Hadji's and said, "Jake, I have fixed you. When we're dead, you won't be able to get close to my grave. What's more, I can roll over and spit down on you."

He took Jake out to the cemetery and showed him the cement wall and the raised plot. The next day, Jake hired the same contractor to fill in his plot, so that his grave would be as high as Paul's. But he couldn't do anything about the wall. So there they were, side by side, with Paul's wall between them so Jake couldn't get up in the night and dirty his grave.

Somebody else nudged me. I turned, and it wasn't Naz this time. It was Krikor Arakelian, an Armenian who had made millions with one of the biggest wineries in the world, at Madera, California. We nodded. When the services were over and we were walking back to our cars, he said a little sadly, "Not many people at the funeral, were there?"

"K," I said, "let this be a lesson to you. Before you kick the bucket, you'd better start doing something with all your money, or nobody'll go to your funeral, either." We walked a few more steps. "They'll not only stay away from the services, they will actually go afterward and spit on your grave."

He shook his head. "It sure is funny," he said. But you could tell from the way he said it, he meant just the opposite.

198

He must have taken it seriously. Not long after, he donated $300,000 for university scholarships. He helped the Armenian-American Citizens' League buy its own headquarters, and gave it $50,000 to establish a fund for an old folks' home. He also set aside thousands of dollars to build a fine chapel for the home. So some good came out of the Kaftarian funeral, after all. It was too bad that Mr. Kaftarian had to be punished, but it got results.

Meanwhile, my faith in myself and in America and in life was growing so big it seemed as though I couldn't tell enough people about it all. There weren't enough hours in the day. There was a war in Europe, and here in the United States many were afraid. They thought we were going too far with our rearming and our draft. I wanted to shout to them all that they could believe in America and the strength of her people, and reassure them that the freedom she guaranteed was the hope of all the people in the world.

The telephone rang in the restaurant one day, and it was an agency in New York saying that the Columbia Broadcasting System would like to have me appear on *We, the People.*

Naz and I took the train to New York. Several people from Young and Rubicam and CBS met us at the station. With them was one person wonderful to see, because she was from our home town. That was Julie Medlock, who had been a reporter for the San Francisco *Chronicle,* and one of our Mavericks at Omar Khayyam's. We all crowded into taxis and went to the Hotel Pennsylvania.

The CBS man said, "Well, let us check you in and then all go have some cocktails."

I am not a drinking man, and, besides, there was something else I had to do. It was the first thing I always did, whenever I came to New York.

"I'm sorry," I said, "but I have to take Mrs. Mardikian and go to my shrine."

"Shrine?"

"We have to go and see the Statue of Liberty."

From the expressions on the faces of the radio people, I

199

could see that they were thinking, "What is this country boob from San Francisco talking about?" But curiosity got the better of them, I guess, because they all came along.

We went down and got on the regular boat and rode out in New York Harbor. It was a beautiful, crisp autumn day. Out of the five New Yorkers with us, it was the first time that four of them had ever been there.

When we got off the ferry, I stopped at the huge base of the monument. High above us she raised her torch. I thought again of the first time I had seen her in the dawn, and of the millions who had seen her before and since, and of the hope that she stood for in the hearts of those millions.

Slowly I started reading aloud the words of Emma Lazarus' inscription:

> Give me your tired, your poor,
> Your huddled masses, yearning to breathe free,
> The wretched refuse of your teeming shore.
> Send these, the homeless, the tempest-tossed to me;
> I lift my lamp beside the golden door.

Before I finished, I was crying. I turned around and saw that I wasn't the only one. The others felt what I felt, and they were crying, too.

The next day, I had to prepare a very special meal for Niles Trammell, president of NBC, and some of his friends —Lucius Boomer of the Waldorf-Astoria; Ed James, managing editor of the New York *Times;* Clementine Paddleford, *This Week Magazine*'s food expert; Madame Metzelteen, who was editor of *Gourmet*—and other experts and gourmets of the Wine and Food Society and *Les Amis d'Escoffier.*

This dinner was difficult, because I was so far from my own kitchen and supplies. My biggest job, strangely enough, was not getting grape leaves for the *yalanji dolma* and *yaprak sarma,* or special ingredients for the *arkayagan abour,* but finding the right California wines that I insisted should go with the dinner, the right Livermore and Napa and Santa Clara Valley wines.

200

The night of the *We, the People* show, I found out that the script had all been changed. One of the producers who had been with us on Bedloe Island had insisted on writing in the Emma Lazarus quotation and the whole scene of our going and standing there on that lovely November afternoon. Eddie Dowling was the narrator. Even in that big theater filled with people and on the radio from coast to coast, my voice choked when I came to those beautiful words.

They are the words of a great, tender mother, the words that such a mother might say, thinking of her children that somehow had become lost all over the face of the earth.

Eddie was crying, and so was I, and I know that Naz was, there on the stage behind me, and I think that many of the people were, too. Not for sadness, but for the mercy, the tenderness, the wonder, and the loveliness of the hand held out to all the poor and hungry and helpless. "Come to me . . ." she says, and she means all the lost, frightened children, everywhere in the world.

CHAPTER SEVENTEEN

The next thing we knew, we were at war. Pearl Harbor and that December Sunday came, and all at once I was discovering a new America. I was seeing what Americans do and how they act with their backs against the wall. I was very proud to be one of them.

The whole world was passing through San Francisco. This was the impression you got then, and for the next five years. All these people had to be housed. And they had to be fed. Some nights, restaurants couldn't handle the crowds; they had to turn people away.

On a typical wartime night, patrons waited at least two hours for a table. They were always cooperative and considerate. If they were civilians and we seated a serviceman

202

or wounded veteran ahead of them, they always understood and approved. We had made a rule, too, at Omar Khayyam's that all our ice cream went to boys in uniform. Any serviceman back from overseas got all the ice cream he could eat. In fact, when we could, we set up canteens at the transport docks and, as they came off their ships, served ice-cold milk and ice cream to soldiers coming back from the Pacific fronts. Next to girls, this was what they wanted more than anything else in the world.

I wanted to help in every way I could. One thing that worked well for a while was the "Jack Spratt plan."

Everybody said that America needed more ships and planes and guns and bombs to win the war. Well, how could anybody make those things or get them to the fighting fronts without food? So it was food that would win the war. Was this just a chef and restaurant man talking? Perhaps so, but ever since Coffee Dan days I had been shocked by the way people wasted food. Anywhere from 25 to 50 per cent of the food served in restaurants was turned back uneaten and thrown into the garbage can. There would be quite a conservation if a customer could be persuaded to "lick his platter clean," like Jack Spratt, or to order less food, or both.

So in both Omar Khayyam's we used this plan. Patrons who ate all the food served to them and returned their plates to the kitchen absolutely clean were refunded 10 per cent of their checks in war savings stamps. It really made people stop and think before they ordered.

Stories on the Jack Spratt plan appeared in many newspapers and were broadcast on the radio. Schools in different parts of the country used it in their cafeterias. It did just what we hoped it would—helped both to conserve food and to sell war savings stamps.

Sometimes I became a salesman for war bonds myself. In fact, you couldn't keep me away from a war-bond rally if I had the gasoline to get there. The rich Armenian farmers and landholders used to say that I was the burr under their saddles. Whenever I saw one in the audience, I would point to him.

"Mr. Yervant," I would say, if that was his name, "I remember you, and I'm sure you remember me, when we were working for twelve and fifteen dollars a week. Today, I have several business enterprises. You have maybe 200 acres of fine grape land. And a big packing house. And some government food contracts.

"Now, Uncle Sam, who gave us all this, needs money. Mind you, he's not forcing us to give it to him, the way the Czar of Russia or the Sultan of Turkey forced our fathers and grandfathers. Instead, he's actually asking us to invest in him.

"And remember one more fact: if anything happens to Uncle Sam, and anything goes wrong with his credit because people like us don't help him out, then all your acres and all your packing houses and contracts won't be any good either."

As an appeal, it never failed.

I had a ranch now in the Imperial Valley, as well as the Fresno restaurant, but the only place I could really go whenever I wanted to was Vallejo. The government had allowed me to buy a new Ford and all the gasoline I needed for these trips, to supervise the operation of the Northside Cafeteria. Fenner Fuller, who managed the cafeteria, and his wife, Esther, and Marie Stoltenberg from Omar Khayyam's in San Francisco—all of us, working together, really proved that we could give Mare Island Navy Yard workers good, substantial food at a reasonable cost, even if we were at war.

In their own ways, other patriotic Armenian-Americans were doing their share. There was an elderly lady from Bitlis. She was gray-haired, wrinkled, and toothless; yet whenever she met Grandma Chalikian on the streets of Fresno, she always bobbed her shawl-covered head and cackled, *"Pari loyce, Nana,"* which means in Armenian, "Good day, granny." This made Grandma Chalikian furious. She would toss her head and look down her nose. "To you I am not *nana*. I am Mother Chalikian."

Anyway, Grandma told us once that she overheard the old lady praying in the Holy Trinity Church. The old lady thought she was alone, but Grandma was in the pew behind her.

204

"Oh, God," said the old lady—she was kneeling and raising her clasped hands—"I hear that airplanes are flying over the cities, and bombs weighing thousands of pounds are falling from them, and they are killing thousands of women and children, and are wrecking some beautiful buildings and old monuments, even churches.

"Now, God, you listen to me. Do something about all this trouble. Put a little sense, a little understanding, a little love in the hearts of men. But if all that doesn't work, for heaven's sake, don't send your Son down again to straighten things out. You come Yourself. This time, it's a man's job. Amen."

Also, there was Kersam, the owner of the Arax Grocery. The store wasn't far from the house Mother Ruzvanian moved into, after we all left the Hotel Sequoia.

One day she came into the store to buy some meat. There was Kersam, in back of the butcher's block, cutting a shoulder of lamb with a big knife. He was singing and whistling. On his head he wore a shiny white helmet.

Mother Ruzvanian studied the helmet. "What is that you're wearing, Kersam?"

Kersam was a big, muscular fellow, but too old to go to war. He shrugged. "Oh, it's nothing. I'm working for Uncle Sam now. I'm an air-raid warden."

As time went on, Mother Ruzvanian learned what happened with Kersam and the drill master. These wardens were trained in discipline every other day at the armory at Kern and L Streets. Kersam was like a bull you are trying to lead by the ring in its nose.

"This is all foolishness," he said. "I don't need this training. I know what to do."

But on it went. The sergeant put them in formation and shouted, "Left! Right! Left! Right!" Always when the sergeant called, "Left!" big, ungainly Kersam would put out his right foot. When the sergeant called, "Right!" Kersam would put out his left. Finally he pulled Kersam from the line.

"Listen, you big ox," he said. "You better learn which is left and which is right."

Kersam got red in the face. He was mad through and through. "Let me tell you something, you little peanut. I don't savvy this 'Left! Right!' stuff. But you just give me a Jap"—he raised his big knee and brought his fists down, as if he were snapping a stick of wood—"and I break him into half!"

All over the Armenian colony of Fresno, the people smiled and chuckled when they heard about it. "That's our Kersam," they all said. And they couldn't help it; they were just a little proud of him.

No one ever saw him without his white helmet. All the people began saying that he wore it to bed. One day Mother Ruzvanian asked him, "Kersam, suppose there was an air raid. What would you do?"

"Don't you worry about Kersam," he said cheerfully. "I know where all the best bomb shelters are. I'd run as fast as I could and be the first one there."

I loved to visit Fresno. I had never seen such hustle-bustle in the town. Never had the farms and ranches looked so well. There were many olive groves that I remembered as run-down and neglected. All of a sudden, with the rise in demand and the increase in olive prices, the groves became as well groomed as tree nurseries, with the rows beautifully cleaned and the trees strong and healthy and watered all the time.

But my trips there grew less and less. Too many other things had to be done. One of these duties, and pleasures, became an important part of my life, and this was the beginning of it. Camp Roberts was a huge training base—one of the biggest in the world—about a hundred miles south of San Francisco. Its commanding officer was Brigadier General Eugene W. Fales.

General and Mrs. Fales were having dinner at Omar Khayyam's one evening, and we were talking together over brandy and coffee, and he said, "George, Camp Roberts is a great installation—one of the best. But there's one problem we can't seem to lick. We can do everything Uncle Sam asks but turn out good food. How about giving us a hand?"

206

A few days later, I found myself in the broiling heat of the lower Salinas valley, staying with General Fales, visiting the mess halls and talking with GIs and all the cooks and mess sergeants. I went into it with all my heart. Here was a chance to help America when she needed it most. You'll never know how proud and happy I was in the army kitchens at Camp Roberts with my sleeves rolled up, and doing what had always been part of me and my special heritage, ever since the days that *Shishko* had burned his fingers on his mother's cook stove, in her kitchen in Scutari.

One of the most important improvements was not up to me at all, but up to General Fales. I discovered first of all that many men in the army kitchens were on "KP duty" because they were being punished for breaking some rule. They hated it, didn't care what kind of job they turned in, and couldn't wait until it was over. Who could blame them if they didn't take pride in what they were doing? And if they didn't, who could expect the food to be worth eating?

After two or three days, I said to General Fales, "All the help in the world won't do any good unless you put men in your kitchens who really enjoy their work, who can work and sing at the same time. Take away their greasy uniforms and give them shiny white ones, and chefs' hats. The Army has a lot of stripes to spare. Well, put an extra one on the cook's sleeve. Give him a little pride and dignity."

There was still conservation to think of. A big part of this problem was not only the tasteful preparation of food, but giving it eye appeal. If food looks good, and then tastes good, you are not going to have any trouble getting people to clean their plates.

At Camp Roberts the most wonderful zucchini squash was delivered by the ton. Most of it ended in the garbage can because all the chefs did was boil it, then sling it down in front of the men. It was my job to prevent this. I fried some onions and added tomatoes and salt and pepper, then stewed them all together with the zucchini. They changed its color and gave it a pleasant aroma, so that it now both looked and smelled as though it would be good to eat.

The chefs were amazed. They had never thought of cooking it that way before. Right there, I could see their minds opening up. I smiled to myself. It wouldn't be long before they would be inventing dishes themselves. The first step was to break out of the routine way of thinking about their job. Then they would be on the way toward singing while they worked, toward working with eagerness and love.

"Look," I said, "here is another method."

I cut the zucchini into strips lengthwise and fried them, and then poured a little vinegar over them. This made the zucchini into a tasty and different appetizer.

"And here," I said again, "is still another method."

I cut some more into strips. Then I dipped the strips into egg batter and fried them.

"You think, maybe, that you have a lowly job in this war. But without men like you in the kitchen, how could the glamorous fighter pilots get off the ground?"

This wasn't original, and they had probably thought it to themselves a thousand times. But I know it did their hearts good to hear someone else say it.

Anyway, that was the beginning of my actual work for the armed services. Before another twelve months were up, I had done the same thing at Fort Ord in Monterey, and at nearly every other army training camp on the Pacific Coast.

But in wars, life is no different; you give and you take. It's just that sometimes it happens quicker and goes deeper. One evening I went out to Vallejo. I went to the Northside Cafeteria and carried out some business there and then went on to a speaking engagement. I was giving a talk before some university women, most of them navy officers' wives, on the conservation of food in wartime.

Their husbands had been away from home for probably a year or more, out in the Pacific, and I felt a strong bond with them that evening. In my pocket was a War Department telegram. "Wars are so horrible," I said, "there is no one who is not affected." And I told them that I had received word that Khoren, my sister Baidzar's strong young son, was

208

dying of spinal meningitis, which had developed while he was at the naval training center at Great Lakes.

After my talk, a dignified lady approached me and asked if I or anyone from my family was going to Khoren. I said yes, Khoren's sister, Mary, my wife, Naz, and I were leaving the next morning. We would have left that very evening, but I had not wanted to disappoint this group of navy women.

"My son-in-law," she said, "is a navy captain. He is in charge of the Great Lakes Naval Hospital. I am going home now and telephone him that you are coming. I know he'll do everything he can."

The next day Mary, Naz, and I flew to Chicago. We finally reached the training station and the hospital. Sick and wounded were everywhere. They made us wear white jackets and put masks on our faces and took us to see Khoren.

He opened his eyes and recognized his sister and me. "Where—where is Aunty Naz?" I had written that Naz was coming with us. But at the last minute the doctor had asked her to remain outside, so Khoren wouldn't have too much excitement all at once.

The physician was a navy doctor from Minnesota. He told us that the commanding officer, the captain, had called on Khoren and cheered him up. So once more, bread on the water had come back. I'm sure that this attention helped Khoren's morale and strengthened his will to live, because he did come out of it alive.

That year, 1942, I closed the restaurant to regular patrons at Thanksgiving and Christmas and had as dinner guests wounded men from military hospitals in the San Francisco Bay area. Even on other days no wounded man in any uniform ever paid for a meal at Omar Khayyam's, but on these two days they came in their wheel chairs and on their crutches and with their canes from the hospital wards.

With them came their commanding officers—generals and admirals—and celebrities from Hollywood or New York entertained them, as they ate their holiday turkey. Among those who came steadily to help over the war years were Rudy

209

Vallee, Jane Pickens, Al Pearce, and others just as gracious and famous. They were always happy to help, no matter how big or how busy they were.

On Thanksgiving, 1943, for example, Leopold Stokowski was in San Francisco for a concert. He said he would come to our dinner for the wounded servicemen, but he added that he could stay for only twenty minutes.

When he walked down the restaurant steps, the boys clapped loudly. Twenty minutes went by, and another twenty. By the time he left, he had been there two and a half hours. He had stopped at all the tables and scrawled his unusual autograph, which covers a menu page 9 by 12 inches in size, for all the GIs that asked for it.

One Christmas we had as guests a number of "basket cases" from the army and navy hospitals. They came with their nurses, and police closed the whole block of O'Farrell Street to traffic so their cars and ambulances could pull up to the restaurant door.

One thing we always did was offer them the free use of our telephone, to call home. It was surprising how few of them thought of telephoning. I guess they had forgotten how simple it is. One very young soldier was on the telephone getting a call to his mother in Salt Lake City. He was an amputee—without legs. He was sitting in a wheel chair. I heard the clicks in the receiver, then a woman's voice. "Hello, Mother—" he said.

They talked happily for a minute. Then all at once he began to tremble. "Have—have I grown? Is that what you asked, Mother?"

His mother said something. He put his hand over the mouthpiece and pushed the telephone at me. "Talk to her for me. Say good-by—say anything—"

I took the phone. I tried to put a smile in my voice. "Madam," I lied, "your son is in perfect health. He is enjoying his dinner here in San Francisco with a lot of his friends." Army regulations, I told her, wouldn't let him speak to her any longer. But, "Don't worry about him. He's all right, and he'll be coming home to you soon."

The soldier pressed my hand and thanked me, and the nurse wheeled him away.

Three months after that, I was called from my office to the restaurant. A young man insisted on seeing me. I went there, and there he was, standing straight as an arrow.

"I couldn't leave for Salt Lake City," he said, "without coming in to say good-by, and to thank you, and prove that you didn't tell a lie to my mother, after all." He looked down at his legs. "The Medical Corps' best. But I'm here. I can walk. I'm in perfect health. And I'm even an inch taller than I used to be!"

How can you beat a spirit like that?

Then, at the Christmas party in 1944, there was a youngster that had been shot through the jaw. It was in a cast, and he spoke with difficulty. We tried to seat him with some of his friends. He grinned with his eyes. "What's the use?" he said. "I can't eat, anyway."

So he had a great time, walking from table to table, kidding with the entertainers and even with the admirals and generals. Then, as they were all leaving to go back to their hospitals, he came up to me.

"Mr. Mardikian, I've got four buddies in my ward. They're a little shot up and couldn't get here today, but their jaws and stomachs are in good shape. I was just thinking—they'd love a Christmas turkey sandwich from Omar Khayyam's—"

I called Bart over, and Peter Gagoush, my two managers. "Get the biggest roast turkey we have in the kitchen, wrap it up, and bring it out."

They came back with a 32-pound roast Fresno turkey. A male nurse from the hospital offered to take it, but the wounded boy insisted on carrying it himself. Bart and Peter and I and the rest of the staff and the entertainers sat down at the tables. It was our turn for Christmas turkey.

We were eating away, talking about the fine party, when I looked up. Across the restaurant, at the foot of the steps, stood the boy with his jaw in a cast. He had a funny look on his face. A dozen possibilities flashed through my mind. An accident—something wrong at the hospital. I hoped he

211

wasn't in trouble for accepting the turkey. I hurried over. His blue eyes grinned again. "I was so happy and excited about the turkey, I—well, I forgot to thank you. So I left the turkey at the hospital and found a taxi and came back—"

He reached into his pocket and took out a package of PK chewing gum. He handed it to me. "Here, I can't use this very well. And I understand it's hard for civilians to get. Will you take it, with thanks, from me and my buddies—?"

I took the little package. "God bless you, Son," was all I could manage. Because this hurt and weary boy had forgotten to say, "Thank you," he had come all the way back—the taxi probably cost five or six dollars—to make up for it, to show me that he was a gentleman and a courteous American soldier.

To this day that package of chewing gum makes me think of all the gallant men—the men with hope and courage and ideals—that America has given to the world. I keep it under an overturned glass in my office. I show it to people and tell them the story. I'll never part with it for anything, as long as I live.

CHAPTER EIGHTEEN

There was one personal trip to Fresno that we had to make in those wartime years. That was for the funeral of Grandma Chalikian. She was nearly ninety, and even "the duchess" couldn't hold out forever against old age.

We hadn't been able to enjoy her company as much as we would have liked during the past ten years, but Mother Ruzvanian, who herself seemed to be failing a little, gave us news of Grandma. Although her tongue had lost its sting, Grandma had been proud and spirited to the end.

We of Armenian background are as sad as anyone else when friends and relatives die, but somehow we recognize death as part of living and accept it as natural, as God's way of doing things. So, when someone dies, he is frequently more vivid and alive to us than he was before. It is that way sometimes in life, when a person leaves the room. Then you are suddenly able to appreciate him and his qualities, because you see what a gap, what an emptiness, he leaves behind.

So it was that even at Grandma's solemn funeral service something funny happened that made us who knew and loved her remember the old-world naïveté that went along with her poise and dignity.

It happened that working for me in Omar Khayyam's in Fresno was a faithful cook. His real name was Mushek Mushekian, but because he was so small we all called him Shorty. He was always doing something for others, and was really a very sentimental man. So, when Grandma died, he sent her the biggest and finest floral piece that anyone had seen in Fresno for many years. It was a huge white cross made of gardenias. On top of the cross, with its wings spread, sat a stuffed dove.

While our heads were bowed and the priest was in the middle of the funeral sermon, Naz nudged me in the ribs. I looked up. She was staring openmouthed at Shorty's cross, up by the altar. It was tipping over.

"Vush!" whispered Naz. *"Vush!"*

It was hard to keep from smiling. *Vush* was the Armenian word Grandma always used to keep away the Evil Eye. But it did no good. The floral piece, dove and all, crashed to the floor. All the mourners were startled and lifted their heads to see what was going on. The priest stopped his sermon and bent over and, with the help of the deacon, tried to stand it up straight. But it was big and hard to handle and tottered back and forth, and everybody was afraid the dove was going to come loose and fall off.

At last they got it up straight, but while they were struggling with it, Naz and Lucie and even Mother Ruzvanian and I held ourselves in. We couldn't help shaking with laughter. We hid it the best way we could behind our hands. Without any of us saying it, we all knew we were thinking the same thing: somebody in the congregation had praised

214

the beautiful floral piece and so had put on it the Evil Eye. If Grandma had been alive, it never would have happened. She would have cried, *"Vush!"* and touched her bottom, and the spell would have been broken. It was remembering the way she used to do this that struck our funny bones. And if she could talk, Grandma would have been saying to us, "See what happens the minute I'm gone, and can't touch my bottom to keep the Evil Eye away?"

Just how fierce Grandma's pride was we learned at the *hokotz djash*, the "feast of the soul," which is the Armenian wake. One of the mourners was Mrs. Arousiak Moradian, who had been a friend of ours for a long time. "I couldn't before," Mrs. Moradian said, "but now that she's passed away, I can let you in on a secret about Grandma Chalikian." And she sat down beside Naz and me and began her story.

Almost thirty years ago, she had rented one of the little houses Grandma had bought when she sold her tobacco ranch in Exeter to the American Tobacco Company. She lived in this little house with her two little boys, Raffi and Yeprad, who was named for the Euphrates River and whom everyone called for short, Yeppi. Raffi was eight years old then, and Yeppi was four.

One day Grandma went next door to Mrs. Moradian's with a post card. She handed it to Mrs. Moradian. "What does it say?" she asked.

Mrs. Moradian read it. "It says you have a package waiting for you at the post office in Exeter."

The next day, in a bitter March dawn, Mrs. Moradian, Grandma, and little Yeppi walked down to the Southern Pacific depot. Grandma had arranged for someone to take care of Raffi and for someone else to take Mrs. Moradian's place at Gottschalk's Department Store, so she could go along and help get the parcel.

They took the milk train and rode the 40 miles south to Exeter. Here there were a couple of stores, the post office, a hotel, and the station, and that was all. It was raining and cold, and a quarter to seven in the morning. Nothing was open. Shivering, they sat in the depot. Yeppi whimpered and sniffled. Grandma sat straight as a ramrod on the bench and tried to ignore him. On the dot of eight, they were at the post office.

The postmaster raised the glass window. Mrs. Moradian poked Grandma. "Give him your notice." Grandma handed him the card. He looked around and found a thick, flat package and then passed it through the opening. Grandma put it under her arm and walked out. Mrs. Moradian pulled Yeppi after her and followed. They went back to the station, for the long wait for the next train north to Fresno.

"After all this trouble, aren't you going to open it?" Mrs. Moradian asked.

Grandma held the package tighter and looked down her nose. "I don't want everybody knowing my business," she said sharply. They got to Fresno late that afternoon, after dark. Even so, Grandma looked up and down the street before they started walking home. She didn't want anyone to see them.

Every day after that, Mrs. Moradian's curiosity grew bigger and bigger. "What was in that package, Grandma Chalikian?" she would ask. Grandma would always look down her nose. "It's none of your affair."

Finally Mrs. Moradian said, "Grandma Chalikian, it's my right to know what was in the package. I took you down to Exeter and brought you back. I lost a whole day's work at Gottschalk's. Yeppi has had the sniffles ever since."

That evening, Grandma called Mrs. Moradian to her kitchen. She locked the door and turned out all the lights except the one over the kitchen table.

"Raise your right hand," she said solemnly.

Mrs. Moradian raised her right hand.

"Swear—swear on the lives of Raffi and little Yeppi—that you will never tell anyone as long as I am alive."

"I swear," said Mrs. Moradian.

Grandma went to a cupboard. "If anyone knew I went all the way to Exeter at five o'clock in the morning for this, I'd be a laughingstock," she said. From a shelf she took a thick, heavy book. Red-faced and embarrassed, she put it down on

216

the table in front of Mrs. Moradian. Mrs. Moradian stared down, with her mouth open. It was a Sears, Roebuck catalogue.

We thought that we wouldn't lose any more of our family for a long time, but a year or two passed very swiftly then, and it seemed as though no time at all had gone by before Naz and Lucie and I stood once more under the mulberries of Ararat, this time for Mother Ruzvanian.

Both Naz and I felt somehow at peace. Our gracious and kindly and beloved Mother Ruzvanian wasn't lonely any more, the way she had seemed, sometimes, after we left Fresno. She was joining her mother and my mother, her brother Yeghia, and Hagop, her husband. Someday we would all be together again. . . .

So these were memories of the war years—these sad trips to Fresno—and we came back from them and threw ourselves even harder into the humdrum, never-ending jobs that went with keeping the home front.

One thing I did was to make a constant round of appearances before women's groups and clubs, to give them a wartime cooking message.

Over and over I harped away on the same things. I wanted them to break the habit of boiling vegetables and throwing away the juice, the best and most nutritious part of all, and then serving their families what was left, which many chefs call "pulp," because it is not much more than that.

Also, I told them, "The war should teach us to make combinations of foods. Now, your average dinner might consist of a meat course, when you can get it, with perhaps several different vegetables, each cooked by itself. In wartime, we shouldn't use that much gas or electricity. And we shouldn't use all the time and energy it takes to wash all those pots and pans. That fuel and that time and energy should go toward the war effort."

I was really arguing for one-dish meals, which thrifty Europeans had been cooking for many generations, and I was wishing for a better way of doing this, or of reaching more people, when my answer fell from the blue. If you want

217

to do things for others, life sometimes shows you the way. One of my customers at Omar Khayyam's was Pascal Covici, an executive of the Viking Press of New York. I told him what I was trying to do and what the problems were. When I was through, he said, "I have just the solution."

"What is that?"

"Write a cook book. Maybe we'll publish it for you."

I couldn't help smiling. Me?—Write a book?

But the next week, I was hard at work. Before I knew it, the book was finished, the proofs were read, and *Dinner at Omar Khayyam's* was on the stands. That was in November, 1944.

But an even prouder moment came. Early in 1945, when the rumor started that the European front was cracking, the people of the free world decided to hold the United Nations Conference in San Francisco. Naturally, I thought right away about the problem of feeding delegates from fifty or more countries, with all their different creeds and customs. Some would come from countries that had only the minimum food requirements. Men from England, for instance, wouldn't have eaten one egg a month. Also, many delegates would be cosmopolitan and intellectual and well-traveled. They would expect a great deal from our American cuisine.

The more I thought about the food problem, the more important it seemed. Good food representing the cuisine of their own countries would keep the delegates in a pleasant frame of mind, which would help them think in terms of peace and harmony and good will. But if they got indigestion in a strange land far from home, the result might turn out to be very bad for the world.

Members of the Golden Gate Restaurant Association agreed. At a special meeting they voted to give the delegates the red-carpet treatment in their restaurants and asked me to explain their feelings to Mayor Roger D. Lapham, who was in charge of municipal arrangements for the conference. I worked and worked over a letter and mailed it to him.

I wrote:

218

How men eat very definitely influences their judgment as well as their digestion. Empires can be built or destroyed at the dinner table. Peace in our time can well depend on whether we soothe or insult the gastronomic tastes of our guests. . . .

The delegates will come from more than fifty nations. They will be accustomed to as many different types of cuisine. What is going to be their state of mind if they sit down to tasteless, commonplace food, prepared without thought of their individual national preferences?

We want the friendship and respect of these delegates from all over the world. How can we win it more surely than by catering intelligently and understandingly to their palates?

It is our duty as citizens to give this matter the gravest consideration. A good dinner will put any man in a conciliatory frame of mind. A bad one will make him quarrelsome. From this viewpoint, we restaurant men, whether we like it or not, must bear the heaviest kind of responsibility for the success or failure of the conference.

To my amazement this letter was released to the press by Mayor Lapham and was printed in newspapers and magazines all over the country. Next to love, I guess few subjects have more human-interest appeal than food.

It had already been decided to operate a public cafeteria in the lower lobby and bar of the War Memorial Opera House, where delegates and press representatives from all over the world could buy a well-balanced, appetizing lunch for one dollar. For breakfast and dinner, they were free to go to the city's restaurants, but this was the one, all-important meal in the middle of daytime working hours.

Only a week or two before the delegates were going to arrive, a difficult situation developed. The San Francisco unit of the American Women's Voluntary Services had offered the all-out cooperation of its membership in the operation of the cafeteria, and had even organized the personnel for it. But Mayor Lapham and State Department agents did not want to place the responsibility for feeding two thousand people a day on the shoulders of these willing ladies; the spirit and desire were there, but it was a job for professionals. When it came to finding a professional, however, State Department men discovered that San Francisco restaurant operators had their hands full running their own establishments and getting them ready for the avalanche of visitors.

My next door neighbor in our Powell Street apartment house was Dr. Henry F. Grady, who had been Cordell Hull's Assistant Secretary of State. He and I discussed the problem of feeding conference personnel, and I know that he talked it over, too, with the State Department people.

The week before the conference opened, one of the agents, Arthur Hazes, called on me. He asked if I would be San Francisco's "official caterer" to the conference, and supervise the cooking and serving at the AWVS opera-house canteen. I told him how grateful I was; but, like the other restaurant men, I had my own wartime obligations toward the public. During the conference they would be heavier than ever.

But that night, before I went to sleep, I thought it over. Of course, I had an obligation to my own patrons and to those who would depend on Omar Khayyam's for meals and much-needed relaxation in the weeks to come. But didn't I have an even deeper obligation to my country?

The very next morning I had a meeting with Arthur Hazes. "I hope your offer of yesterday still stands," I said.

"Yes," he said, "it does."

"Well, I'll be more than glad to accept." We shook hands. "But," I added, "there's one condition."

He smiled. "I'm sure it'll be all right."

"The condition is that the State Department cannot pay me. I can't take money for helping you, or helping America."

We went to work, and to begin with there were only two little stoves in the basement of the Veterans' Building, which is across a broad court from the opera house and where we had to cook the meals for the AWVS canteen.

I found this out on April 23, three days before the conference opened. I telephoned the largest restaurant-supply house in San Francisco. "Come to the Veterans' Building and install some big ranges. You've got twenty-four hours. State

Department orders." The ranges were in and working by noon of the next day.

Then, of course, we faced the problem of getting some two thousand lunches a day from the Veterans' Building to the lower lobby of the opera house. There was a tunnel under the court, but it was hardly big enough for a job like this. We solved the problem with milk-delivery trucks, borrowed from a San Francisco dairy. The personnel, however, could use the tunnel for going from one building to another. Here we passed before the eagle eyes of the military police and FBI agents, and showed identification cards. I always thought it was funny that there I was with my bulky frame in spotless white, with a tall chef's cap on my head, and yet every time they stopped me for identification. They weren't taking any chances on an impersonation, farfetched as it might seem.

The AWVS produced 750 women from all walks of life. I asked each one to help one day a week. They were wonderful ladies, but less than 5 per cent had catering experience. Some employed cooks and maids of their own and hadn't handled a tray in years.

But I was very proud of them, and the city was rightfully proud of them. I gave a little speech on the importance of what we were doing, and how we were acting as hosts and hostesses not only for San Francisco, but for all America. These delegates would form opinions of America and Americans by the food put before them and the people who put it there. The ladies all pitched in to do their best, from the young mother who had to leave her children with the neighbor next door while she waited on tables, to the gray-haired matron driven to the Veterans' Building in a chauffeured limousine.

I'm sure the whole world was holding its breath that afternoon of Wednesday, April 25, 1945. I remembered that it was raining that afternoon. It fell in drenching sheets in Van Ness Avenue as the big black limousines, tires singing on the wet pavement, drew up to the awning that stretched over the opera-house steps and out to the curb. And the

221

heart of everyone there filled with hope as Secretary of State Edward Stettinius formally opened the United Nations Conference for International Organization.

With him on the platform, straight as arrows, were several young men and women of the armed forces, and Governor Earl Warren, who welcomed the delegates for the State of California, and Mayor Lapham, who greeted them for San Francisco.

Then, over the radio loud-speakers, we all heard the stirring words of President Truman, speaking from Washington and reminding us and the rest of the world that, "If we do not want to die together in war, we must learn to live together in peace."

When the delegates and all the spectators crossed the marble-floored lobby and pushed out through the doors, we found that while we had been inside, a miracle had happened: the rain had stopped, the storm clouds had broken up and were blowing away, and the sun was shining all over the beautiful city. Across the street, the dome of the City Hall glistened and gleamed, and the spring flowers were bright around the sparkling fountains of City Hall plaza. Everyone thought it was a magic omen. After six years of darkness, light was coming back to the world.

CHAPTER NINETEEN

The conference opened on a Wednesday, but it was actually the following Monday, April 30, that the delegates rolled up their sleeves and got down to work. I remember that the Sunday we were getting ready for the first real week of work was a long, exhausting day for all the behind-the-scenes workers. None of us was sure where things were, where they went, how to work together—just like any team where the members are new to each other and their duties not fully worked out.

Late that night, after twenty hours at the Veterans' Building, the opera house, and Omar Khayyam's, I went home and collapsed into bed. The next thing I knew, Naz was shaking me. "George! George! Wake up!"

223

The bedside light glared into my eyes. My traveling clock said long after midnight.

"The pains have begun. You have to leave right away for the hospital."

I shook the sleep out of my head. "Hospital?" Then I remembered. It was time for Lucie's first child. Haig, her husband, was in Southern California. She had been living with us, and everything was all arranged with St. Mary's Hospital. Still groggy, I piled out of bed. Five minutes later, Lucie, the nurse, and I were in the car and on our way.

Halfway down the Powell Street hill a cry from Lucie brought my heart to my mouth. We were too late! "What's the matter?" I asked, and started to pull over to the curb.

"The gas gauge. Look at it!"

Sure enough, it stood at "E." But I was relieved to find out the trouble wasn't what I thought it was. All the downtown garages were closed and dark. "Shall we change to a cab?"

"We'll do no climbing in and out of cars," the nurse said briskly.

We were lucky, and made it. I left them at the emergency entrance. Lucie made me go home. "It'll probably be hours," she said, as a nurse put her into a wheel chair. I found a garage open on Stanyan Street and bought some gas and drove back home to get some sleep. Naz met me at the door. She was in tears. My heart sank. Something terrible had happened at the hospital.

"Naz! What is it?"

"I just talked to Lucie on the telephone—"

"What did she say? Why are you crying?"

Naz threw her arms around me. "Lucie had a baby girl," she sobbed.

"But isn't that just what we've been waiting for? Sweetheart, why are you crying?"

"Because I'm so—so happy!"

Well, I guess it was a familiar scene for many Americans. And probably the exact words, in many cases. I must admit that I felt like crying, too. Naz and I had never been blessed

224

with children of our own. We knew that this little girl was going to bring new happiness and new life into our family.

And that is what she did from the moment she was born. It was my privilege to name her. I chose the name Unita, which was very close to Mother Ruzvanian's name, Anitza, and added to it Naz, for my wife, making Unita Naz. This was appropriate, because to me it meant "United Nations." Now, since that Monday was the first real working day of the conference, I like to think that the United Nations and this dark-haired, brown-eyed, beautiful little girl came into the world on the same day.

Another still more personal reason why the little girl was so important was that she turned all our minds from the sadness of the death of Mother Ruzvanian. You might think that this death and birth made the words and formalities of the conference seem to have little to do with our personal lives, but actually they made the conference more important than ever. These men were there to try to bring peace to the world; what they were doing could affect the lives of millions, many of them wise and wonderful ladies like Mother Ruzvanian and many more of them helpless infants like Unita Naz. I really wished that each delegate, with his Homburg hat and brief case, could have gone to his morning meeting straight from the maternity wing of St. Mary's Hospital, where the babies cried and slept, and trusted the grownups to make a happy world for them.

As the days passed, we had our problems at the canteen. For instance, turkey is the king of American foods; there was such a demand for it that we had to cook sixty-four a day. But with the ranges we had we could roast only sixteen at a time.

And I soon learned, to my distress, that many Catholic delegates must have received special permission from their priests to eat meat on Fridays. I had ordered for the first Friday luncheon 550 pounds of roast beef and 350 pounds of salmon—and worried whether there would be enough fish to go around. An hour after the cafeteria opened, the beef was all gone. But in the ovens and on the steam tables

225

was more than half my supply of salmon. It went unordered and had to be given to charity.

Another time, a young State Department attaché with horn-rimmed glasses told us that certain members of an Indian delegation, because of religious regulations, could not eat food cooked in the same pots that were used to cook food for Christians. I would have to buy new pots for these delegates and see to it that their food came from those and no other pots.

Well, I thought that this was a great deal of trouble to go to, when we had all the other delegates to take care of, and press representatives as well. So I bought the special pots, but in reality cooked all the meat in one huge pot, just the way we had been doing it. Then, when it was done, I transferred the Indians' share to their special pots for warming and serving. This saved a lot of time, trouble, and range space.

But my conscience bothered me. Finally I pulled a Catholic chaplain to one side. "Do you think I am doing a bad thing, Father?" I asked. "Will God forgive me for fooling these Indians like this?"

He was a practical man. "As long as they don't know, I'd say it is all right. They have done their religious duty as best they can. As for you," he said with a smile, "well, maybe with all these mouths to feed the good Lord will excuse you. Anyway, we can call it a hardship case, and hope for the best."

On the whole, though, I think all the delegates knew that everyone was going out of his way to make them feel at home, as far as their meals were concerned. There were, for example, some talented Italian women who cooked spaghetti and meat balls for the Latin delegations. Most of the AWVS ladies at the canteen on Wednesdays were Armenian-Americans, who worked hard over other old-country dishes and delicacies. And at Omar Khayyam's, after the day at the opera house was over, I had a wonderful time cooking for delegations from the Mediterranean countries and the Middle East. For the Saudi Arabians I made *lah majoun;* for the Egyptians I cooked *foul,* made of dried horse beans, and

226

lula kebab, which is highly seasoned meat broiled on a skewer; and for the Syrians I prepared *kebba,* a baked dish made of *bulgour,* or cracked wheat, and meat, Damascus nuts, and currants.

Almost every evening, the Turkish delegates came to Omar Khayyam's for dinner. Some of my Armenian waiters still had not forgiven the Turks for the massacres of 1915 and other years, so I instructed Bart to see that they were served by waiters of other nationalities.

One night, when the restaurant was particularly crowded, Bart forgot. He assigned Hovagim, the most patriotic of all the Armenian waiters, to the Turks. Everything went well until the last course. The chief delegate called Hovagim over. "Waiter, five Turkish coffees."

Hovagim stood beside their table, arms folded like an Armenian Patrick Henry, and gazed sternly at the wall above their heads. The delegates took no notice. "Waiter," repeated the chief delegate, without looking up, "we will have five Turkish coffees, please."

"Sir," said Hovagim loudly, "in this restaurant we do not serve Turkish coffee. If you mean the dark, thick coffee made with powdered grains, that is cooked and served in a *jazveh* and sometimes drunk by people of your nationality, we have that. But we refer to it as 'Armenian' coffee."

The Turk, a real diplomat, bowed slightly. "Thank you. Then we will have five Armenian coffees."

The next day, he saw me at the canteen. He put his hand on my arm. "My dear friend—" he said, and told me in an amused way about Hovagim and the coffee. Then he said, "We don't mind your taking some of our favorite dishes and calling them Armenian, but"—he wagged his finger playfully—"you should leave our Turkish coffee alone."

As if I were a professional diplomat myself, I nodded and agreed, and he walked away smiling. I shrugged to myself. What was the use? Why tell him that during the Armenian captivity in Turkey, the Armenians took up the drinking of Turkish coffee, made it 100 per cent better than it was before, and gave it back to the world as "Armenian" coffee?

227

But points like this seldom came up. Jan Masaryk, for instance, thought it appropriate that he, a representative of Czechoslovakia, and I, a native of Armenia, should meet and talk at this conference where men from the most powerful lands on earth were gathered together. In the guest book at Omar Khayyam's, he signed his name. Then he wrote, "One small nation feeding another small nation is rather a nice idea."

The question that seemed to bother him was whether the United Nations could really work. Was it too ideal? "It sounds wonderful," he would say, "but can it actually be that way?" His enemies never gave him a chance to find out. Less than three years later, he committed suicide.

That was a sad thing. With Madame Pandit, it was happier. Her mission was to do what she could to gain independence for India. While talking with her one evening, I couldn't resist telling her an Armenian story.

Once, during my boyhood, the Armenian patriarch Father Khrimian attended an international conference in Berlin to appeal for Armenian independence from the Turks. When he returned to Istanbul, the Armenians gave a huge banquet in his honor. After it was over, he rose and said:

"I went into the hall where representatives of all the nations in the world were present—the conquerors and the conquered. And at the dinner table in this hall, they served us a large bowl of *harissa*—just as it was invented centuries ago by the Armenian monks.

"Everyone had a wooden or metal ladle or spoon, except me. I had a ladle made of paper. It wilted under the weight of the *harissa,* so that I could not even taste the delectable dish of my people."

All of us interpreted this to mean that Father Khrimian's pleas for Armenian independence were "paper" pleas, useless at tables where everyone else had implements of strength and force. As it turned out, maybe we have grown more civilized. Madame Pandit's pleas were paper pleas, too. But today India has her independence.

With all that we had to offer, I think the most popular

dish at the canteen was eggs—fresh, boiled eggs. I used to see delegates leave the food counters with five or six on their plates. The fact that they were only charged a dollar for as many as they could eat was one of the wonders of America.

In spite of all this, we headed toward a serious crisis in about the third week of the conference, when local OPA officials notified us that we had run out of red-meat ration points. From then on we would be able to serve only fowl, such as turkey and chicken, and other foodstuffs that were nutritious, but for the most part plain and unappetizing.

With this on our minds, it didn't make us any happier to learn that a Soviet steamer had arrived in port loaded with vodka, Scotch, and American bourbon, and with spring lamb and stall-fed beef for *shashlik* and beef *à la Stroganoff*. We went to the OPA and demanded 500,000 pounds of beef we knew they could get in Canada and have shipped to San Francisco in the matter of a few days. The answer was, "No."

How could they do this when it was a question of prestige and "face" for the United States, and also a question of the physical well-being of these men who were trying to bring peace to the world? Everyone had cooperated beautifully until now. Even the union representatives, who weren't easy to get along with at times, looked the other way while we used AWVS ladies to do jobs ordinarily done by the members of the culinary union. But in the San Francisco OPA office was a real martinet. He was going to show his authority.

Before the crisis became grave, and before most of the delegates knew that it even existed, Mr. Stettinius telephoned the OPA office in Washington. The very next day, top-ranking OPA officials flew to San Francisco and broke the deadlock: they gave us permission to use all the meat we needed, without any red points at all. And so, as the papers put it, the "culinary generalissimos" of San Francisco avoided a "gastronomic Waterloo."

What we were operating in the opera house was a real American cafeteria. Many of the patrons had never carried a tray. Secretary of State Stettinius, Senator Vandenberg,

229

Commander Stassen, Anthony Eden, and all the other members of the American, French, and British delegations ate there, and so did the representatives of all the other nations, except one. Never did we see Molotov and his cohorts in our dining room.

The most glamorous delegates were the Saudi Arabian princes and sheiks. With their flowing robes and their air of far-off sands, caravans, and romantic places, they fascinated everybody. One afternoon, at the request of Kenneth Bechtel, I served a meal for the princes. The host was the Standard Oil Company of California, and it took place on a tanker Marinship had built for Standard Oil, during the vessel's trial run in San Francisco Bay. I asked Standard Oil officials how much they wanted to spend.

"Twenty-five dollars a plate," they replied.

"And how many will there be?"

"Two hundred."

Naturally, for such a feast I could not depend on the tanker's galley stove. Most of the food was prepared at Omar Khayyam's, driven across the Golden Gate Bridge to the Marinship pier at Sausalito, then taken up the gangplank to the ship.

It was a picturesque affair. We had prepared more than twenty native Arabian delicacies for the princes. These were served at tables set out on the tanker's main deck. To protect the diners from the California sun, we had hired a gaily striped tent, like a tent of the Bedouins, and had it slung over the tables. It saved the day, and the dinner, because in the middle of the meal a pouring rain set in. The Bedouin tent kept us dry.

An orchestra played under the tent. On the deck below was still another ensemble, to please guests who were strolling about the ship between courses. Toward the end of the meal, during the *paklava*, Prince Faisal leaned over. He habitually spoke Turkish; on this occasion, I was his interpreter.

"I wonder," he said, "if this good man here"—he nodded

230

toward the orchestra leader—"can play a special tune for me?"

"I'm sure he would be happy to, Your Highness," I replied. "What is the name of the tune?"

The Prince wrinkled his brow. "Alas," he said, "I cannot remember its name. It was a sentimental little song that a beautiful, blonde *chanteuse* sang for me in Paris, four years ago."

I said to the orchestra leader, "Play some Parisian love songs for His Highness."

After each one, the Prince shook his head. "No, that is not the one."

Finally the leader asked, "Can His Highness hum the tune, to give us a hint?"

Before I could translate this into Turkish, Prince Faisal interrupted. "No, no. I do not remember it at all. I have been racking my brain—but keep on playing anyway," he said. "These tunes make me very nostalgic for Paris and its delights."

Later, when the orchestra had stopped, I said, "Your Highness, I was under the impression that you did not speak English. Yet you understood the orchestra leader perfectly and replied to his question yourself."

He put his lips close to my ear. "That was a slip. I very seldom do that, because speaking Turkish and having an interpreter gives me more time to think about what I am going to say."

To me one of the most beautiful sights of the conference was the delegates of the little countries. For the first time in history they sat on the same platform as the representatives of the most powerful nations in the world and spoke without fear of the consequences. This conference was giving them something priceless—their dignity as human beings.

Even the Armenians, through the Armenian National Committee, were able to be heard. The committee presented a memorandum to the conference, asking a review of the status of Kars and Ardahan, two states turned over to

Turkey by the U.S.S.R. Traditionally and historically they belonged to Armenia and the Armenians. The committee wanted them to be returned to their rightful people and possessors. But I guess that civilization has not progressed far enough for this yet, because nothing has been done about it.

It was thrilling to see, for instance, all the Near Eastern delegates having lunch around the same table every noon. Some of the nations they represented had been bitter enemies for centuries, wanting only to slaughter and wipe each other from the face of the earth. Here, politely passing the bread and sugar to each other, were delegates from Egypt, Syria, Irak, Lebanon, Transjordania, Greece, Turkey—all talking together in peace and good fellowship.

I spoke to Dr. Charles Malik, who today is ambassador of Lebanon to the United States. "Dr. Malik, may I ask how this has been done, how all of you have become so friendly?"

He explained that many of the delegates were graduates of, or connected in some way with, the American University in Beirut. There they had absorbed democratic ideals.

I thought it over. Here was an American institution able to get across to these people the idea that they can live in peace, like civilized human beings, without being at each other's throat. And also that they have a right to think, act, vote, and worship as they please. And this institution was thousands of miles from America.

Suddenly I had an idea. If this could take place among educated adults, in an institution so far from America, what would be the effect on the impressionable minds of young men and women—in an institution on American soil? Wouldn't they learn a lesson in democracy they would never forget?

And so I thought, I will establish a scholarship. Every year I will bring a student from the old country, and let him live among the American people, let him go to American churches and libraries, let him play American sports and see all sides of American life. Then, when he went back

232

home, he would call his father, mother, sister, and relatives together and would say:

"Dad, Mother, and the rest of you—I think that we people living in this part of the world have been a bunch of fools. Imagine! I went to America, and I saw a Jew working with a German. I saw an Armenian working with a Turk, and I saw a Pole working with a Russian, without having the least idea of killing each other!

"Their children were all going to the same school, and they were all getting along fine. If that can happen in America, why couldn't it here in our own country? Why can't we stop hating each other, and try to act like civilized human beings?"

With this as my hope and ideal, I worked out a scholarship plan. I would pick a student from the Near East and pay all his expenses—in short, let him go to college on me. But there would be one or two catches.

For example, what usually happened with such scholarships? Just what you'd expect. The United States turned out to be so wonderful, none of the students ever went back home to tell about it.

Well, I would do it differently. I would give him, say, fifteen hundred dollars a year for four years at the American university of his choice. Every time I gave him fifteen hundred, he would sign a note. At the end of the four years, he would owe me at least six thousand dollars.

Then I would say to him, "Go back to your own country. Tell your people all you have learned about America." If he refused, then he owed me six thousand. He would think twice before starting out in life with such a debt. But if he agreed, then he owed me nothing. I would tear up the notes.

There would be still another catch. The scholars would have to promise to learn something beneficial to their country's economy. I would accept none who wanted to be doctors or lawyers; these professions could be learned at home. Rather, I would ask for those who wished to study American engineering, agriculture, or science.

233

During their years in America, these students would live in an American community and see for themselves how people of many classes and races get along together in peace and harmony. Maybe, I thought, the American way will make such an impression on their minds and hearts, they will spread the idea of fellowship and good will wherever they go.

Since then, many of these students have come to America. But, as I foresaw, the hardest thing is to make them return to their native lands. Once they see what it is like and what it would be like for their children, they all want to stay. Who can criticize them?

Almost before we knew it, it seemed, the conference came to an end. President Truman came to San Francisco, and it was all over, and the delegates started saying good-by and leaving for their homes in the distant corners of the world.

I'm sure we all felt the same way, we who were staying behind and those who were going back across the seas. We all had a prayer in our hearts. We all felt that maybe peace was not a dream, after all. Maybe out of the world's bitter experience and tragedy, lasting peace was coming.

Anyway, the world was talking about peace. If enough people believed that there was actually going to be peace and went around saying so, then nothing would stop peace from coming.

234

◇◇◇◇◇◇◇◇◇◇◇◇◇◇◇◇◇◇◇◇◇◇◇◇◇◇◇◇◇◇◇◇◇◇◇◇◇◇◇

CHAPTER TWENTY

That August the war ended, and there were some wonderful moments as the Americans came back home. It seemed to me that the one thing I could do was serve them satisfying, strength-giving meals. I did this whenever I could, either at home in the Powell Street apartment or at the restaurant.

The "Angels of Bataan" were pale and emaciated, and their hair was snow white from their terrible years in Santo Tomas, but in spite of this, how beautiful they were, in their army nurses' uniforms, as they sat around our table and enjoyed themselves.

Everybody loved and admired them. I had called the manager of Blum's and asked for sixty-eight boxes of Al-mondettes, a popular and hard-to-get candy. "Haven't you

235

heard of the sugar shortage?" he wanted to know. "Two boxes are the most we can give any customer."

"But," I said, "these are for the Angels of Bataan."

The sixty-eight boxes of candy were at our apartment within the hour.

From the letters they wrote to Naz and me afterward, they thought the dinner was marvelous. They loved the California fruit and the Armenian pastries. They would never forget the candy from Blum's. But deep down in their hearts, what meant the most was the thrill of being back in an American home. This was what they thanked God for—an American fireplace and four American walls.

Not long after that, General Jonathan M. Wainwright, the hero of Corregidor, came back home after those terrible years in a Japanese prison camp. He was coming to Omar Khayyam's for dinner. The general's son, Commander Jack Wainwright, and our mutual friend in the Quartermaster Corps, Brigadier General Milton O. Boone, wanted this to be a very special dinner. It was to be General Wainwright's home-coming feast, his first meal on American soil.

In the restaurant, no one but Bart and Peter Gagoush and I knew that the general was coming. If we had let the news leak out, the hundred and fifty people waiting in line for dinner would never have been seated, because none of those already at tables would have moved.

As the general came down the restaurant stairs, excitement filled the room. The three hundred diners stood up. The thin, tired warrior stopped a moment at the bottom of the steps and looked into their faces. They broke into wild applause and cheering. Tears streamed down their cheeks.

The general was speechless. He tried to say something. His lips made no sound. Finally he said huskily, "Thank you. God bless you." I led him to his table and told the general how honored we all were by his coming.

Because of OPA restrictions, everyone could not have all the meat, steak, and *shish kebab* he desired, I said. But in

236

his case, it was different. I would get him anything he wanted. Privately, I had made my mind up that if this hero asked for anything I didn't have, I would certainly get a six-shooter and go out and bring it back!

"Tell me, General Wainwright, what have you been craving in the way of food?"

He smiled. "Well, for the last four years, I have been dreaming of a wonderful steak about this big"—he indicated the size of the platter—"and this thick"—he held his thumb and forefinger as far apart as they would reach—"not too well done—nice and crispy black on the outside and red and juicy on the inside."

I said, "I know exactly. Now, how about some nice appetizers?"

"No," said the general.

"Or salad?"

"No—just the steak."

Then I said, "I'm sorry, General, but there is something else you must take. It is *arkayagan abour*—royal soup."

He consented graciously. As he ate it, I told him how I had discovered the recipe at San Lazzaro and how appropriate it was for his dinner.

"The Armenian legend goes," I said, "that when a hero went to war and came back victorious, this soup was served in honor of his home-coming."

Next, I asked the general what his favorite potatoes were. I didn't dare suggest our specialty of rice pilaff; I could picture myself in his place, limited to a handful of rice as a daily ration, month in and month out.

"What will it be—baked, roasted, hash brown, German fried, cottage fried, or French fries?"

"French fries. And lots of them."

"And another vegetable?"

"Canned peas," he grinned. "Just plain, old-fashioned canned peas, with lots of butter."

I cooked everything myself, and watched with pride the enjoyment with which he ate every bite. By the end of the

237

steak, he was hitting his stride. He topped the dinner off with four scoops of ice cream and four or five pieces of *paklava*.

To make the occasion complete, Naz and I invited the party to our home. There we sampled more Old World delicacies that Nevart, our cook, had prepared for the general. Best of all, and what he appreciated most, was the big silver tray of fruits from our ranch in St. Helena, in the Napa Valley—four kinds of melons, skinned and cut into wedges; beautiful peaches, apricots, plums, and about five varieties of grapes. It was like a California horn of plenty.

Late that evening we took the general back to his hotel. The following day he began his round of parades and personal appearances, and the day after that he flew on to Washington.

But we had personal problems, too. I could see that something had to be done about the Fresno place. It was getting too complicated to handle two big restaurants so far apart. After a long family conference, Arshag and I decided to sell out in Fresno. He and Minnie could move back to San Francisco, and he could manage Omar Khayyam's in San Francisco, and free me for other enterprises.

All of us had been proud of the Fresno restaurant. We had been happy building something there, and it had been a big steppingstone. So its last night, New Year's Eve in 1945, was a sad night for us all. When we sang *Auld Lang Syne* at midnight we really meant it, because we were singing out the old year, and all the old years, too, all the way back to 1935 and even before that, to the little place in Mariposa Street, where everything began.

The restaurant had never looked so beautiful, all decorated for the holiday celebration. I wasn't the only one who felt sad. "Now," Naz said, as the people sang and kissed each other and wished each other a happy new year, "I know how a mother must feel, when her daughter gets married." I squeezed her hand. I knew what she meant.

Food was very scarce that year. Working for the government food-conservation programs, I traveled all over the

238

United States, asking housewives to be more careful—
UNRRA was doing its best to feed a world that was starving.
"Plant a garden patch and grow your own vegetables," I
told them. "Eat less wheat bread every day. Eat less meat.
Make French toast out of day-old bread. Throw nothing
away. Save. Conserve. You will save the lives of starving
people."

Sometimes when I was through with my talk, I would go
through the audience with a tin pail. "Eight cents for food
will save a child's life. Eight pennies—"

And so it went until late summer, and I received a letter
postmarked Kronenberg, Germany. It was from General
Boone, whom I had last seen at the dinner for General Wainwright. He said he had been appointed chief quartermaster
of ETO, the European Theater. The Army was having serious food problems in storage, distribution, and preparation.
Things were going to be a lot worse that winter. He knew
about my work at Camp Roberts and other army installa-
tions. If it were cleared in Washington, could I go to Europe
and give them a hand?

I wrote back and said I would be proud and happy to
go. As with the conference canteen, I would accept no money
from the government. I still owed America my life and liberty
and all my happiness, and if what I had to give in return
was work and the best of my heritage and experience, then
she would have it for nothing, and with all my heart and
soul in it.

Early in October I received another letter—from the
quartermaster general, Major General Thomas B. Larkin.
He said I was in the Army now; I should proceed immediately to Washington. Before a week was over, I had my
affairs in order and went to Suisun Field, north of San
Francisco. There I was assigned a flight to Washington.

Naz was nervous about the flying, especially at this time
of the first mountain snows. I tried to calm her. "Honey,
today we fly over storms. We are not traveling by oxcarts."

Nevertheless, when all the passengers were taken into
a projection room and shown a moving picture, I was feeling

a little nervous myself. This movie showed a big plane, like the one warming up in the runway, having engine trouble, and then plunging down and splashing into a heavy sea. Everybody climbed out of the cabin and put on his Mae West. The man showing us the movie told us to take special note of the way you inflate Mae Wests, because when your plane ditches in the ocean, they sure come in handy.

I didn't tell Naz about this movie. But when we came out, it was time to go. Many of my helpers were there— Bart and Alice Rustigian, Peter Gagoush, Little Jeff, and Jimmy the Greek philosopher. I kissed them all good-by. It was like leaving on a pilgrimage.

I said to Peter, "Didn't you bring the *harissa?* You'd think I was a pilgrim."

It was a bad joke, but it took the edge off the parting and got me into the cabin of the plane without crying, which is something I'm always likely to do when I'm saying good-by. But when I go away, I want people to remember me laughing, not crying.

The next day I was in Washington, talking with General Larkin and Colonel Kester L. Hastings, personnel chief of the Quartermaster Corps. General Larkin told me about the problems. He gave me a title: expert food consultant to Secretary of War Robert B. Patterson. Colonel Hastings gave me letters to embassies and commanders. The following morning they put me on a C-54, and we took off and flew out over the Atlantic.

A few hundred miles west of the Azores, I felt a heavy bump. I looked out the window. One of the propellers on the left side was slowing down. The captain came back from his cabin. He was smiling, just like the captain of the plane I had seen in the Suisun movie. I felt fine until I saw that smile.

"Don't worry," he said calmly. "Everything is going to be all right. We just have to trim the ship a little. We're going to move all the heavy weight forward."

With that, the crew started taking all our baggage from
240

the rear of the plane and carrying it to the front. Meanwhile, the propeller had stopped completely. Rain beat against the windows. The plane began to pitch and buck. We passengers looked at each other. Our faces were growing as white as the finest rice pilaff that we had ever served at Omar Khayyam's. The look in everyone's eyes said, "This is it."

By this time the crew had finished with the baggage. There were some empty seats up front. I stood up. I tried to sound calm, as if I were an old hand at ditching in the ocean 100 miles from land.

"Gentlemen, there is still considerable weight to move forward. You keep your seats. I alone will shift from the back to the front, and that will be sufficient to save the plane."

With that, barely able to squeeze along the narrow aisle, I inched my 240 pounds forward. It broke the tension. Everybody relaxed and took the emergency in stride. The captain fought the storm all the way and brought us safely to the Azores.

We arrived in Paris on a Sunday. I sent Naz a cable, telling her we were safe. The next evening General and Mrs. Boone met me at Frankfurt, where his headquarters were. We took the heartbreaking drive through the ruins to Waldhauf. Along the way we drove by Kronenberg Castle, where there was that daring postwar jewel robbery. I admired its gardens, and most of all, its chestnut trees. Many evenings after that I ate the good chestnuts from those trees. General Boone's German chef, who had once cooked for the Kaiser, picked them and roasted them for me.

We wasted no time. The following morning, at my meeting with officers from G-4, the section in charge of supply, a rugged, square-shouldered Irishman stood up. He was Lieutenant Colonel Patrick H. Buckley. He had received his training in the Army Cooks' and Bakers' School at the Presidio of San Francisco, and he was ETO's food-service officer.

He looked me straight in the eye. It was almost impossible, he said, to keep trained men in the kitchen and mess halls.

241

They all wanted to get out of the Army and back home as fast as they could. Most of them hated KP work. The food they turned out showed it. Discipline had grown lax.

Then the Colonel got a cold note into his voice. "Mr. Mardikian, we have seen many people like you come and go in this theater, but we haven't been able to profit much from their visits. This is a military operation. We don't have all the needed utensils and foodstuffs and merchandise. We have to make out with what is at hand. We're not complaining. We're doing the best we can. I'm sure we're all happy that you want to help. But, frankly, I don't think we're going to get much out of it."

I made a fast tour of the occupied zone, to get oriented. The problems were the same everywhere, and not much different from those in Camp Roberts and Fort Ord. I reported back to General Boone and said I was ready to get down to work. But first, I wanted him to let me have Pat Buckley. He would make a good guide and assistant. Also, I asked for a car and driver, so we could go wherever we wanted. Finally, I said, I didn't want the posts told that we were coming. I didn't want any red-carpet treatment. General Boone agreed to all this.

Pat and I and our driver left right away. In the next six weeks we crisscrossed back and forth over occupied Germany and Austria two or three times. When we reached a new town and a new post, I called a meeting of everybody connected with food, from generals in charge of supply to mess sergeants. I told them that mostly they were feeding kids away from home for the first time in their lives. They were in competition with everybody's mother.

"You have to be mothers. American soldiers love Mom's cooking, even if it kills them, and some of it will. But the way he remembers it, it was wonderful. He liked it because it had some color to it. It was served to him hot. And it was served with pride and a smile."

As at the army camps of the West Coast, I tried to get them to feel good about their jobs. I said they ought to give chefs tall white hats and spotless uniforms every day. Mess

242

sergeants ought to have another stripe and mess officers another bar. Then, after talking to them, I sat down and ate with them.

They were receiving cheese from Denmark and celery and apples from Italy, in addition to the supplies from home. There was enough food, and it was being stored carefully and well. The mistakes were being made in the kitchens and mess halls.

Even a meal at Maxim's in Paris or the Chambord in New York would lose its appeal if, as you ate, you faced a wall poster warning you against venereal disease. Yet in nearly every mess, the walls were covered with these VD posters. There was a very real fight to wage against VD, but dining halls were not the place. I went to Lieutenant General Clarence R. Huebner, ETO's chief of staff.

"General, please—I agree with you 100 per cent that this VD situation is very tough to cope with—but for the love of Mike, can't we take those horrible signs out of the dining rooms? The boys see them everywhere else they go. Can't we leave them in peace while they're eating?"

To my amazement, the general agreed. In one mess hall after another, all over the occupied zone, the signs came down off the walls.

Commanding officers everywhere were very concerned about this problem. Giessen, for example, was a large depot housing many colored troops, the backbone of the Quartermaster Corps. Not far from town was one of those beautiful German forests, with rich, tall, lovely trees.

The commander at Giessen was angry and at the same time helpless about the climbing VD rate among his men. You would think it was his personal fault, he said, the way headquarters was riding him about it.

"It's that damned forest," he said. "These girls come and set up tent villages in it. That's where all my men are going and getting their VD. Some day, I'm going to set a torch to those trees and burn them all down."

But in his heart, I think he knew the forest wasn't to blame. Most of those girls were war widows and the mothers

243

of starving children. It's easy to blame people, until you put yourself in their place, and try to understand why they do what they do.

Sometimes ingenuity was needed more than anything else in the army kitchens. Pat Buckley and I visited the big kitchen of the base at Darmstadt. It was a few minutes before the evening meal. The head cook was tearing his hair out.

"What's the trouble?" Pat asked.

The cook swore hard. He had promised the boys apple pie. Now, he discovered, there wasn't enough shortening. Pat thought for a moment. He caught sight of a lot of heavy custard cups stacked on the kitchen shelves. "How much shortening have you got?"

"Half as much as I ought to have."

"Use your custard cups," Pat said.

The cook was puzzled. "Custard cups?"

"Make little individual pies—deep dish. Then all you'll need is the top crust."

That night the entire company ate Pat's deep-dish apple pies. They were a sensation. And this was just the spirit, the ability and willingness to try new combinations of old ingredients and materials, that someday was going to make the GI the best-fed soldier in the world.

Pat was stationed at Darmstadt. Early in December we were on our way back to Waldhauf for the weekend, for a rest and further orders. We were driving up from the south.

"Come into my place at Darmstadt for coffee," Pat said. "Then the driver can take you on to Waldhauf."

It was very cold. Steaming coffee sounded good.

He lived in a nice house. We went inside. It was warm and comfortable. He lived with a Darmstadt family. He had phoned ahead that we were coming, and their pretty blonde daughter, Sofia, had made us some sandwiches. She served us these, and then brought in some delicious little German cakes and hot coffee.

"I'm glad we got back," Pat said. "Now I can go hunting. I try to do that every weekend."

I was surprised. I asked what he shot.

244

"Deer and boar," he said.

"What do you do with all that meat?"

Sofia, coming into the room with more coffee, gave him a soft smile. Pat smiled back. "Shall I show him?"

Sofia nodded. Pat got up and led us to the kitchen. He opened the door to the back porch.

"My refrigerator," he said. "I call it my walk-out icebox."

There, on the porch, were two wild boar and two deer, skinned and cleaned, but standing, frozen stiff, on their four legs.

I couldn't understand how he and this family could use all the meat. "What do you do with this, Pat?"

"They're for my orphans," he said.

There was a Catholic orphanage in Darmstadt. Pat had found out that its food supplies were very limited. Sometimes the children went without meat for weeks. He decided that every weekend he would go hunting for them. The Lord must have been on his side, because he always came back with something. That was my "tough" colonel, Pat Buckley.

That winter of 1946–1947 was the worst in a hundred years. All these countries were in ruins. The cities were like great wounds. Now in the bitter cold and snow, they were cities of the dead, ghost cities, with silent streets and buildings open to the winter sky, and mile after mile of crumbling brick walls. In one night's bombing at Darmstadt, I was told, we had killed thirty thousand men, women, and children. It was strange that in the middle of all these ruins stood a Russian church. The people of Darmstadt had built it many years ago, they told me, out of friendship for the Russian people, because two babies born in Darmstadt had grown up to sit as Czarinas on the Russian Imperial throne. Among scores and scores of blocks that had been flattened to the streets, it was the only building left. Its steeple was intact. Not a fragment of its lovely stained-glass windows was broken. Why was this?

All the cities except Heidelberg were huge dumps of concrete and bricks. The people walked in a daze. They were punch-drunk, wandering around, lost, starving, freezing to

245

death. To be hungry is bad enough. But to be hungry and blue with the cold . . .

This sight I saw in the streets of Berlin. I couldn't believe my eyes. A coal truck came by. Thirty women appeared from nowhere. Half of them threw themselves in front of the truck. The driver had to stop, or he would run over them. The women, gasping and screaming like maniacs, swarmed over the truck. They pulled the driver from the cab and beat him to the street. Children ran from blasted buildings and climbed up beside the women. Nobody stopped them. They stole every piece of coal. The women carried it off in the bosoms of their dresses and coats. In ten minutes they were gone. There, on the deserted street, stood the empty truck. The driver lay prone on the pavement, bleeding. Soon MP's arrived and gave him first aid.

I had the best of everything. But I got so cold every night I felt like crying. I sent back home for so much money, Naz and Archie and the others wondered if I had lost my head and was gambling. But I wasn't.

I went with four new suits. Before December I had given them away and had only my Army uniform. I couldn't help giving when I saw those beautiful children with those large, pleading eyes. They were always shivering, and I knew that the unnatural shine in their eyes was from tuberculosis.

Maybe they were the children of Nazi soldiers and fliers, but were we going to take it out on them?

The more I thought about this, the more I realized something. Every time we read or hear about an ambassador, we picture a dignified, impressive man, who knows everything about world affairs. And very wise and tolerant and strong, like Benjamin Franklin. That is the way it should be; he is representing our President and all the people of America.

But with all due respect to our State Department officials, and many of them are personal friends, I think that the finest ambassadors America ever sent anywhere are our GIs and officers like Pat Buckley.

Almost every one of them acted, not like a conquering soldier, but like an American. Many times I saw them go

246

through a PX and buy all the candy, chewing gum, cigarettes and cigars their pockets would hold. By the time they had left the exchange a block behind them, it was all gone— given away to candy-starved youngsters and working men who craved a smoke.

The GI couldn't tell you in words how he felt or why he felt that way. He just looked at those children and those famished men and women and held out his hand to them and gave them everything he had. It was like the fight in Golden Gate Park. One boy knocked the other down. Then he bent over and helped the beaten one to his feet, and put his arm around him, and comforted him.

CHAPTER TWENTY-ONE

The important and far-reaching things in life begin very casually. Nothing tells you that they are the start of something big. Nothing prepares you for what is coming.

Lieutenant Colonel John R. Deane, Jr., of San Francisco telephoned me from a post near Kronenberg. He was homesick and wanted to talk about his relatives and his home town. With General and Mrs. Boone's consent, I invited him to dinner.

During the conversation after dinner, Colonel Deane said to me, "Mr. Mardikian, you have been to Funkerkasserne, of course."

The name was strange to me.

"The displaced-persons camp," Colonel Deane said. "Near Stuttgart."

248

My business was with the Army, not DP camps, I said.

"But all the DPs at Funkerkasserne are Armenians. Almost two thousand of them," he added quietly.

I couldn't believe my ears. "You must be mistaken. This is one war Armenians had nothing to do with. How would they get there, in a DP camp?"

"They were taken prisoner by the Nazis and put to forced labor."

"But now the war is over," I said. "Why don't they go home?"

"Their homes are in Russian-held territory. They're afraid to go back. They might be killed or sent to Siberia. So they stay there, at Funkerkasserne."

"What do they do there?"

"Hope—and pray."

I had been scheduled to go to Berlin the next day. Instead, I got in my car with Pat Buckley and Colonel Deane, and we drove to Stuttgart and then to Funkerkasserne and a meeting with two thousand Armenians that would change the rest of their lives, and mine, too.

It was a typical day of that winter. The bitter cold sank into your bones. We had let the British director of the camp know that we were coming. More than a thousand of the DPs met us at the camp gate. In the distance, under the gray skies, lay the camp parade grounds, the bare brick barracks of the former Nazi army post, and the high barbed-wire fences. The DPs ranged in age from little children to gray-haired great-grandmothers. They were all thin, with large dark eyes, and bundled in rags.

The British director helped us out of the car. He introduced us to the UNRRA chief, who was the head of sixteen DP camps in that region. UNRRA was going out of existence soon, and these people were terrified. They would be turned loose to freeze and starve to death. When the world is like that, even a concentration camp represents a haven.

The DPs watched our arrival in deep silence. They saw important officials treating me, a countryman, with respect.

249

Perhaps for the first time in years a real hope—not a false hope or a daydream—stirred in their hearts. I do not know. But suddenly I heard them whispering, like wind in the mulberry trees of home. Then they began to cheer. They broke into cries that grew stronger and stronger. *"Barov yegar, hazar bari!* [Welcome! A thousand welcomes!]"

I tried to say something. I waved. A little girl stepped forward and handed me a bouquet of flowers that someone must have nursed carefully, in a pot, in the barracks. They were wilted with the cold. A troop of boy scouts, in uniforms made out of American blankets, led me to the main camp office. The barracks, which had been badly hit by American and British bombers, had been made into a Polish DP camp and had finally been given to the Armenians.

A new auditorium of raw timber had been built by the unskilled hands of the Armenian prisoners, who had been merchants and professors, musicians, poets, and artists. We went there, and all the DPs crowded in after us. On the stage with me was Mr. D'Orte, the director; Pat Buckley and Colonel Deane; and the *Vartabed* from the Mechitarist monastery in Vienna, who lived with them and gave them spiritual comfort and strength.

I was introduced, and they waited for me to speak. I got up and started to talk. In these careworn faces turned up to me, I saw four thousand years of Armenian history. I saw centuries of terror and oppression. I saw centuries of struggle and yearning for freedom. I saw fear and disillusion and bitterness. Yet, at the same time, miraculously—as miraculous as life itself—I saw a light of hope. They were looking up at one of their own, who spoke their own tongue, who shared their ancestors and their heritage. And he had come to them—from America! He was a messenger from God's country. What could he bring but good news?

I talked to them for an hour and fifteen minutes. I warned against expecting too much. All I could do was see that they would be taken care of after UNRRA went out of existence and then return to America and see what help I could get for them there. I told them about the Armenian-

250

Americans—the artists, the doctors, the teachers, the ranchers in California. They were patriotic and generous men.

"I can solemnly promise you this. I will see to it that our people in the United States are told about you. It is their duty to help you, to give you a chance to find homes for yourselves so that you can start building your *ojakhs*—your hearths and firesides—all over again. If it takes all of my fortune and all of my life, I will help you—"

When it was over, we drove in silence to our rooms in the Hotel Graf Zeppelin in Stuttgart. I looked out the car window into the dark, wintry streets. I thought of all the upraised faces, all those beating hearts, all those lives. I didn't say anything to Colonel Deane or Pat, all the way to the hotel. They were quiet, too. I think they must have known that I wasn't just looking out the window. They must have known that I was praying.

I still wanted to do the best job I could for the Army, but now I was anxious to finish, so that I could keep my promise to the DPs of Funkerkasserne. I wrote long letters to my well-to-do friends in California and all over the United States, telling them to organize so they could send medicine and food.

When I had done all I could in the ETO, I got papers to work with the occupational forces in Italy. Pat Buckley was traveling part of the way with me, and this particular day we started out from Frankfurt and headed along the *Autobahn* for Munich. It was so cold that two German cars froze under us on the road. We abandoned them and transferred to still another. We passed through Stuttgart late that night and kept going. About 40 miles south of Stuttgart, the car coughed, bucked along the road for a hundred yards or so, and stalled.

Grim-faced, our weary sergeant-driver got out once more and lifted the hood and tried to find out the trouble. As cars passed, we flagged them down and asked them to tell army authorities ahead to send help. Finally an army truck stopped. Two GIs got out and walked over, blinking flashlights.

"Maybe we can fix it, sir," they said to Pat.

"Go ahead and try," Pat said.

While they worked over the engine, Pat and I walked up and down, swinging our arms to keep warm. The beam of the light from one of the torches happened to fall directly into the faces of the GIs. I stopped in my tracks and stared, and went back—fifteen years back. . . .

In that spring, only a few months after we had opened the first Omar Khayyam's on Mariposa Street, next door to Doc Corcoran's optometry shop, a little boy about eight years old came and stood in front of our door every night. He was selling the Fresno *Bee*, the local afternoon paper. All through the evening, he never stopped shouting, "Bee-ee-ee! Frez-z-no Bee-ee-ee!"

I couldn't help liking him for his determination and endurance, but he was very annoying to the patrons inside who wanted to carry on a quiet conversation during dinner. And so I would go out and see the lad.

"How many papers have you got?" I would ask. He would say, "Three," or, "Four," or whatever it was, but there were very seldom more than seven. Then I would buy every one. Before he went home, I would invite him in for a sandwich and a glass of milk, or, in cold weather, for a bowl of hot soup and crackers.

On one particularly stormy night, I went out a good deal earlier than usual. We stood there in the pouring rain. I said, "How many, Sonny?"

"Twenty-three."

"Come with me. I will buy them all. Then you can go home and get out of this storm."

While he stood beside me at the cashier's desk, rain dripping from his coat and newspapers, I told Alice, the cashier, to give him $1.15. Alice, a natural business woman, disapproved. "Mr. Mardikian, do you realize how many dinners we have to serve to earn $1.15?"

"It's just this once," I said. "Give him the $1.15."

For the next few minutes, I was very happy over my boy-scout good deed for the day. The customers began to arrive.

Then, all at once, above the sound of the storm, I heard, "Bee-ee-ee! Frez-z-z-no Bee-ee-ee!"

I boiled inside. I ran out the door into the rain and grabbed the boy by the arm and shook him. "You little liar! What is the matter with you? I buy your papers all the time so you can go home and study your lessons. Tonight I buy more than ever, so you will not have to stand in this awful storm, and now you come back with more to sell!"

I forgot to mention that the newsboy was cross-eyed and that he had a beautiful Italian face. As I yelled at him, his dark eyes filled with tears that matched the raindrops.

"I'm not a liar!" he shouted. Then he threw his papers at me and started running. I ran after him, but I couldn't catch him.

By nine o'clock, I was the most miserable person in the world. I had to find the newsboy and talk with him. But all I knew was that his name was Tony. Searching for a "Tony" in the Italian district of Fresno would be looking for a needle in the haystack.

Finally I called the newspaper. They told me where to find Tony's distributor. The next morning, the distributor told me Tony lived on E Street. I jumped into my car and drove to the boy's home. I introduced myself to his mother and explained how sorry I was about scolding him and told her what an unhappy night I had spent. His mother, an American-born, thought it was all very amusing. But she understood my worry and told me that Tony appreciated my buying his papers.

That night he was back at his old stand in front of the restaurant. I went outside and held out my hand. "Sonny, let's shake hands and forget about last night." He shook hands and grinned. "Yes, sir," he said.

"When you grow up, Sonny, what are you going to be?"

"I want to be a truck driver."

It was such an impossible wish, coming from that little, scrawny, cross-eyed newsboy. I knew, though, where it had come from. As he sold his papers on that corner, he saw the

253

big, husky truckers unloading produce from the San Joaquin Valley ranches. They were his heroes.

Time passed. I lost track of Tony. But I always thought of him, whenever I thought of the little restaurant on Mariposa Street.

All this raced through my mind as Pat and I stood there in the snow, by the *Autobahn,* swinging our arms to keep warm. Finally I stopped and went over to the GIs. Nothing was too fantastic to happen in this world. One of them had a little mustache. He wore a corporal's stripes. I said, "Haven't we met before, Corporal?"

He straightened. He turned his light on my face. His wrench clattered to the fender. "Why—you're Mr. Mardikian!"

"And you're Tony, the Fresno newsboy."

It was true. Here, after all these years, and on this cold, dark road six thousand miles from home, was little, gravel-voiced Tony. His eyes were no longer crossed. And he had reached his goal—by becoming a truck driver for Uncle Sam.

They gave up trying to fix the car on the road and towed it to the nearest snack bar, a few miles down the highway. There, at last, Tony explained what had happened that rainy night in Fresno. The distributor had stopped him on the way home through the storm and told him that if he wanted to keep the stand, he had to put in so many hours every evening. Because I had bought so many papers all at once, he had not been there nearly long enough. The distributor gave him another armload of papers and made him go back. So it hadn't been his fault, after all.

Of course, we had to tell Pat the whole story. We sat there for almost an hour, eating hamburgers and drinking hot coffee and getting warm, and talking about the old days in Fresno, California.

Then I said good-by to Pat for the time being and took a train to Gorizia, in northern Italy, the base of Major General Bryant E. Moore's Eighty-eighth, or "Blue Devil," Division.

It was the same problem here. I had to give the army cooks

254

some kind of pride in their work, and the feeling that they were just as important as the men trained to pilot fighter planes or drive tanks. In some places I had the hardest times, not with the GIs, but with the officers.

One company colonel at Gorizia sounded as though he was "from Missouri." He complained that it was fine for food authorities like me to come and tell them what to do, but how would we feel if we had to cook meals with items that nobody liked?

"Rice!" he sneered.

The poor fellow didn't know that I had made a fortune in San Francisco serving rice pilaff.

"And what can you make out of canned pears—the most unappetizing thing there is?"

General Moore was standing there with us. "General," I said, "if it's all right with you, I'd like to have the colonel give me a list of the things he and his men don't like."

The general agreed.

The colonel started over again. Rice. Canned pears. Fish. "As for creamed corn—" He was so disgusted, he couldn't finish.

"Fine," I said. "Now here is what we're going to do. Get all your officers and all your food-service men, including your sergeants. I personally will cook tomorrow night's dinner out of these items. There won't be a grain of rice, or anything else, left on their plates. That's a promise."

General Moore set up the Armed Forces radio-network microphone beside me in the kitchen, so I could talk to the troops who were unable to take part.

"Beets!" the colonel growled. "What the hell can you do with canned beets?"

I took about six large cans and poured all the beets into one big pot. Then I sliced into rings a great many onions and boiled and shelled some eggs, and dropped all the eggs and onions into the beet water. Then I took handfuls of wholespice, that you use in pickling, wrapped it in gauze, dropped it into the pot, and poured in quite a bit of vinegar. I let it settle all night.

255

My beet dish was served with the dinner the following evening. Each serving had six or seven slices of beets with onion rings over them, and, over all, the sliced boiled eggs. These slices were a pretty tricolor, red on the very outside of their rims, then a shining white, then the rich yellow of the yolk.

Instead of boiling or baking the fish, as they usually did, I fried it a beautiful, crisp gold. And instead of just warming up the despised creamed corn, I made it into corn fritters. With the rice, I cooked a wonderful pilaff by braising it in butter and then mixing it with beef broth and baking it in the army gasoline stove, the M-37 field-unit range, which is one of the finest pieces of kitchen equipment that I have seen anywhere.

When it came to the pears, I got some chocolate pudding mix and made a very soft pudding and poured it over them. This actually changed their texture. Then I got some ice-cream mix and made it into a whipping cream and put that over everything. For the finishing touch—to give this dish, too, that all-important eye appeal—I cut maraschino cherries into quarters and stuck them on top.

Well, everyone was amazed with the dinner and loved it. When the dessert was over, I turned to the colonel. "Colonel, I want you to know that if this creation out of the hated pear were served to you at Omar Khayyam's, I would call it Pear à la Omar and charge you a dollar. Here in the Army, you can get it for nothing."

I had proved my point, and the colonel and I became the best of friends. But—and this was the most important thing of all—alongside of me as I worked were probably fifty army cooks. With their own eyes, they saw how it could be done. I hoped with all my heart that they understood what I was trying to say, that all they needed to create appetizing and eye-appealing dishes was some ingenuity, some extra effort, and, above all, some love for their work. These are the ingredients that every cook must supply from his heart. They are the secret of fine cooking, whether it is in the Army, or a restaurant, or in the home.

Mrs. Moore, the general's wife, was staying in Venice. General Moore suggested that we drive there. The very afternoon of our arrival I found a major with a motor launch and made him take me to San Lazzaro.

As we got close to the island, we could see the Mechitarists running back and forth on the landing. The sergeant at the wheel grinned. "They see our uniforms. They probably think this is an invasion."

I called a greeting. "*Gettza Hayastan!*—Long live Armenia!"

Almost twenty years had gone by since I had been there on my trip around the world. It still looked the same as it had the day I left. There were the same old buildings, the same terrace, the same trees. Unbelievable as it seemed, I heard my name.

"Mr. Mardikian! Mr. Mardikian!"

A little father on the landing was jumping up and down and clapping his hands. It was one of the monks who had worked with me in the archives. As we tied up the launch, the abbot-general himself arrived. Laughing, chattering in Armenian, shaking our hands, they pressed around and welcomed us to their island.

In the old reception room of the monastery, we sipped the cordial that they make of the cherries that grow on the island, and drank Armenian coffee. I told the abbot-general that I had visited the Mechitarist monastery in Vienna.

"They showed me where Franz Werfel stayed with them, after the First World War—"

The priest nodded and smiled. I didn't have to say any more. Every Mechitarist knew how Werfel had gone there for sanctuary after that war and how the monks there had told him about the Armenian tragedy at Musa Dagh, in the Near East near Aleppo, and how he had been inspired to write the beautiful and masterly novel *The Forty Days of Musa Dagh*.

The next day, General and Mrs. Moore went back with me. The Mechitarists were very moved by the American general's visit. In his honor they opened their vaults and

257

brought out golden vestments and Bibles that had been written in Armenian more than a thousand years ago.

We had more cordial, and Armenian coffee in shining copper *jazvehs,* and you can imagine how those rooms and those manuscripts brought back the precious days that I had spent there so long ago. The timelessness of the place and the work these fathers were doing, and of the fathers themselves, brought a lump to my throat. Some I remembered as middle-aged were old men now, smaller and thinner, with gray hair and beards. Think of all that had happened in the world since then! Yet here they were, just as if none of it had ever taken place, quietly writing and collecting and preserving, and doing work whose true benefits would not be realized or recognized for a thousand years.

I hated to leave San Lazzaro, and I shall always hate to leave Venice. But with each passing night it was growing harder to sleep. The burning eyes of the children of Funkerkasserne stared at me out of the darkness. The most pitiful sound in the world—the sound of old people sobbing—haunted me. How could I sleep, when I had to get help for them?

◇◇◇◇◇◇◇◇◇◇◇◇◇◇◇◇◇◇◇◇◇◇◇◇◇◇◇◇◇◇◇◇

CHAPTER TWENTY-TWO

For the next few weeks, I spent most of my time packing or unpacking and on the move, either by car or train or plane. I went to Milan, then to Genoa, then to Laverno.

The food-service officer there was a Colonel Nelson. When I arrived, the two problems in the depot were some kind of epidemic and the disappearance of enormous amounts of food supplies.

"Every time I look out my office window," he said, "a hearse is going through the gates. It's followed by Italian mourners, all weeping and wailing as if they were burying their best friend."

To stop the pilfering he had strung electrified wires around the storehouses and had put all the military police on the

259

alert, but still somebody, somehow, was getting away with a large stock of food.

Finally, one of his officers, with a funny look on his face, said, "Colonel Nelson, would you let me call the post hospital and find out about this 'epidemic'?"

"Go ahead," said the colonel.

The officer put in his call, and the cat was out of the bag. There wasn't any epidemic. No one had died on the post for months. The next time the funeral procession plodded solemnly past his office, the colonel stepped out his door and politely brought it to a halt. His men threw open the hearse doors. It was loaded to the roof with American food supplies.

After visits to other army depots in southern Italy, I had a private audience with Pope Pius XII. We talked about the children of the world. His Holiness, whose concern over the suffering and troubled times showed in his low, quiet voice and in the lines of his beautiful face, said that he knew America would help them. I left feeling very humble, and feeling, too, that this holy man was a wonderful friend to the United States and to the democracies of the world.

One of the ladies in my office in San Francisco was a great admirer of the philosopher George Santayana, who was living near Rome in the convent of the English Blue Sisters. She had made me promise to call on him and see if I could do anything to make life easier for him.

I found him smiling, and very gentle, and apparently very contented. Except for one thing. "I like biscuits with my tea," he said. "The sisters here are very kind, but they don't serve enough biscuits."

The next day, I got several large cartons of crackers and cookies at the Army PX and took them to him. "You know," he said confidentially, "my publishers in New York are really very good to me. They send me everything I ask for—but they take it out of my royalties."

Soon after this I boarded the *America* in Cherbourg and sailed for home. The voyage was just what I needed. It gave me time to rest up for the tasks that lay ahead.

Naz and Julie Medlock were at the pier in New York to meet me, and there was almost a full day of interviews with newspaper people. I told them generally what I had found and some of the things that should be done.

Wherever I found officers interested in the quality of the food their men were getting, the meals were exceptional. Kitchen personnel were on their toes. At the posts where the commanding officer didn't know or care anything about food, the men were served poor meals. I had found great need for improved morale among the cooks and mess officers. I hoped that they would receive more recognition and appreciation.

"It's just the way it is in your homes. Tell your wife what a wonderful cook she is and how good her dinners are, and she'll work her fingers to the bone to please you and make special things for you. But if you take her meals for granted and never pay her a compliment, pretty soon you will be getting mediocre meals set before you."

I told about the trouble with the VD signs and said I hoped the Army would eliminate the word "mess" and use "dining hall" instead. Then I suggested the establishment of a catering corps at West Point, or something like it. Somewhere in their training, I thought, future officers should learn about food and kitchen problems. Robert Ruark, the Scripps-Howard columnist, was there. A day or so later, he discussed my remarks in his column. It was headed "Dough foot's Pal."

In his informal way, Bob wrote:

George's No. 1 recommendation to Gen. Ike will be to establish a new military department—"A culinary corps, or catering corps," George says. "Everything else is specialized, and it's time they got around to specializing food." . . . George says that until the Army sets up a cooking corps, with talented personnel who receive commensurate rank and money for their work, Army chow will continue to repulse a buzzard in some messes, and succeed only in maintaining life in others.

I had not been this blunt; still, it was not far off the mark. General Larkin was disturbed. He ordered me to Washing-

261

ton to square it with General Eisenhower. Naz and Julie went with me.

When General Larkin and I walked into General Eisenhower's office, he stood up and met me and shook my hand, and smiled so warmly that all my five months of weariness seemed to disappear. He had already read my report to General Larkin, and he had read what I told the newspaper people, including Bob Ruark.

"I'm sure you're on the right track," he said, smiling. "We're going to do all we can to put your recommendations into effect. Now—how about lunch?"

We walked to the Chief of Staff's private dining room in the Pentagon and sat down with General Larkin and the other members of General Eisenhower's staff. General Eisenhower told me two things I've always remembered. One is that he wanted to be known as the Chief of Staff who, after all these years, really did something about improving army chow. The second was that his hobby was cooking.

I had known that his brother Edgar was a national authority on all sorts of omelettes and an artist at grilling trout and salmon. But I didn't know that the urge to cook ran in the family.

"What are your specialties, General?" I asked.

"Potato salad," he replied. "Potato salad and vegetable soup."

I thought this was a very curious coincidence. I told him about my own personal interest in potato salad, ever since the time I crossed the continent on the train and couldn't order anything else, because it was the only item on the menu I could read. Then I gave him the recipe for my own potato salad that I had developed as a delicacy for special occasions. He wrote it down and was happy to have it.

Finished at last with my reports in Washington, Naz and I flew home to San Francisco. It was getting toward the end of March. Three months had passed since I had made my promise to the DPs of Funkerkasserne. Suren M. Saroyan, my old friend and San Francisco attorney, met us at the airport. The airport then was a thirty-minute drive from

262

Nob Hill. Before we were back in our apartment, Suren and I knew what we were going to do next.

The following week, we got together some of the most prominent Armenian-Americans in California in a San Francisco auditorium. I told them about Funkerkasserne, about the men, women, and children I had seen there. I begged for money. By the time the afternoon was over, we had organized the American Committee to Aid Homeless Armenians, or, as we called it, ANCHA. I was chosen president; Suren was elected vice-president and secretary. In addition, we raised enough cash to establish ANCHA and to begin the long, complicated task of helping the displaced Armenians.

The job grew bigger and bigger. Before we knew it, Armenian DPs had turned up at other camps in Germany, Austria, and Italy. The total rose from nearly two thousand to more than four thousand. But as we kept finding more and more of them over there, so the response broadened over here.

Naz and I went east again, to raise more money. By July we were back in New York. The Armenian Relief Society was holding its national convention. On one of the hottest summer days I spoke to its members in the basement auditorium of the Armenian Church on Twenty-seventh Street.

There were about two hundred delegates, and unanimously they voted twenty-five thousand dollars to ANCHA. If they had more, they would have given it. They also promised to represent ANCHA in their communities, and so give widespread aid in gathering food, supplies, and clothing. On its own, ANCHA could never have supported the organization they made possible. We always say that the ladies of the Armenian Relief Society were the ones who really helped us get aid on its way to our DPs.

Within a few months, we were able to take emergency steps to keep matters from growing worse, and to catch our breath and see what we could give in the way of permanent help. We were all hoping and working for the day when ANCHA could bring the DPs to a new life in the New World

263

—in Canada, the United States, and South America. That was our dream.

It looked as though the Lord was being extra good to us, when we learned of the retirement from active duty of Brigadier General Haig Shekerjian. Armenians the world over knew General Shekerjian and respected him. He was the first of their nationality to graduate from West Point. With fingers crossed, we asked him if he would go to Europe as the official director of ANCHA.

I don't know whether he ever knew how much it meant to us, but he said yes. By the end of that year, 1947, he and his wife, Helen, had established headquarters at Stuttgart and were receiving and distributing ANCHA food and clothing, and General Shekerjian was attending all the meetings of the IRO—the International Refugee Organization—in Switzerland.

Finally, I had to go back myself. That is the way I am, and I'm sure it's a serious fault. In the days before the war I could seldom take a vacation from the restaurant. It was almost impossible for me to spend an evening at home without taking down my hat and saying to Naz, "Well, honey, I guess I'll go down to the restaurant for a minute, just to see what's doing there. They may need me for something."

Now it was the same way with this new responsibility. The only hope for freedom for more than four thousand was depending on ANCHA. Maybe there was something over there for me to do. I could take Naz with me, and at last keep the promise I'd made that Christmas morning, sixteen years ago, when I had given them all the Christmas cards and the checks that would be good some day. We sailed from New York late in March, 1948.

I still had more work to do with the Army, so I left Naz in Paris and went on to Germany. Naz caught up with me in Heidelberg. Before leaving home, we had decided to take back a refugee boy and girl, to adopt and raise as our own. We had written to General Shekerjian and asked him to find us two youngsters. Now, we left Heidelberg to see whether he had been able to do this.

264

Funkerkasserne looked almost the same as it had that cold and terrible December day when I had seen it first, with Pat Buckley and Colonel Deane. The same prisonlike brick barracks, the same barbed-wire fences. But on this day the sun was shining, and spring was in the April air.

General and Mrs. Shekerjian met us with happy smiles of welcome. "We have found two beautiful children for you," the general said. "They are brother and sister. They have lost their mother and father and live here at Funkerkasserne with their grandmother."

We spent the rest of that afternoon and evening discussing ANCHA affairs. Early the next morning the four of us and the Armenian camp director went to the small barracks room where the children lived. General Shekerjian knocked on the door. The old lady opened it.

The general bowed. "May we come in?"

The woman stood aside. We entered the room. At a table in the corner, their heads raised from the book they had been reading, sat her two lovely grandchildren, with their dark, curly hair and their dark, sad Armenian eyes. The boy was nine, the girl eleven.

They gave their chairs to Mrs. Shekerjian and Naz. The grandmother sat on a handmade stool. She sat straight, with great dignity, and waited to hear why these people had come to see her and her two jewels. The general had thought it wise to wait until we were there to tell her, so we could all discuss it together.

"Madam," began the camp director, "we are here to tell you of a great piece of good fortune that has come your way."

He described our plan to adopt her grandchildren and take them back with us to America, to give them a home there and all the advantages that American children enjoy.

"It is an honor, indeed," he said, "that out of all the homeless Armenian children in Europe, Mr. Mardikian, the founder and president of ANCHA, has chosen your grandchildren to raise as his own, in his own home, as if they were members of his own family. . . ."

As he talked on, I couldn't help noticing the effect of his

265

words on the grandmother. She sat absolutely still, looking at the director, at the general, at Mrs. Shekerjian, at Naz, at me. She didn't say a word. Her face was blank and expressionless. But there was something in her eyes that carried me far into the past, to the unhappy days of my own childhood, in my own tragic Armenia, which she must have known even better than I. Somehow, because of those far-off days, and the bitterness of them, I knew what she was saying in her heart:

"Why, you foolish people. All I have left in the world are this boy and this girl—these two precious children—left to me as a sacred trust by my own son.

"And you come here, pretending to be benefactors, and want to take them away from me—the only things I have to live for. Do you imagine for one minute that I will let you have them? Do you dream for one minute that I would stand here, and say good-by to them, and let them go with strangers, to a strange land? Before I would do that I would die."

I reached out and touched the director's sleeve. He stopped. "We'll forget about all this, Director," I said.

I got up and went over to the old lady and took her hand. "Don't worry, *Nana*. We are not going to take your *tornigs* —your dear little grandchildren—from you. Some of us, with the best of intentions, make mistakes. We try to help people—the wrong way. Sometimes I think that we Americans have much to learn about helping others."

As we walked away from the barracks, General Shekerjian said, "I'm sorry it turned out so badly."

"But it's going to turn out wonderfully, General," I said. "We're going to take all three of them back to America with us."

And that is what we did. But instead of separating them —the children with us and the grandmother somewhere else —we found them a home in Philadelphia where they could live together, just as the grandmother had promised her son they would. As this is written, they have been there for the last six years. Old as she is, the *nana* cooks for different fami-

266

lies. The boy is a healthy, happy young fellow who is crazy about baseball, and the little girl is one of the brightest students in her class in high school.

We had been getting calls for help from DPs in Italy. They were afraid to stay in their homes or even live in hotels because they thought the Italian police would arrest them and turn them back to the Russians. For years, even when Russia was ruled by the czars, this fate has filled the Armenians with terror. They would rather submit to Turkish torture than the living death of Russia. The saying was, "Better to die physically in Turkey than spiritually in Russia." The mere sound of "Russia" struck panic into the hearts of these DPs.

So we drove to Milan and arrived at the time of the Italian elections. We sat in our hotel windows and saw the hammer-and-sickle flags of the Italian Communists flying in the streets. The red flags, the marching, and the Communist slogans plastered all over the city took me vividly back thirty-one years to the Bolshevik uprising, when every soldier in the Russian army was rushing to Moscow to claim the Czar's crown or get his share of the royal jewels.

As I saw Italy and the Italians in that crisis, I saw how America could lead through strength and money and power —through its big fleets in the sea and the air and through its atomic weapons—but I don't think that is the best way. I think our best leadership will be through our hearts. Our hearts must be so filled with love for human beings that we can give in the Christian way of giving, without expecting or thinking of getting anything in return.

Just to be able to give is a blessedness, and speaks for our way of life. But it is an unusual way of giving, one which the people of many lands cannot understand, unless we go out of our way to show them, to demonstrate in action that there are no strings attached. It is theirs. We don't expect anything back. Our gifts are to get them on their feet. It is the way of the strong boy helping the weaker boy off the ground. It is helping those people to help themselves.

My Uncle Krikor had escaped to Milan. Army friends

had seen that he got food, clothes, money, and transportation from Bucharest to Vienna, and then to Italy and safety. So we had a wonderful time at our reunion. Naz, who had heard so much about him, met him for the first time. And both of us for the first time met Uncle's wife, Siranoush, and their seventeen-year-old son, Dro. It would only be a matter of a few months before they would all follow us across the sea to America.

But now we had to be on the move again, to get back home and somehow get more help for the DPs. We drove down to Rome, where we met and dined with the Armenian cardinal, Patriarch Gregory Agajanian of Cilicia, and then went on to Naples. We arrived there on a sunny June morning, and that afternoon boarded our steamer for the passage west.

The *Saturnia* was carrying many immigrants to America. They were on every deck, from steerage to promenade. Nevertheless, as we steamed up New York Harbor, all of them, crowding to the rail and straining to see ahead of them, looked very much alike, no matter what deck they stood on. They were all trying to get a glimpse of our Lady of Liberty, just as I had more than a quarter of a century before. I knew how much she meant. The same feeling burned in their hearts—hope, and thanksgiving for peace and freedom at last.

I turned to Naz by my side. She was looking up the harbor, toward the statue and the magnificent skyline. "Now, honey, what is the matter?"

She held tight to my hand. "You've been telling me for years how the Statue of Liberty is a shrine, and what it stands for. I—I believed you, but—but I didn't know what you were saying. You have to see her like this—at the end of a long journey—the way she is waiting for you, in the New World, across the sea—"

I put my arm around her, and we stood there watching the tugs come down the bay to meet us.

CHAPTER TWENTY-THREE

Suren Saroyan had come to New York, and we went to work for ANCHA immediately. For a long time, life was one village, one town, one city after another, an endless round of hotel rooms and motel meals, club rooms and Armenian-American halls, all filled with thousands and thousands of intent, upturned faces.

We knew now that there were at least thirty-nine hundred displaced persons of Armenian descent in the barracks and muddy cantonments of Germany and Italy. To save them all, we needed money, more than $250,000. We needed it to make sure there would be enough food and medical supplies in the DP camps until we could find a way to bring them to the New World. In addition to money, to meet the

Federal entry requirements, we had to see that there would be proper housing for them on their arrival and to find sponsors to guarantee jobs and living wages.

Many times in these days I thought of something Cardinal Agajanian had said in Rome. "Yes," he observed quietly, "I am firmly convinced that it is easier to get into Heaven than into the United States of America."

"How is that, Your Eminence?"

He smiled gently. "Well, when a man dies, we say a little prayer for him, and I'm sure God forgives him, and lets him through the gates. Can you say the same of your immigration officials?"

But that was our task, and in the last six months of that year we crossed the United States eleven times. When we were through, ANCHA had offices in sixty-two cities and towns. Each office was manned by five, six, and sometimes seven workers. None accepted a penny for his work.

This was one of the reasons we were so successful. All our workers were volunteers, and it was all work from the heart. We weren't in it to get our pictures in the paper. We were in it to save lives. If we didn't rescue those Armenian DPs, no one would, and if no one did, they were lost forever.

There was even a mascot bringing us good luck—Unita Naz's one-year-old baby brother, Haig, Jr. He had been born in San Francisco, July 3, 1947, while Naz and I and Suren Saroyan and his wife, Naomi, were in Boston raising funds for ANCHA. We had wired Lucie our congratulations and thanked her for the good omen, which is the way Armenians regard the birth of a boy.

Another priceless contribution came from General and Mrs. Shekerjian in Europe. How intelligent they were! Never once did they make the mistake of painting America as a paradise, where the DPs could be lazy and take it easy for the rest of their lives.

Instead, they described the hardships that went along with the good things America offered. It was a beautiful and free country, but you had to work for what you got. It was the land of opportunity, but you had to recognize opportunity when you saw it. Sometimes you had to hunt for it. And when you found it, you had to grasp it and make the most of it, to the best of your ability. That's the kind of country the Shekerjians talked about.

By the first part of the summer of 1949, more than two thousand had been rescued from the DP camps and brought to America, as our ANCHA slogan said, "for liberty and a chance." Two hundred more reached New Orleans in the middle of August. The Travelers Aid Society ladies saw them safely to the trains that were taking them to Southern California ranches near Fresno, Bakersfield, and Los Angeles.

Mechanics, engineers, whatever they were, they pitched into their daily tasks. Doctors picked grapes and cotton. A composer and professional zither player worked as a grocery clerk in the daytime and gave recitals in the evening. A former judge worked in a candy plant. A one-time art director was a sign painter's assistant. Each day they added three English words to their vocabulary. Every moment of their lives they thought and lived and worked so that when the great day of their naturalization arrived, America would be proud to make them citizens.

In October, another group arrived in San Francisco after a three-day trip across the continent in a chartered bus. Among them was a tiny old lady who, according to immigration authorities, was the oldest immigrant ever to enter the United States. She was ninety-nine-year-old Mrs. Mariam Mateosian.

Mother Mateosian was a grandmother, and had lived through almost an entire century of change and history in the Caucasus and the Balkans. She had survived two Turkish massacres, the Nazi invasion of the Crimea, the Russian conquest of Armenia, two Nazi concentration camps, and the displaced-persons camp where General Shekerjian found her.

On the morning of their arrival in San Francisco, we spread a feast for them at Omar Khayyam's. She sat in her wheel chair like one of those miniature peasant figures carved

271

of wood. Once, as I served her some *lavash*, the traditional Armenian cracker bread, she reached out and touched my forehead.

"*Asdvadz tsezi yergar gyank da* [May God give you long life]," she whispered.

That afternoon, we put them on the train for their future homes in the San Joaquin Valley. Mother Mateosian spent the entire journey with her wrinkled face pressed to the train window, looking out at the unbelievable richness of the beautiful valley. It was the crushing season, and you could smell, even in the train, the odor of grapes from the huge crushers of the valley vineyards.

She was weeping quietly as Ted Ashjian and my brother, Arshag, took her from the train. In her gnarled fingers she twisted the only thing she owned—a worn gold crucifix.

"Why are you crying, Mother?" Ted asked.

"I am crying for happiness, my son. I have cried so much in sorrow, I have tears left only for happiness." At her side was one of her grandsons, Kazar Mateosian, forty-four years old and a shoemaker by trade. He had brought with him his wife and their four little sons and daughters. On the station platform, as the train pulled out and left them there in the city that would be home forever, Kazar put the lap robe over his grandmother's knees. She was still weeping.

"I have seen America," she said. "Now I can die happy."

Mother Mateosian became one of the best-known citizens of Fresno. She touched the heads and foreheads of any American man, woman, or child who came near her. It was a gesture that both honored and thanked them. She did this, she said, because every American alive played some part, whether he knew it or not, in helping her and her grandson and grandchildren come to this country. She used to sit all day long in a rocking chair on the front porch of the little cottage Kazar bought and make the sign of the cross and bless everybody that went by. Many Fresnans parked their cars there and passed her house on foot and smiled to her, just to say that they had received Mother Mateosian's blessing.

272

In January, 1950, a little less than three months after her arrival, Mother Mateosian was one hundred years old. ANCHA gave a birthday party for this wonderful old lady in Fresno Memorial Auditorium. She had a cake with a hundred candles on it, and everybody who dropped a donation in the collection box for DPs still in Europe was offered a piece. In fifteen minutes the cake was all gone. Not one donation made a sound as it fell into the box. All the money was paper bills—more than four thousand dollars.

Next to the cutting of the cake, the most stirring moment was when members of a local American Legion post unfurled on the stage a beautiful American flag. It was the gift of former DPs in the Fresno area to the new Veterans' Hospital in Fresno. After this, there was a concert by the Armenian-American Citizens' Club band, Old World dances by some of the DPs, and regular dancing. For a very few minutes, Mother Mateosian was able to take some sprightly steps on the dance floor. I was one of the honored ones with whom she danced.

I don't think either one of us was supposed to be on a dance floor. As far back as the breakfast for Mother Mateosian and the others at Omar Khayyam's, and perhaps a month before that, I had been having sharp pains in my back. Standing up made them worse. When I was making ANCHA appeals and would have to talk for an hour or more, Suren Saroyan would get a couch ready behind the curtains of the speaker's platform, so that when I couldn't stand it any longer, I could close my appeal and lie down, and someone else could take my place. I think my suffering really helped the cause, in a way. Armenians, as you may have guessed, are emotional people. They cry, and they give, and the more they cry, the more they give. My tears would start them crying, but sometimes my tears would be those of pain, not of pity or sympathy.

Finally, toward the end of October, I went into the hospital. My physician, Dr. Emmett Allen, said I would have to have an operation. I had to protest. "I am very busy, doctor. There is a great deal to be done."

273

Dr. Allen's face was serious. "You can count on being in this hospital bed for the next five weeks. We have to remove a kidney."

I had been under observation for a few days, and they were setting the time for my operation, when a message was delivered to me in my hospital room. It was a cablegram from General Shekerjian. It said that a Brazilian refugee commission was on its way to Italy to see whether to allow DPs into Brazil. It was important for me to go to Washington at once, to discuss the matter personally with the Brazilian ambassador and persuade him to use his influence to help us send more of our own DPs to freedom in Brazil.

As I lay there in my room, with the beautiful October sunlight flooding through my window and with General Shekerjian's cable in my hand, I hesitated. Perhaps General Shekerjian could fly back to Washington from Europe.

I lay back and closed my eyes. The voices within spoke up. "You're weary and sick. Let General Shekerjian do it." And the reply: "The general is on our front lines. He's needed there every minute." Still another voice said, "Tell Suren to go—"

I knew that Suren would be eloquent and persuasive. The DPs would have a sturdy champion in him. But as I was about to accept this idea, I remembered the faces and the tragic eyes of the DPs of Funkerkasserne. I had made a promise to them. I had given them my word that they could believe in freedom again. Three years had passed. Some were still there. Others were living like animals in the alleys of Milan and Rome, afraid of the very light of day, because it might betray them to the death-in-life of the labor battalions.

And now at this moment the silent appeal in those eyes came back to haunt me. I had seen it. Suren hadn't. I had felt its truly terrible power. Suren would be speaking from his head. I would be pleading with all my heart—

I reached for my bedside telephone and called an airline and made a reservation for a night flight to Washington. I called Western Union and wired ANCHA officials in Washington to arrange an interview for me at the Brazilian Em-

274

bassy for the next day, if possible. Then I threw back my covers, got my street clothes from the closet, and began to dress.

My nurse came in and saw what I was doing and left. The phone rang. It was Dr. Allen. "You mustn't do this," he said. "You are a sick man."

I couldn't help smiling. I felt wonderful. "Doctor," I said, "God has had a lot of chances to kill me off. First with the Turks, then with the Russians, and three years ago with the winter cold in Germany. But He let me survive them all, so I guess He wants me around for a while. I'll be back, and then you can carve me up all you like."

I was in Washington the next morning. The talks I had at the Brazilian Embassy during the next few days won us the opportunity to bring over three hundred of our DPs to Brazil.

The second week in November, more DPs arrived in New York aboard the *General Muir*. I went to meet them. One was a white-haired grandmother of seventy. Before I could stop her, she knelt before me on the wooden planking of the pier.

"God will give you long life," she said, pressing my hand, "for saving us."

"*Nana,*" I said, as gently as I could, "I am not a savior. I am just a very stubborn man."

CHAPTER TWENTY-FOUR

At no time have I meant to give the impression that I went through all this by myself. No man ever gets anything done alone. There were all the kind, unselfish people I have mentioned, and many more that I have not been able to tell you about. Also, there was one other. He wasn't there in person, but every day his presence was near to me, giving me strength and courage.

As I have written, I knew about Herbert Hoover even before I came to America. In Armenia in those early days of the First World War, he was to us a sort of messiah, holding high a star—the white, shining star that was the emblem of Near East Relief. He was a symbol of generosity and kindness, sent into a world filled with terror and tragedy, to save us from famine.

So my devotion to Herbert Hoover and my love for him go back a long time. They go back to when he was saving the lives of thousands of homeless and starving, when his name all over Europe and the Middle East stood for an outstretched and helping hand.

As time passed, because of the miraculous way things happen in America, I got to know Mr. Hoover. We became personal friends. Every year in July, at the annual two-week outing of San Francisco's Bohemian Club, I went to the Bohemian Grove in the California redwoods and personally supervised the cooking for "the Chief" and the other members of his section, Caveman's Camp. As still more time went by, he chose me as one of the eleven members of his Subsistence Task Force. Our assignment was to find ways and means of cutting Federal expenses in the procurement and storage of foods for all American Armed Forces and the Veterans' Administration. We hoped to be able to save American taxpayers millions of dollars a year.

So in those moments when I lay on the cots or couches that Suren Saroyan fixed for me and listened to the other speakers carrying on out front, I used to close my eyes and think of Herbert Hoover in that terrible winter of 1946. He was then an elderly man, in his seventies. At his government's request, he was traveling through Europe, trying, as he had thirty years before, to find some way America could help the suffering people of Europe.

They say that after he had been out in freezing weather all day long, seeing one heartbreaking sight after another among the starving men, women, and children, he would return to his hotel room. It, too, would be freezing cold, because there was no fuel. He would sit there long past midnight in the candlelight, trying to write his report with his overcoat on, and woolen gloves on his fingers—this American hero with a lifetime of service already behind him. But age, weariness, bitter cold, scenes of untold suffering and despair, and the smell of death that hung over all of Europe that winter—nothing stopped him. He sat there in his hotel room and wrote his reports.

277

Early in the June of 1950 Dr. Allen and other specialists said that I couldn't go on. The operation had to be performed. If not, they said—well, there were simpler ways of killing oneself, such as going off the Golden Gate Bridge. And they were serious.

I went to the ranch Naz and I had bought, *El Rancho Silverado*. It was north of San Francisco, in the Napa wine country among the Mayacama hills. There, the doctors said, I should sit in the sun, and build my strength for the operation to come.

One Saturday evening my brother, Arshag, and his wife, Minnie, drove up from San Francisco to see me. We talked about restaurant affairs and about our DP problems. Arshag had a little 20-acre ranch in Fresno. He spent quite a bit of time down there and, with Ted Ashjian and the others, was very busy with the San Joaquin Valley DPs.

After dinner, Arshag and I went out on the lawn in front of the ranch house and sat in the deck chairs. My sheep dog, Omar, lay on the grass beside me. The soft, warm light of early evening was closing in on the valley. Down the hillside came the tinkle of sheep bells from the ranch's little flock. We talked about the operation.

"Are you worried?" Arshag asked.

In the peace of this twilight, how could I worry about myself or my life or death? "No, Arshag. No matter what happens, it will be for the best. It will be God's way, and that is the best way."

We sat in silence. I'm sure we were thinking the same things, sharing the same feelings, going back together down the years of our lives. I was seeing him again the last time I had seen him in Scutari, before I left for the Caucasus; I was seeing him that night in Powell Street, when he and the others met me there by Aram's tailor shop, and that other night at the door of his house, when he wanted me to walk home with the girls, and that morning on the deck of the *President Wilson*, when I was going so far away. . . .

And so we sat in the quiet evening, with the dog and the

278

sound of the sheep bells, and closer together than ever before.

At last it was time for them to go. He said good-by, and said he was going to Fresno. This was a surprise to me. It was Saturday night, three days before my operation at St. Francis Hospital in San Francisco. Fresno was a long, hard drive, especially on top of his trip to St. Helena. I wanted them either to stay there at the ranch and start out the next morning, or at the most, return to San Francisco and then drive on to Fresno on Sunday.

But he wouldn't listen. "I don't want to spend Sunday on the road. I have a lot of things to do in Fresno tomorrow. It would be better if we went down tonight."

When did he plan to come back?

He clapped me affectionately on the shoulder. "I wouldn't miss the operation for anything in the world. I'll be here Monday evening, to drive you down to the hospital."

So they left and went to San Francisco, and they drove all the way to Fresno that night. Sunday morning he did a lot of ANCHA business. Then he came home for Sunday dinner with Minnie. When the meal was over, he got up from the table, crossed the room, sat down in an armchair, and smiled at Minnie. The smile froze on his lips. He fell over sideways. Even before Minnie reached his side, his overworked heart stopped beating, and he was dead.

I woke up early the next morning to find Naz and my doctor and nurse beside my bed. I saw that Naz had been crying. I could always tell.

"Honey, what is wrong?"

"You have to be brave, sweetheart—"

I looked at the doctor, at the nurse. What had happened? Was it Unita Naz? Little Haig? Lucie? Their faces flashed across my mind. My heart began pounding.

Naz buried her face in her hands and turned to one side. "It's Arshag—"

Then they told me.

I was so weak, I broke down. I couldn't help crying, not

279

only for Archie and Minnie and their son, but because I felt I myself was so tired and exhausted, I would not pull through, and now Arshag wouldn't be there to take care of all the family affairs.

My own condition was worse than ever. That afternoon the ambulance came down the long drive to the ranch house, to take me to the Seventh Day Adventists' Hospital in St. Helena.

Naz was upset and had to stay inside, but Lucie and Nevart, our cook, and Unita Naz and little Haig came out to the driveway as the attendants carried me to the ambulance.

Haig was wearing a toy fireman's helmet and carrying a toy cowboy pistol. As the attendants closed the ambulance doors, he began to cry. The ambulance started up and slowly circled the turn-around.

"Bring my uncle back!" called Haig. The ambulance kept on going. "You bad men! Bring my uncle back!" And he ran down the road after us, until he saw that he could not stop us.

Dr. Allen and Dr. Thomas Gibson, the surgeon, postponed my operation. I insisted that I had to go to Arshag's funeral in Fresno. They nearly had to tie me in bed to keep me from going. Finally I couldn't resist them any longer and gave up.

Two days after that, I was driven in the ambulance to San Francisco, to St. Francis Hospital. I remember being rolled into the operating room, and the nurses and Dr. Gibson smiling down at me.

I said the Lord's Prayer and talked to the Lord. "Lord, take me if you think it's best. But if you think I'm needed here, keep me here a little longer, until my work is through—" My eyes were closed, and these were the last words that I remember before I went to sleep.

I came out of it all right and started my long, slow recovery. The children came to see me all the time and made the days pass quickly. Naz and Lucie and all our friends and the boys from the restaurant kept my room filled with flowers, and it was a bright, sunny, cheerful room.

One morning after he examined me, Dr. Gibson stayed by the bed. It was about three weeks after the operation. "Do you mind," he said, "if I sit down for a while and talk? You're getting well now."

I said, "Not at all, doctor. Please do."

He pulled a chair to the bedside. He had been working hard. His face looked drawn and tired.

"There is something I have to tell you," he said.

What was it this time? I wondered. I was still tired from everything. Part of me didn't care. I waited for him to go on.

He rested his elbow on the bed and shielded his eyes. Whatever he was going to say was already affecting him.

"In all my years in medicine," he said, "I have never had such an amazing experience as I had the morning of your operation. We would have told you this before, but you had to be past the shock of Arshag's death and the operation."

On a table across the room was a bowl of roses. I kept my eyes on them, while he went on talking.

"Very early that morning, a little after seven, just about an hour before you went into the operating room, a group of foreigners entered the downstairs lobby of the hospital.

"They could not speak English. They were very excited. They spoke in emotional bursts and seemed to be making some kind of request or demand.

"Then one of the nurses came into the lobby—a German girl who had come to America after the war. The reception-ist called her over. Maybe she could understand what the visitors were trying to say. The nurse spoke in German. Several of them answered immediately and told her what they wanted."

He raised his head from his hand. "Do you know who they were?"

"I can't imagine—"

"They were Armenian DPs."

281

I stared at him in astonishment. "But where did they come from? What were they doing here?" I was afraid they had caused trouble.

He read my thought. "Don't worry. They were all right. But neither I nor anyone else in this hospital has ever heard of anything like it. They seem to have come from the San Joaquin Valley, from some of those little farming communities. Somehow, they had heard about your operation. They didn't know whether a person could live with just one kidney, so they wanted us to pick one of them, drawn by lot, and remove his kidney and transplant it to you, so that you would be sure to live. As far as they knew, it was a death sentence for one of them. But every one was eager—even more than that—they were fighting for the chance to give their lives, so they could save yours."

My heart was so full, I couldn't speak. Neither of us said anything for a long time.

"Of course," Dr. Gibson said at last, "we had to tell them that they could do nothing. None of us could do anything, but hope and pray. It made them very sad. You had done so much for them—"

He stood up and put the chair back in its place and reached for his bag. I was still so moved I hardly knew what to say. I tried to make a little joke.

"Well, doctor, I suppose you will be taking all the credit for the wonderful operation you performed—but just between you and me—we'll know that a little group of Armenian farm hands did a little something, maybe, to keep your hand steady—won't we?"

He nodded and turned away. Both of us believed in his scalpel and his skill, but we both believed in praying, too.

When it came toward the end of July, I begged Dr. Allen to let me go to the Bohemian Grove. Finally he consented to take me there himself for the final day of the summer encampment. We went right to Caveman's Camp. Somehow the news went ahead to the Chief that I was slowly making my way along the trail on my doctor's arm.

We came around a bend in the trail, and there he was,

282

smoking his pipe, tanned, relaxed, dressed in comfortable clothes, eyes twinkling with good humor. The moment he saw me, he stood up and came over and helped me to a chair.

"Sit right down, George," he said, "and take it easy, and tell us all about it—" We sat there under the redwoods and talked for a long time.

Early one morning after the end of the summer, all of us got into cars and left San Francisco and drove across the bridge to Oakland to meet a train—my sisters, Baidzar and Alene, with their husbands and children; Minnie in a black mourning dress, and Gregory, the son that Arshag had left behind; Lucie and Unita Naz, with her dark, sparkling eyes, and little Haig, with his cowboy pistol and endless questions, and Naz and I.

The train slid in under the long shed behind its whining diesels and stopped there in front of the big clock. Before I knew it my arms were around the heavy, familiar frame of my Uncle Krikor. At his side were his wife, Siranoush, and their son Dro, whom we had seen in Milan.

My mother, Uncle Krikor's sister, should have been there, and Arshag, who had missed Uncle Krikor so much and had been looking forward so eagerly to seeing him happy in America. And they had had to leave behind Sebouh and Christine, their other son and daughter, who hadn't escaped from Bucharest and into Italy in time to qualify for entry under the first Displaced Persons Act and would have to wait five more years before they could join us.

But we were thankful for what we had. It was good to have someone here as the head of our families, in the sense of a patriarch—someone we could look up to for strength and wisdom, someone to whom we could give the respect we would give a father or a grandfather. Now here he was, with his gentleness, his warmth, his solid strength. As I stood there and listened to the greetings and saw the tears and the laughter of our family all crowded together on the platform beside the train, suddenly, amid all the noise and confusion, I was happier than I had been in a long while. I would have to go back over a lot of years and times before I could remember being happier than I was then.

A few days later, it seemed as though a long passage in our family history came to an end. Uncle Krikor wanted to make this trip, so all of us, in several cars, drove down the San Joaquin Valley to Fresno. It was a hot, sticky autumn day. The sky was low and gray over all the valley. The windmills stood still.

The plots in Ararat Cemetery were our destination. We drove the nearly two hundred miles and turned in through the cemetery gates and went down under the trees and stopped the cars and got out.

Uncle Krikor slowly walked to the graves. The rest of us stood together a little apart. Arshag's *hoghagoyd*—his earth-mound—was still fresh.

In his sadness for his sister and his nephew, whom he had seen for the last time so many years ago, Uncle Krikor seemed smaller, older. And in his sorrow, I loved him more than ever.

He bowed his head. The rest of us bowed our heads with him. We stood in silence under the low, gray sky and prayed.

CHAPTER TWENTY-FIVE

There was more work to do for the Army in Europe, and there were more DPs to take care of. On St. Valentine's Day in 1951, Naz and I boarded the big plane in New York, and General and Helen Shekerjian met us in Frankfort.

General Eisenhower had kept his word. Five years had made an amazing difference. Nearly all the changes we had worked for had been put into effect. The old army "messes" were really dining halls now. Bright curtains decorated the windows. Vases of cut flowers stood on the tables. Gone—and I hope forever—were the pin-up girls and the VD signs, which had always seemed such a strange combination for army-post walls. In their place were these gay touches which gave the halls a warm, wholesome, and even homey atmosphere. I inspected all the camps from Berlin to Vienna. As far as their food and dining halls were concerned, they were happy places.

Now all the food was piping hot, and the cooks were always trying for eye appeal, whose importance I drummed into every army cook and baker that would ever listen to me. They worked hard for appetizing dashes of color on the plates—in gravy, sauces, various greens and vegetables, salads, fruits, and desserts. The cooks, with their taller chefs' caps, strutted around their kitchens like prima donnas; they had realized at last that they were just as important as the man behind the gun, or the man in the Sabre Jet. Many of them knew that jobs in some of America's finest hotel and restaurant kitchens were waiting for them when they got out of service. It made me feel good to see them with this pride in their work, this sense of their real value. I knew that it would be passed along to the GIs in the form of better food.

Nearly five hundred Armenian DPs still lived in the camps in Germany. ANCHA had not been able to bring them to the United States or Canada or South America because they were suffering from tuberculosis or some other illness, or because they were ineligible for some other reason.

After a few weeks, when I was through with my army inspection assignments, General Shekerjian and his wife and Naz and I went from camp to camp, where our DPs were living, and took a complete census. We made arrangements to do what we could for those who needed money for food and clothing and medical treatment. Then we drove to Geneva, for talks with J. Donald Kingsley, head of the International Refugee Organization. He was very friendly and cooperative, and you can imagine our deep feeling of relief when he promised us that the IRO would take care of our DPs who had to stay behind in Europe.

So here, after four long years of work, we closed ANCHA's books in Europe. There remained now several hundred DPs who had made their way to the Orient or had escaped

286

from Red China. Until we rescued and relocated them, ANCHA in America was still in business.

We left Geneva and flew over the Alps to Italy and then on to Greece. The plaza in the center of Athens was filled with citizens strolling arm in arm. It reminded Naz and me of Courthouse Square in Fresno, on the evenings of the band concerts.

There are almost ten thousand Armenians in Athens. They are all that are left of the thirty thousand who fled for their lives in 1922, when the Kemalist Turks overran Smyrna and set fire to the city. They fled to Athens, where the League of Nations built huts for them, in the section known as Kokino.

They still live in these huts. They are honest, hardworking people who are trying to bring up their children to believe in the democratic way of life. There is not enough farm land in Greece to support them. Nevertheless the Greek government has shown them mercy and understanding, and we are all hoping that some day some friendly nation will open its doors to them. Until then, they do the best they can. Their boy scouts are well-trained, proud, and alert. On Sundays their churches are filled to the doors.

The biggest heroes of all are the Kokino schoolteachers. They have never fought in battles, but they have devoted their lives to bringing up these ragged and often hungry children to believe in the ideals of decency and democracy. Thanks to them, these children are growing up to be loyal friends of America. The dream of their lives is someday to go there.

Our last day in Athens Naz went to every supply store she could find and bought out their stocks of school books, crayons, pencils, and paper and had them sent to the school children of Kokino.

We crossed the Mediterranean to Cairo and then went on to Beirut, the home of Jemaron College, whose buildings were donated by the Palanjian sisters in memory of their brother, and also the home of my favorite of all institutions,

287

the American University of Beirut. This wonderful school has been making friends for America in the Near and Middle East for almost a century.

Among our guides and friends in Beirut were Movses Der Kaloustian and his lovely young wife, an Armenian from Alexandria. Kaloustian is a tall, distinguished-looking member of the Lebanese Parliament. Even more than that, he is the Gabriel Bagradian of Franz Werfel's great novel, *The Forty Days of Musa Dagh*. If you have read this book, you will remember the heroic, life-or-death stand of three thousand Armenian peasants against the Turkish army, on the summit of Musa Dagh, the Mountain of Moses, some three or four hundred miles north of Beirut. In real life, Kaloustian was their leader. Today, thirty years later, he has become a living legend in the Near East.

They took us to Azouniye Sanatorium, which Armenians all over the world help to support. Then we drove across soft, spring-green hills, and came at last to Aindjar.

Aindjar is like Kokino in Athens. Its houses are huts built by the League of Nations. The people who live there are the survivors of the forty days of Musa Dagh, and their children and grandchildren. They were brought there in trucks by the French, when the French government turned the state of Alexandretta back to the Turks in the late 1920s. It was the middle of winter. There was little food and no sanitation. So two-thirds of them died there in famine and misery.

In the little square of Aindjar, in front of their ram-shackle church, I stood on a platform with Movses Der Kaloustian and said what I could to help them: no matter what happened, we of Armenian descent all over the world remembered them and were proud of them; they had proved to the world that Armenians did not always go like sheep to the slaughter. On Musa Dagh, and still farther north in Van and on many other historic battlegrounds, they had fought against hundred-to-one odds, and won the victory. Because of them, Armenians everywhere held their heads high.

288

Then I told them that Naz and I would help them and particularly their church. (Since then, the San Francisco branch of the Armenian Relief Society has sent materials and money for the Aindjar school.)

Two Swiss women, the Aenishanslin sisters, were living in Aindjar. They were graduate nurses who had devoted their lives to Armenians and the Armenian cause. Like the rest, they were living in a hut. They had divided its one room by a curtain. They used the front as a reception room.

Before we left, Naz spoke to the elder in Armenian. "Sister Hedwig, is there anything we can do for you—anything we can give you?"

They were very pleased. But they were very shy, too. They ran behind their curtain and whispered in German. At last they reappeared.

"Mrs. Mardikian—our dear friends—" Sister Hedwig said in perfect Armenian, "we don't want anything for ourselves. But in the whole village of Aindjar, there isn't a single clock. We have three thousand people here, and not one of us ever knows what time it is."

I told Sister Hedwig that she should write immediately to Geneva in her native Switzerland and tell the clockmakers there to send the biggest, four-sided clock that they make. Then she should go to Beirut and have the finest architect design a tower for this clock. Then she should have the tower built and the clock placed in it, and it would be a gift to Aindjar from Naz and me. Every citizen, from then on, would always know the time of day.

So that you will know what happened, I will tell you that almost three years went by before the Aindjar clock was installed in its tower. To the wonder and amazement of all the villagers, the clock not only tells time, it plays a beautiful tune on its own chimes every hour of the day!

Bishop Zareh, the spiritual ruler of all the Armenians in Syria, is in Aleppo, and we visited him. Also in Aleppo is an Armenian school named Karen Yeppe College, in honor of the brave Danish woman who defied the Turkish *saptiehs*, or guards, and with her arms across her door stood between their sabers and the Armenian refugees she had hidden in her home at Urfa. Before we left, Naz gave the college a completely fitted chemical laboratory. Ninety per cent of the hundred thousand Armenians in Aleppo are survivors of the 1915 massacres and Turkish "deportation" orders. The Arabs have treated them well, and they and their descendants have become useful citizens.

It was early May and very hot in Baghdad, and it seemed as though every one of the city's four hundred thousand people slept on the housetops. We spent much of our time with Armenian doctors from the staff of the Government Hospital. Their favorite pastime was moonlight *sequifas* on an island in the middle of the Tigris River, which runs through the city.

A *sequifa*, which means "broiling," is a fish barbecue. The fish which is cooked is the *shabut*. These are Tigris salmon, and you buy them alive from Baghdad fishermen who catch them and string them through the gills and keep them in the river. Another necessity is the wood of a special bush, which burns with a quick, hot flame and gives the fish an exotic flavor.

The fish are split lengthwise and cleaned. Then they are put on pronged sticks, and the sticks are pushed into the ground in a circle around the fire. A man tends the fire with a long pole and keeps it from scorching the fish, and also adds more brush when the flames die down.

When the fish are cooked just right, they are taken off the sticks and put on a huge, round tin platter. Over them are spread chopped tomatoes, curry powder, and a chutney-like pickle mixture. The platter is placed for a few minutes on the coals. Then the meal is ready. Everyone serves himself with his fingers, or with the help of a thin Baghdad bread called *koobus*.

After the meal everybody sings in the moonlight. It is very romantic, with the ancient river flowing past, and the moon shining on the spires and turrets of the city of "the Arabian nights."

The fountain of Omar Khayyam in Sanjalak Park in the

heart of Teheran was finished while we were in Beirut, but Dr. Grady, now Ambassador to Iran, and Mrs. Grady had decided not to hold the dedication ceremonies until we could be there. Mrs. Grady and the Shah's sister had designed the fountain. It was made of Iranian marble, and, in addition to a spray of water playing into a pool, it had several drinking taps. Naz and I were very proud of it.

The Gradys met us at the airport, and the next day we dedicated the fountain. Before turning the water on for the first time, I spoke to the crowd gathered about the marble pavilion.

First, I said that this fountain should be a symbol of America's friendship toward the people of Iran. I hoped that their relationship would always be as clear and refreshing as the water flowing from the fountain's pipes.

Secondly, I thought it very appropriate, and the least I could do, to dedicate the fountain to the memory of the great Persian poet, Omar Khayyam. Whatever success I had enjoyed with my American restaurants, I thought much of it was due to the fact that they had been given his name, and an atmosphere inspired by the immortal *Rubaiyat*.

The audience applauded. As the fountain splashed on, they crowded forward, and praised Allah for such a beautiful gift.

The newspapers called me "the Sultan of America's *Chellow Kebab*," which is the way our papers would say, "America's Shish Kebab King." Two brothers named Tajvidi read these newspaper interviews and came to see me. They were painters who had done a series of illustrations for the *Rubaiyat*. These paintings appealed so much to Naz and me, we bought them. They hang today on the walls of Omar Khayyam's.

So we found these paintings in Teheran, and also a painter. Several days after we got there, we went to an elaborate garden reception. Ambassador and Mrs. Grady and many Iranian military and civil officials were there.

During the afternoon, we were shown an impromptu gallery, hung with many paintings of Iranian village scenes

291

and landscapes. They had a fresh, original quality, a naïve strength. "Is the artist here?" I asked.

Our host, Alek Aghayan, went to a corner and pulled toward us a young boy twelve or thirteen years old. He was poorly dressed. His shoes were worn and broken. His eyes shifted and rolled with embarrassment. We couldn't help feeling sorry for him.

"Here," said Mr. Aghayan, "is the artist."

This boy was one of the many children of a peasant family that lived in an Iranian desert village. His mother had died. His father was barely able to make a living. A Teheran artist, Haroutun Minassian, offered to give the boy room and board in exchange for odd jobs.

One morning, Minassian found the boy making pictures —finger-painting them with oil paints on canvas. He had a picture in his mind, he said, of his native village. Something made him try to make a painting of it, the way he had seen Minassian make one.

Only he thought he could do better with his fingers, because he didn't know how to hold a brush. Minassian was astonished, and he began to teach the boy. These pictures were the result. Looking at them, we were certain that the boy was a prodigy.

The next morning, Naz and an Armenian Relief Society worker took him to the clothing markets and bought him two new suits, new shoes, socks, and underwear. You should have seen the effect! He stood with his head up, and he looked everybody straight in the eye. Everywhere they went, he tried to draw attention to Naz, as if to say, "See? I have a protector!"

We decided to take the responsibility for this boy and send him to the school of the Mechitarist Fathers of San Lazzaro. He has been there now for more than three years. Hardly a month passes that I do not receive letters from him written in beautiful Armenian, in Italian, and also in English. He signs his letters and all his paintings "Mardik."

Still another surprise was waiting for us in Teheran. On our last day there, Ambassador Grady had a telephone call from Monsignor Abgar, Prelate of the Catholic Armenians of Iran. The monsignor said that the sisters and the students of the Immaculate Conception School would be very disappointed if we did not visit them before we left.

We stopped packing at once and drove to the school. High, thick walls surrounded the convent buildings. As we passed between the iron gates, several hundred students stood at attention in the courtyard. The mother superior came forward. The nuns stood together at one side.

The mother superior greeted us, then turned back. Suddenly she stopped, and at a signal from her, a sister left the group and stepped forward.

"Mr. Mardikian," said the mother superior, "I am introducing to you Sister Shooshan. She is from Xanta. Her mother was a member of the Mardikian family. For many years Sister Shooshan has prayed to St. Anthony, asking for a relative. In you, with your name, her prayers must be answered."

I stared at Sister Shooshan. She looked just the way my sister Baidzar had looked, years ago. And I must have reminded her of someone in her own family, because she ran and embraced me. It was a dramatic moment. With the happy looks on the faces of all the sisters, it was as if the sun had suddenly come out from behind a cloud.

We went inside the convent, and Sister Shooshan dried her tears and told me her story. She had been born in Xanta, my parents' native village. While she was still a baby, her family had left Xanta. When she was five, her mother and father were taken away by the Turks. The last thing her mother had said to her was "Your name is Mardikian. Remember—Mardikian, Mardikian." As they dragged her away, her mother kept calling back, "Remember!—Mardikian!" She never saw her mother or father again.

After the First World War, Armenian Relief authorities took many Armenian orphans to Istanbul. My mother, like many others, visited the asylums regularly on the chance of finding a missing relative.

"One day when I was nine years old," Sister Shooshan said,

293

"a lady came to the orphanage where I was living. I'm sure she was your mother. She said her name was Mardikian and asked if there were any refugee children from Xanta. For some reason, they turned her away. When I heard about it, I ran to the front yard to find her, but she had gone. After that, I began praying to St. Anthony to bring her back."

A year or so later, she entered an Armenian Catholic convent. Eventually she took the vows. She had been very happy. All she needed to make her happiness complete was to know that somewhere in the world, someone was alive who was related to her and her family. Now, even this had happened.

At the end of our visit, the mother superior said good-by. She presented to Naz a lovely bouquet and a beautiful embroidered tablecloth. "For you, Mrs. Mardikian," she said, smiling, "the queen of our hearts."

A few hours later, in the flat, dazzling sunlight of the Iranian May, we said good-by to Ambassador and Mrs. Grady and Sister Shooshan, who had come to the airport to see us off. Our plane took off and circled Teheran and headed south for Isfahan.

High over Iran I closed my eyes and pictured thousands of years of Persian dynasties, the builders of the Persepolis, conquerors of Armenia many times, warriors who had fought the Greeks all the way to Athens. I also pictured the soldiers of Tamerlane swarming to Isfahan and those of Alexander marching across these deserts and mountains to India.

Also, this was the land of Omar the poet, philosopher, and astronomer, whose name was as familiar to me as my own. In fact, many times, tourists have come up to me after dinner at the restaurant and have shaken hands and said, "Thank you, thank you, Mr. Khayyam, for the wonderful dinner." I never have the heart to tell them that I am not Omar Khayyam. So, as I looked down and saw the Persian desert under our wing and falling slowly behind, I felt sad at leaving the country that had given so much to me and to all the people who had ever had a good meal and enjoyed themselves at Omar Khayyam's.

We flew to Karachi, and on to Bombay and Calcutta. A

few days more, and we crossed Thailand and flew north to Hong Kong.

Here there was much ANCHA work to do with the American consular service and with William N. Collison of the IRO. The problem here was the same as it had been in India: getting Armenians out from behind the Bamboo Curtain and to safety in other places.

Early on a June morning we landed at last in Tokyo. We were met by General Hastings, who had become chief quartermaster of the Far Eastern Command. As such, he was also the first Quartermaster General of a United Nations Army. After the conference in San Francisco, I could sympathize with him. He had his hands full trying to satisfy the dietary requirements of the soldiers of so many different countries and nationalities.

I left immediately on a tour of army depots with Colonel Coy Baldwin, chief of food service. In an army car we visited every American post from Sasebo in the south to the very tip of northern Japan.

After that we went toward the fighting in Korea, and at Seoul I presented my Washington credentials to General James Van Fleet. While I was visiting the Korean front and seeing what the GIs were getting to eat, I did what I could to improve their diets and help the cooks prepare the food in the front-line field kitchens myself. Many of my friends thought I was crazy or didn't know any better. But when I knew they needed help with their food, how could I sit behind my office desk in San Francisco and dictate recipes to send them?

Some of the sights would have made you feel good. The greens and vegetables, for instance, that were grown in the army gardens in Japan—big, beautiful heads of lettuce and large, healthy bunches of radishes and onions. The moment they arrived on the planes the GIs carried them to cool caves and cellars they had dug in the Korean mountainsides to keep the vegetables crisp and fresh.

Once Colonel James Lamont, the Eighth Army quartermaster, borrowed a jeep from Colonel Dan Gilmer, commanding officer of the Seventh Cavalry, and we got in it and

295

rode as far as we could. Then we got out and continued on foot to the Greek contingent, which was 20 miles north of the Thirty-eighth Parallel and trying to contact the enemy. It was hard going.

The Greeks were wonderful to see. As we climbed the hillside where they had made their headquarters, we were met by their commander, Colonel Dionyssios Arbouzis, and about twenty other officers, and a Greek Orthodox priest and the correspondent of an Athens newspaper. Around their headquarters tent they had constructed arches of boughs and wild flowers. Lettered in blossoms on one of the arches were the words, "Welcome, *compatriotes.*"

They had set a luncheon table, and there was good Greek food and bottles of *ouzo* and *mastika* and *regina* wine. This was King Paul's name day, so we drank many toasts to the Greek monarch. Machine-gun fire rattled close by. Mortar shells whined overhead and thumped home up front.

All at once we heard a commotion by the colonel's tent. Down the short trail toward us came a Chinese Red with his arms full of flowers. Two Greek soldiers prodded him toward us with their rifle barrels. They had gone out to get flowers for the luncheon table. In the field they had captured this enemy sniper, disarmed him, and made him pick the flowers and carry them to the colonel.

The colonel smiled at me. "Both the flowers and the prisoner are yours."

"Thank you," I said. "You keep the prisoner."

I dried the flowers carefully and took them back home and sold them to my friends. With the money I bought a case of Greek cheeses and olives and sent them to Colonel Arbouzis and his men. I know they enjoyed them, because the colonel told me so. When the Korean War was over, he passed through San Francisco on his way to the War College at Fort Leavenworth. Naz and I were happy to entertain him and his friends. We went to the Greek quarter and bought some *ouzo* and had it ready for them when they arrived.

My last day in Korea I saw something to think about; maybe you will think about it, too. I went to the cemetery in Pusan. You could tell from the moon-and-star emblem where the Turks were buried, and you could tell from the crosses where American soldiers were. You could see where the French and the British were, and the Abyssinians and the Greeks, and all those who had proved to the world that their nations were united not only by words and pacts, but by dying. There they lay together, under the Korean sky.

That was July 3, and that afternoon I flew back to Tokyo. In Japan, as they had been in Europe, the GIs were still the best ambassadors America ever had. You can tell how you stand with people by the way their children act, because they act spontaneously, the way they feel. In Korea and Japan, the youngsters' faces, no matter how tired or hungry they were, broke into smiles whenever they saw American soldiers going by in jeeps or trucks or trains. They waved and shouted, and you could tell how glad they were to see the GIs. "Hello, Joe!" they'd cry. "Hello, Joe! Hello, Joe!" And the soldiers always waved back.

Tough and battle-worn as many of them were, their hearts went out to the children—the four-, five-, six- and seven-year-olds who are always the innocent sufferers in wars, and the years after wars are over. No matter where you see them —in Athens, Berlin, Milan, Aindjar, Pusan, or Tokyo— the children break your heart. You have to do something for them, to help them, because they are so helpless. And because you don't want them growing up to be soldiers.

The tour ended. I turned in my reports to General Hastings and flew to Honolulu. It was a wonderful feeling to be on American ground, in an American city again, and to relax on the warm sand with Naz.

We stayed at Waikiki for three days and then flew over the Pacific to San Francisco, the city we loved more than any other because it was home.

But it wasn't only coming home that made it good to get back. The yearly outing in the redwoods of the Bohemian Grove would begin in a few days. I wanted to see the Chief and the others at Caveman's Camp. I had to tell them about the help that people and children needed in different parts of the world. And then, after that, we all had to try and see that they got it.

297

CHAPTER TWENTY-SIX

I t was strange that in working so hard for the freedom of others, I lost more and more of my own freedom. But I still believed that nothing is ever so real and so alive and so valid as when you are giving it away.

So it was just and right, and I was very happy, when the Bohemian Grove outing was over, to welcome General Shekerjian back from Europe and to visit with him all the DPs we had relocated in the United States, to see how they were getting along.

General Shekerjian had been with ANCHA for four years, and it was as though God had really sent him to help us. His retirement from the Army had come exactly at the right moment.

General Shekerjian had done a magnificent job in Germany. While he worked day and night to push the DPs through the consulates, past the DP commissions and through the review boards of the IRO, his wife, Helen, taught the refugee grownups and children how to speak English and things about American history and ways of life that would make them better citizens.

I don't think I have told you how General Shekerjian became the first Armenian-American to go to West Point. He himself never told me this story. I heard it from one of his classmates.

When Haig Shekerjian was sixteen, he lived in a town in Connecticut. In the daytime, he attended high school. At night, he held down a job to support himself, his mother, and three sisters. One morning a big house caught fire. Haig, on his way to school, stopped in the crowd. He heard a woman screaming. The firemen frantically poured tons of water into the flames. They wanted it under control before they sent in their rescue squad.

But Haig had to act quicker than that. Before anyone could stop him, he pushed through the crowd, disappeared into the flaming building, and a minute later carried the woman to the street. She broke free and tried to run back into the house.

"My child! My baby's in there!"

Haig went back in. Flames crackled along the eaves. Smoke billowed from the windows. The crowd stood fascinated. Two minutes went by. Three. Then, choking and gasping, Haig stumbled from the house, with the baby safe in his arms.

Haig was a hero. The following Saturday afternoon the whole town joined in a Haig Shekerjian Day celebration. The mayor and the fire chief and other officials made speeches. Then they turned to the guest of honor. As a reward for his valor, the town was ready to give him a car, a home, a trip to California—anything his heart desired. All he had to do was ask.

"There's only one thing in the world I want," he said.

"Name it," they said, "and it's yours."

Haig said, "I want to go to West Point."

The city officials saw to it that, when Haig finished high school, he received his appointment. That is the story of how General Shekerjian went to West Point.

On this trip, we saw our DPs—almost thirty-six hundred of them. They were all proud; they were all self-supporting; and their hearts were filled with gratitude toward America. For them, she had opened her golden door.

Not one wanted to go back. While it was true that they were amazed at the height of the Empire State Building, and were awe-struck by the trains and swarms of automobiles and the food and clothes that Americans have, what they were most grateful for, and what they loved the most was this: they left New York and went all the way to California, or they left New Orleans and traveled days to reach the State of Washington, and not once did men with helmets and bayonets and guns step across their path and say, "Where is your passport? Where are you going?"

This was freedom that they had never known; they would cherish it until they died. And, deeper than that, we knew that once it was theirs, they would lay down their lives for it, if necessary, and they would do this eagerly and gladly.

Do you know what the last words of Mariam Mateosian were? That beautiful old lady passed away in Fresno when she was a hundred and three years old. She had lived here for four years. On her deathbed she whispered, "Tell all my American friends—God bless them and keep them, for making it possible for me to come to a free country to die."

After our trip, I knew that all of our DPs felt the same way.

Armen was with me now, and Uncle Krikor, too. Bart and Alice Rustigian had gone back to Fresno, to open a fine restaurant of their own. But some of the DPs and Armen and Uncle Krikor were helping me with my real estate and other enterprises, and Peter Gagoush and Dro, my nephew, were helping me with the restaurant. Thanks to them, I was able to make my tours and trips.

300

As it had with Mr. Hoover, life completed another circle when I tried to help the children. I had seen schools in Greece with no books or desks, and children going to them barefooted, because they were hungry to learn. I had seen schools in Beirut and Damascus made of flattened 5-gallon tins; I could imagine them in the heat of the Syrian sun.

I had seen the starving ophans of Korea, and I was more convinced than ever that Stalins and Hitlers and Mussolinis are not born that way; they are creatures of cold and hunger, oppression and fear. Children that get enough to eat and are warm enough do not grow up with chips on their shoulders.

And so I came full circle to Dr. John Voris, who had spoken to us there on the windy parade ground of Alexandropol more than thirty years ago.

The letter that Vahan Tcheraz had written for me and that I was unable to deliver when the *Meghali Ellas* reached New York I had given to Dr. Voris long before this, when our paths had crossed once in Fresno. But meanwhile, Dr. and Mrs. Voris had started helping homeless and destitute children in the mountains of Kentucky and in the Ozarks. Then, with World War II, this work spread to include children who had been made orphans by Nazi bombs. After Normandy and the occupation, food, clothing, medical supplies, and money had to be sent for the children of France, the Low Countries, and Scandinavia.

Dr. Voris and his associates formed an organization. They called it the Save the Children Federation. It worked principally through service clubs, parent-teacher groups, colleges, and high schools.

So now Dr. Voris and I began working together. We sent thousands of blankets and tons of clothing from California to the child refugees of the great Pusan fire. Soon Dr. Voris asked me to be the northern-California chairman of the Save the Children Federation. I accepted, and now I am the chairman for all of California. If I had another life, I would devote it all to trying to help the children, for there is no end to this work, and there is no work so important.

Naz and I were invited to President Eisenhower's inauguration, so we went to Washington. I was not feeling well. During most of the preliminary events, I stayed in our hotel rooms at the Hotel Statler, watching them on television. But when noon of Inauguration Day was getting nearer, and our grandstand tickets were right on the bureau, I couldn't lie there any longer. Fever or no fever, I turned off the television and got out of bed and dressed, and we went there to the east side of the Capitol.

It was an unforgettable hour. I think we all felt joyful that we had won the election, and we all felt very proud of the man whom we had worked for and who would lead our country through the next four years. I know it was the first time in my life that I had ever become involved in politics. That was true of many of us.

We believed we were crusaders. But I know that as far as I was concerned, the crusade, if there was one, was for the man, General Eisenhower, rather than for a party platform or a set of political principles. General Eisenhower was a symbol of might and strength, and at the same time a symbol of integrity and honor. There wasn't a person within hearing range of a radio anywhere in the world, or a person who could read, regardless of his language, who didn't know of General Eisenhower and the victories he had won for freedom and democracy. He had earned the love of his friends and the respect of his enemies.

There, beside the beautiful, inspiring building, we heard the Marine band play, and we heard the prayers, and the oaths of office administered to Vice-president Nixon and President Eisenhower, and then listened to the strong, forceful voice of our President, as he delivered his inaugural address.

When it was over, I had to get in a taxi and return to the hotel to lie down, but Naz went on with friends to watch the inaugural parade. I heard band music all the way to my hotel, and even then, as I entered our suite, I could hear it faintly in the distance.

I had only been back a little while in San Francisco when the saddest thing happened. In the evening, after dinner the telephone rang, and it was Captain Spike Wood, the son of my friend Major General Walter Wood, who had retired and was the head of IRO in Washington.

"Mr. Mardikian," he said, "this is Spike Wood—remember me?—and my brother, Tommy?"

I said that of course I remembered them both. Wherever he was, he must come right up.

Spike tried to answer, and then all at once I knew that he was crying.

"We've kept our promise, Tommy and I." His voice was breaking. "We're back—both of us—but he's in a wooden box."

Spike was at the army embarkation docks at Fort Mason, and I told him I would send my driver for him, but he said no, he would get there all right, and I gave him the address of our new apartment on Pacific Heights.

It had only been a year before that Spike had graduated from West Point and had come to San Francisco on his way to the Korean front. Tommy, then in his third year at college, drove out with a classmate to see Spike off to war. Naz and I were moving then, so we turned over our Nob Hill apartment to the three of them. Our staff at Omar Khayyam's kept them supplied with roast squab and turkey and ham and all sorts of delicacies, and they had a gay, carefree time.

And as we were all saying good-by, Spike and Tommy promised that when the war in Korea was over, we would meet again in San Francisco and have good dinners and good wine and talk about old times.

The months passed, and Tommy graduated and became engaged to a lovely girl and followed Spike to the Korean front. Three days after he got there, shrapnel blew him to pieces.

And now Spike had brought him back home, and that is what he meant when he said that he and Tommy had kept their promise.

When he arrived, Naz and I embraced him. I went to my study and called long distance and got his mother and father on the telephone in Washington.

"Here, Spike," I said, "Mother and Dad want to talk to you." Then I closed the study door and left him alone.

303

He was in there for about twenty minutes. Then, very quietly, he came out. Two months later, when I went to Washington, I saw General and Mrs. Wood. They told me that in all those twenty minutes, Spike hadn't been able to say a word. He had just sat there with the telephone in his hand, listening to them say that they loved him and Tommy, and that everything was all right.

Another Korean story reached a happier ending when the great commander of the Twenty-fourth Infantry Division, Major General William F. Dean, came back to life and the living out of the North Korean prison camps.

When we read the wonderful news that he was coming back home, I telephoned Mrs. Dean, who lived in Berkeley and who had never once lost her hope and trust in the General's survival.

"Mildred," I said, "Omar Khayyam's is yours, for a home-coming dinner, or whatever you want."

And this very happy, very thankful wife of a hero gave the answer that any woman would have. "Our first dinner in public, we would love to have with you, I know. But first, George, I want to get acquainted with my husband. I haven't seen him for so long, I just want to look at him. I just want to sit with him and hold his hand and hear his voice."

That is exactly what she did, and who can blame her? But a week or so later they came to the restaurant and broke *lavash* with us, and it was a proud and happy evening in the history of Omar Khayyam's.

Perhaps the coming home of General Dean was a good omen, because a little while after that, my prayers for a chance to pay my debt to America were answered in a way that I never dreamed possible.

The letterhead said, "Commission on Organization of the Executive Branch of the Government," and the letter was dated January 24, 1954.

Dear Mr. Mardikian:—

In the work of this Commission, we are determined to set up an effective Task Force on Management of Subsistence in Federal Agencies. Mr. Joseph Binns was selected as chairman

304

and he informs me that you are willing to serve on this Task Force. This letter is a confirmation of your appointment. I want you to know that I greatly appreciate your willingness to work with us in these problems.

The work of this Task Force in investigation and recommendations is of the highest importance in our problem of reducing Federal expenditures and relief to our over-burdened taxpayers. The dimension of the problem is somewhat indicated by the fact that the Federal Government expends about $4,500,000,000 annually on this service. . . .

Yours faithfully,
[signed] Herbert Hoover, Chairman.

In our long days of rest and relaxation under the redwoods of the Bohemian Grove, I used to like to say, "Chief, many years ago, in the form of relief to the destitute people of Armenia, you cast bread upon the waters of the River Arax. Now, I am in charge of your meals here at Caveman's Camp. So I am seeing that this bread comes back to you, in the form of *daron abour, boulgur* pilaff and *shish kebab.*"

That was trying to be poetic, even joking a little, but underneath I was very serious, and I'm sure that he always knew it. To serve him was one of the greatest of privileges. On July 24, which I still celebrated as my birthday because it was the day I landed at Ellis Island, it always pleased the Chief to make a little speech to the other members and the guests of the camp and tell them my story, so that they would know something about the beautiful, shining thing America is to millions of human beings all over the world. Every year I listened humbly as he spoke. And then, after the outing was over, it was always a pleasure to entertain him for an afternoon or evening at our home in San Francisco. But nothing had ever filled me so much with gratitude or made me so humble as this honor in his letter.

Joseph Binns is the executive vice-president of the Hilton Hotels and the managing director of the Waldorf-Astoria in New York, and about the middle of April he telephoned to notify me of a change in procedure of our Task Force. We usually held our monthly meetings in Washington. But our

May meeting was going to be held the first week of the month, in Los Angeles. Would I please arrange my schedule accordingly?

Just about the time this message came, there was a curious change in the members of my family. Naz, particularly, looked worried, and she was anxious to see that not the slightest thing irritated me. My least whim was humored. My office staff fell all over themselves being polite. Never had I been so petted and pampered. Consequently, I woke up every night in a cold sweat. Dr. Rodney Yoell, my physician, must have discovered something in his recent examination. Everyone knew it but me. They were being kind, but—this must be it. This was the end. I went over and over the details of my will in my mind, to make sure Naz, Unita Naz, little Haig, and the others were all provided for. I myself began to go around looking like a tragedian.

But—you had to keep up appearances. Colonel Harold H. Sheller, commanding officer of the Mira Loma quartermaster depot near Riverside, one of the largest of its kind in the world, invited me to Southern California to talk to his men. He said the date would be May 5. I told him I would be delighted.

Then about May 1, Marshall Chashoudian, the musician and composer, phoned me from Los Angeles with thrilling news. The National Broadcasting Company had accepted one of his compositions. A large orchestra was going to play it on a coast-to-coast television program. Naz and I had to come down and be his guests at the broadcast.

Marshall was a dear friend. He had done great work for ANCHA as its Los Angeles chairman. He and his committee had found homes and jobs for more than a thousand DPs.

"We'll be there with bells on," I said. "When is the broadcast?"

"May 5," he said.

Naz and everybody were still catering to me as if I were the Shah N' Shah himself, but in spite of my gloomy thoughts, I felt fine.

306

So I went down to Mira Loma and made the talk at noon, May 5.

That evening, at about three minutes to seven, Marshall and his wife, Noushig, and I reached the television studio. Marshall took his time about parking the car. I thought he seemed very relaxed for a composer whose music is about to be heard by 20 million people.

"Don't be nervous, George," he said, perfectly at ease. "I'm sure they have seats for us."

As we entered the auditorium, the lights dimmed. An usher escorted us to front-row seats. I pressed Marshall's arm, to reassure him. It was a great moment in his career.

But there was no orchestra on the stage. I turned to a pair of ladies at my left. "Where is the orchestra?" They didn't have any idea. "We're strangers here, too," one of them said.

Then a man came out on the stage and cried, "This—is your life!"

I was amazed to see that it was Ralph Edwards, from Oakland. I had known him for many years. "Marshall," I whispered, "we've come to the wrong studio."

A big searchlight played over the audience. There was a monitor screen high above the stage. You could see the program on it. I looked at it and saw that the spotlight was on me. I heard my own name.

"George Mardikian!"

I thought it was a dream. I must be dreaming this.

Then Ralph shouted, "George Mardikian—*this is your life!*"

Impulsively, I hid my face in my hands. I was thunderstruck. The next thing I knew I was up on the stage. To this day, I don't remember going up there or what happened during those first five minutes of the show.

When the program was over, they had lots of thoughtful presents for Naz and me, but the most wonderful thing they gave me that evening was the looks on the faces and in the eyes of the two hundred DPs that were in the studio audience, and really part of the program. I had seen them at Funkerkasserne. And I was looking at them now, smiling,

307

healthy, well-dressed. And inside, I, too, was saying, "Thank you, America."

You cannot please everyone. The program had been over for some time, and we were leaving the studio. I felt a tugging at my coat. It was little Haig. His face and large dark eyes were filled with reproach. "Uncle—why wasn't I on the show?"

"I had nothing to do with the show, Sonny. It was as big a surprise to me as it was to you."

"But why was Sister on, and I wasn't on?"

I patted his head. "Sister's name is Unita Naz. She was born on the opening of the United Nations. So they thought the people should know that."

He put his finger in his mouth. "What about me? Wasn't I born the night Washington crossed the Delaware?"

"That was a cold, stormy night in the middle of winter. You were born the night before the Fourth of July."

He thought it over seriously. Then he tried again. "Well, if it was the name they were after, you've been telling me all this time that I was named for the first king of the Armenians—King Haig. How about that?"

He had me there. There wasn't anything to tell him. I patted his head again. "That's all right, Sonny. We'll get you on television, some day."

He pulled at my coat again. "And I don't want to be on any kid show like *Howdy Doody*, either," he said, as we went out the door.

We all returned home to San Francisco, and soon the mail began coming in. Among those we heard from was Kerop Arakelian of Mexico, whom we had met in Athens in 1951. He said that he and his wife would like us to visit his brother Gaspar's home in Acapulco. We thought it would be a pleasant change, so we went down there with Suren Saroyan and his wife, Naomi, and Marshall Chashoudian and his Noushig, a name which means "little almond."

After a week in Acapulco, we went on to Mexico City. My office had forwarded my personal mail. In it was an envelope with "The White House" engraved on it.

308

I opened it, and it was an invitation to an informal stag dinner on June 24. "Because of the informality of the occasion, I suggest that we meet at the White House about half past seven. . . . While I am hopeful that you can attend, I realize that you already may have engagements which would interfere. . . . I assure you of my complete understanding. . . ." The letter was signed, "Dwight D. Eisenhower."

I remember that when I was a child my mother used to take us to shrines that meant a great deal to her, particularly after the Turks came and got my father. They were usually little chapels, where we burned candles and prayed for things we wanted. They were always very still and quiet, and filled with an unseen presence, and I always felt very little when I was there in the dimness, beside my mother.

I had been in the White House before. Just the previous November, at Thanksgivingtime, Naz and I and Lucie and the children were graciously shown through by Mrs. Eisenhower. I had been there on other occasions, too. But there was something special, something personal, about this invitation. It touched me so deeply that as I walked up the White House steps that warm June evening, the feeling came back to me that I was entering one of the shrines of my childhood. This was the house of a good and great man, who was the chosen leader of a good and great people, and it was the presence of all these united people that I felt and that made me feel quiet inside, and small.

All of the guests—there were seventeen—arrived on time. I knew most of them, and some were my good friends. We had terrapin soup and individual steaks, and I remember that imported French wines were served. This upset me, because the wine people of California should have seen to it that the White House cellars were stocked with the wonderful Napa Valley and Livermore and Santa Clara Valley wines.

The President discussed his health and his place at Gettysburg and his daily activities and the heavy responsibilities of his office.

At about ten o'clock, some of us made a move to leave.

309

The President smiled and motioned us back to our chairs. "It's not very often that I can spend an evening chatting with my friends," he said. "Please sit down. I'll tell you when to go."

Later on, in general terms, we were discussing world affairs. Several of the guests were military men. One was a former Ambassador to Russia. He told us how the Russian leaders had put up signs all over Moscow saying that religion was a dope, an "opiate of the masses." The President listened carefully. Then he said, "My friends, the biggest, most powerful weapon that America has is not the atomic bomb, or the H-bomb, or even the superb fighting ability of her officers and men. It is the strength—the spiritual and moral strength—of 160 million Americans. No nation in the world can conquer that strength. Remember that, gentlemen, for that is the weapon that America's enemies really fear."

I knew what he meant. I believed it with all my heart. The soldiers in the front lines were always close to God. They talked with Him all the time. So had I, and so, I knew, had the President.

A little after eleven he stood up and smiled again. "Well, gentlemen," he said, "it's just about bedtime—"

He went with us to the door and warmly shook hands with each one of us and said good night. We walked down the steps, and the White House door closed behind us.

The others offered me rides in their cars, but I refused. I thanked them, and they waved good night and drove away to their homes.

I went out of the White House grounds and started down the street. I wanted to walk, and I wanted to be alone. I wanted to listen to something.

On a September day after I had come back from Korea, President Truman had given me the Medal of Freedom, and now in the warm June midnight, as I walked slowly down the deserted avenue, I heard the Sixth Army band playing again, and the officers' shouts across the parade ground at the Presidio of San Francisco, and General Swing's strong, steady voice—

"Citation—The President of the United States . . . has awarded the Medal of Freedom to Mr. George M. Mardikian, American citizen, for meritorious service—"

He read on, and the troops stood on the parade ground at attention, and the bright flag rippled in the wind off the bay.

And I remembered the picture. That hadn't been too long ago. On the day before I left for Alaska on an inspection trip with General Horkan, Naz and I gave a reception for him, and we were so proud to serve him and all the guests our specialty, which was big red strawberries from our ranch on the Silverado Trail, dipped in champagne and then in powdered sugar. While we were eating the strawberries, General Horkan said that he had a surprise for me from Washington. Suddenly, in his hand, was a smiling portrait of President Eisenhower, in a beautiful frame. And he was reading before everyone there, the words that the President had written: "To George Mardikian, with greetings and best wishes and with lasting appreciation of invaluable service to our Armed Forces. Dwight D. Eisenhower."

Then, for the millionth time, I remembered a summer afternoon, when the Chief and some of the other members of Caveman's Camp had come to my home, after the outing at the Bohemian Grove was over. We were all sitting in the living room, and I had a guest book there. Before he left, the Chief said that he would write something in it, and he did, and after they had all gone I read it out loud softly, and they are words that I, who was born in Armenia and saw the Statue of Liberty from a steerage deck, will carry in my heart until the day I die:

"To George—Every time I lose faith in America, I always remember that it made you."

In what other land could it all have happened? Where else but here?

Nothing could describe my pride in America and my love for America and the thrilling feeling inside that I was a son of America, the wonderful land of the free where an immigrant boy, who stepped with shining eyes into the melting pot of New York, could sit down at the White House dinner table thirty years later, as a guest of the President of the United States.

No money could buy that feeling. No country in the world could give it to me but the United States of America, which gives everything decent human beings long for and hunger after.

I went back over the years—the struggling years, the years in Fresno, and the great privilege it had been to start my restaurant during the depression, to put my heart and soul and heritage into it and make it my steppingstone, my gift to America.

Gratitude swept over me, stronger than I had ever felt, and I guess this whole book has been trying to tell you what it was for: for the pioneers who came and built this country, where a man can work in peace and raise his children without hatred and fear and without having to carry rocks in their pockets when they are out at night; for the fine people who kept those ideals alive in their schools and churches, and for the brave heroes who fought and died for them in wars; for the great wonderful blessing that is the goodness, the kindness, and the fairness in the hearts of Americans. For all these things that to me go to make up the Song of America.

In the quiet night, tears came suddenly to my eyes. I kept on walking down the street in the dark, and all the words and the sound of my footsteps and the beautiful, soaring music of faith and dreams blended in my ears and in my heart, and I walked on and on, listening to my Song of America, and wanting everyone to hear it, all over the world.